THE **HARDY BOYS**

UNDERCOVER BROTHERS™

PAPERCUTZ™

THE HARDY BOYS

UNDERCOVER BROTHERS™

#7

The Opposite Numbers

SCOTT LOBDELL • Writer
DANIEL RENDON, PAULO HENRIQUE, SIDNEY LIMA • Artists
Preview art by PAULO HENRIQUE
Based on the series by
FRANKLIN W. DIXON

PAPERCUTZ™

New York

The Opposite Numbers

SCOTT LOBDELL – Writer

DANIEL RENDON, PAULO HENRIQUE and SIDNEY LIMA — Artists

MARK LERER – Letterer

LAURIE E. SMITH — Colorist

JIM SALICRUP — Editor-in-Chief

project sunshine

bringing sunshine to a cloudy day™

Callie Shaw volunteers with Project Sunshine. Project Sunshine is a nonprofit organization that provides free services to children and families affected by medical challenges. We send volunteers to hospitals to provide arts and crafts, tutoring and other special services. For more information on Project Sunshine please visit www.projectsunshine.org.

ISBN-10: 1-59707-034-3 paperback edition
ISBN-13: 978-1-59707-034-8 paperback edition
ISBN-10: 1-59707-035-1 hardcover edition
ISBN-13: 978-1-59707-035-5 hardcover edition

Published by arrangement with Aladdin Paperbacks, an imprint of Simon & Schuster Children's Publishing Division.

Printed in China
Distributed by Holtzbrinck Publishers.

10 9 8 7 6 5 4 3 2

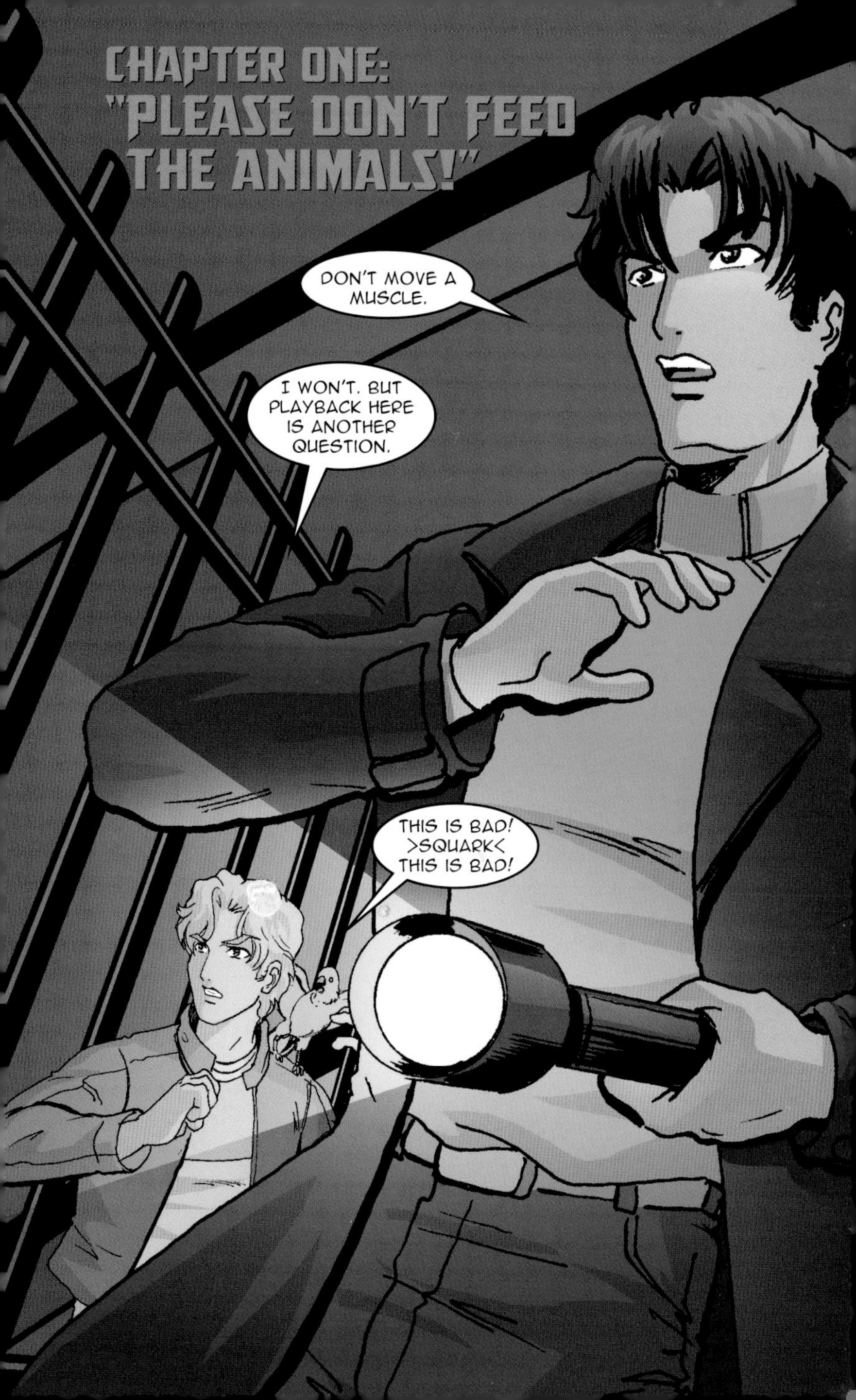
CHAPTER ONE:
"PLEASE DON'T FEED THE ANIMALS!"
DON'T MOVE A MUSCLE.
I WON'T. BUT PLAYBACK HERE IS ANOTHER QUESTION.
THIS IS BAD! >SQUARK< THIS IS BAD!

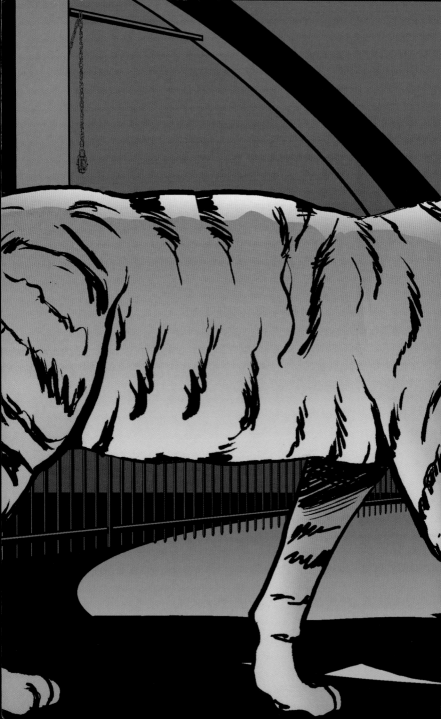

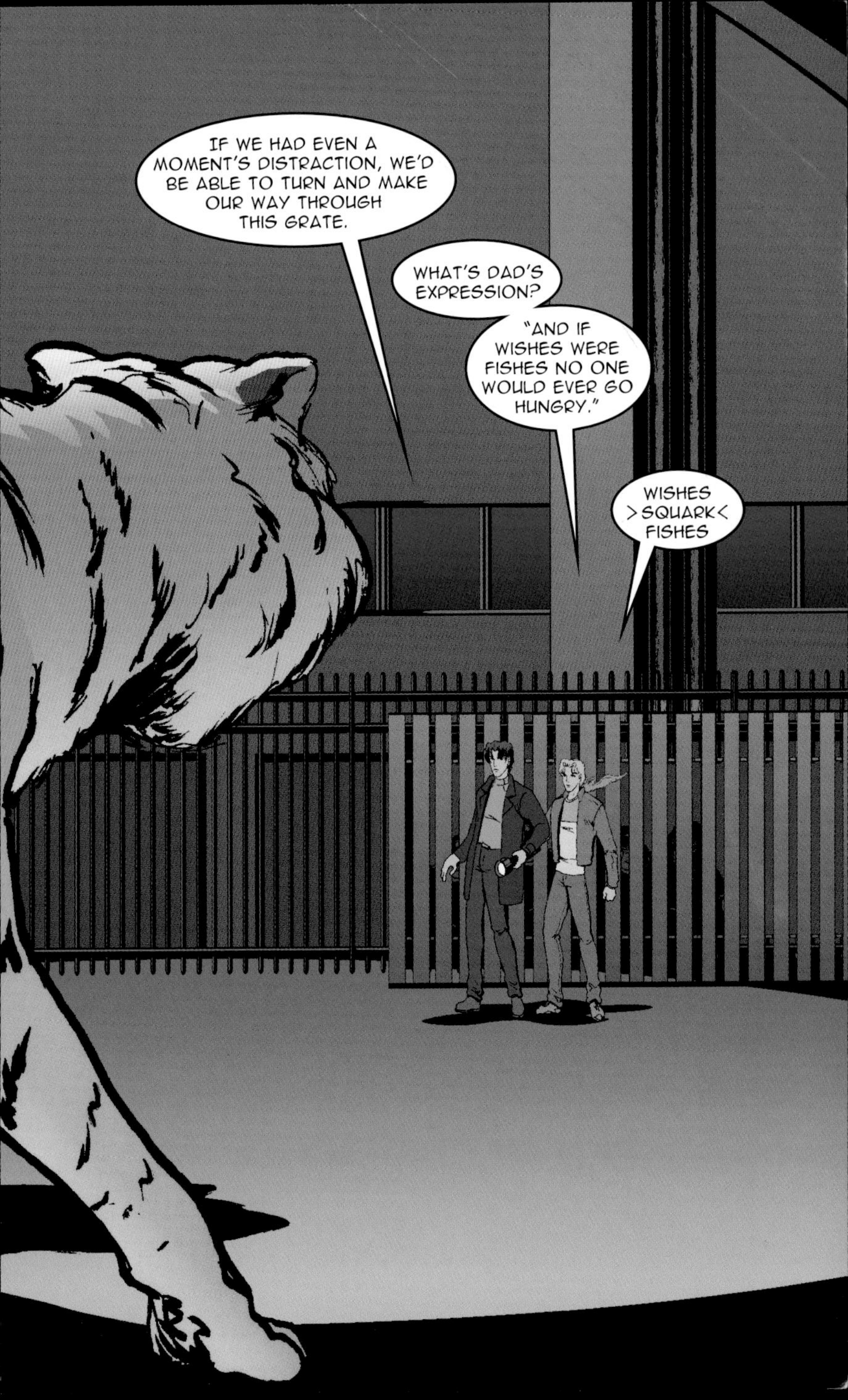
IF WE HAD EVEN A MOMENT'S DISTRACTION, WE'D BE ABLE TO TURN AND MAKE OUR WAY THROUGH THIS GRATE.
WHAT'S DAD'S EXPRESSION?
"AND IF WISHES WERE FISHES NO ONE WOULD EVER GO HUNGRY."
WISHES >SQUARK< FISHES

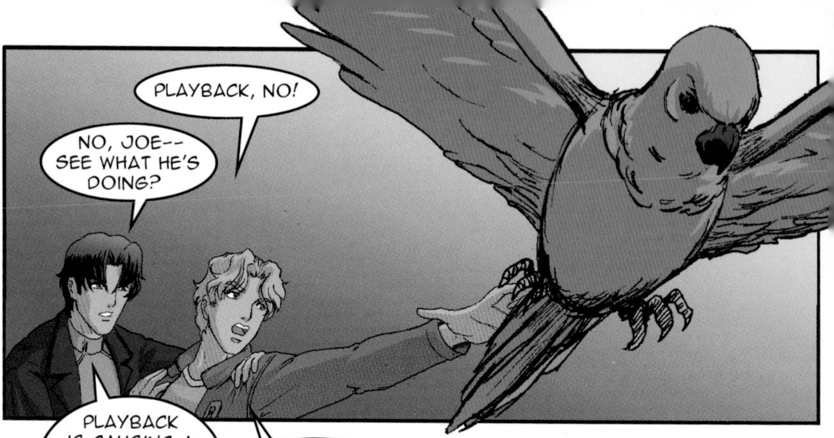
PLAYBACK, NO!
NO, JOE-- SEE WHAT HE'S DOING?
PLAYBACK IS CAUSING A DISTRACTION ALLOWING US TO ESCAPE!
THAT'S ONE SMART BIRD.

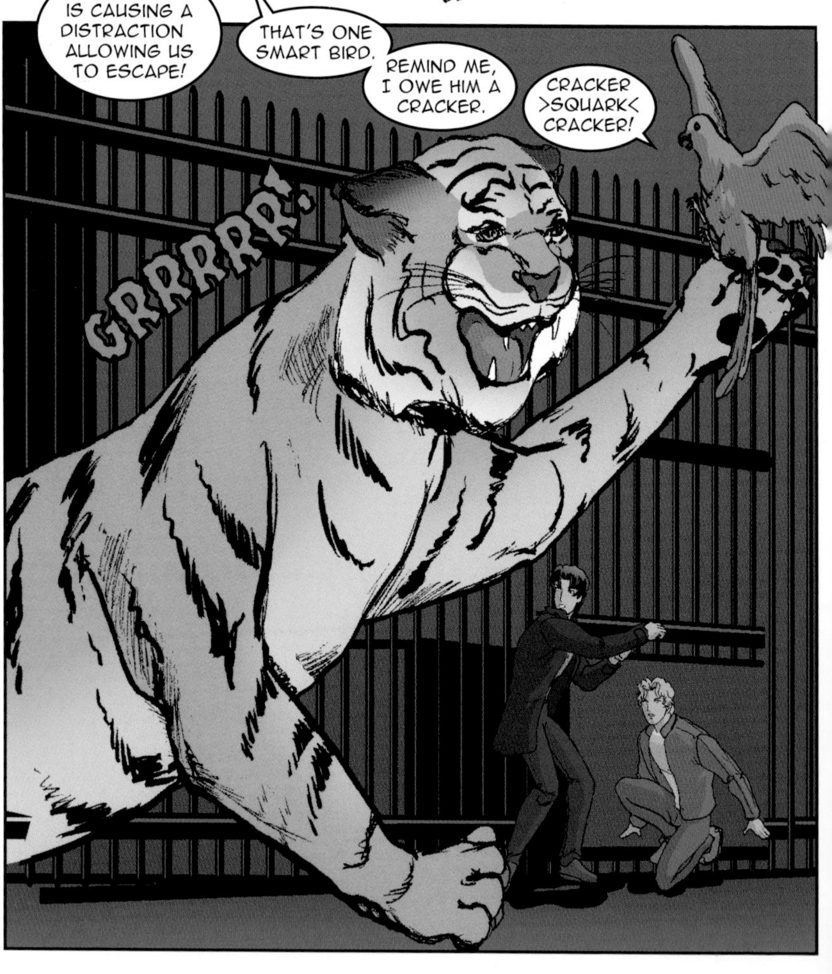
REMIND ME, I OWE HIM A CRACKER.
CRACKER >SQUARK< CRACKER!
GRRRRR!

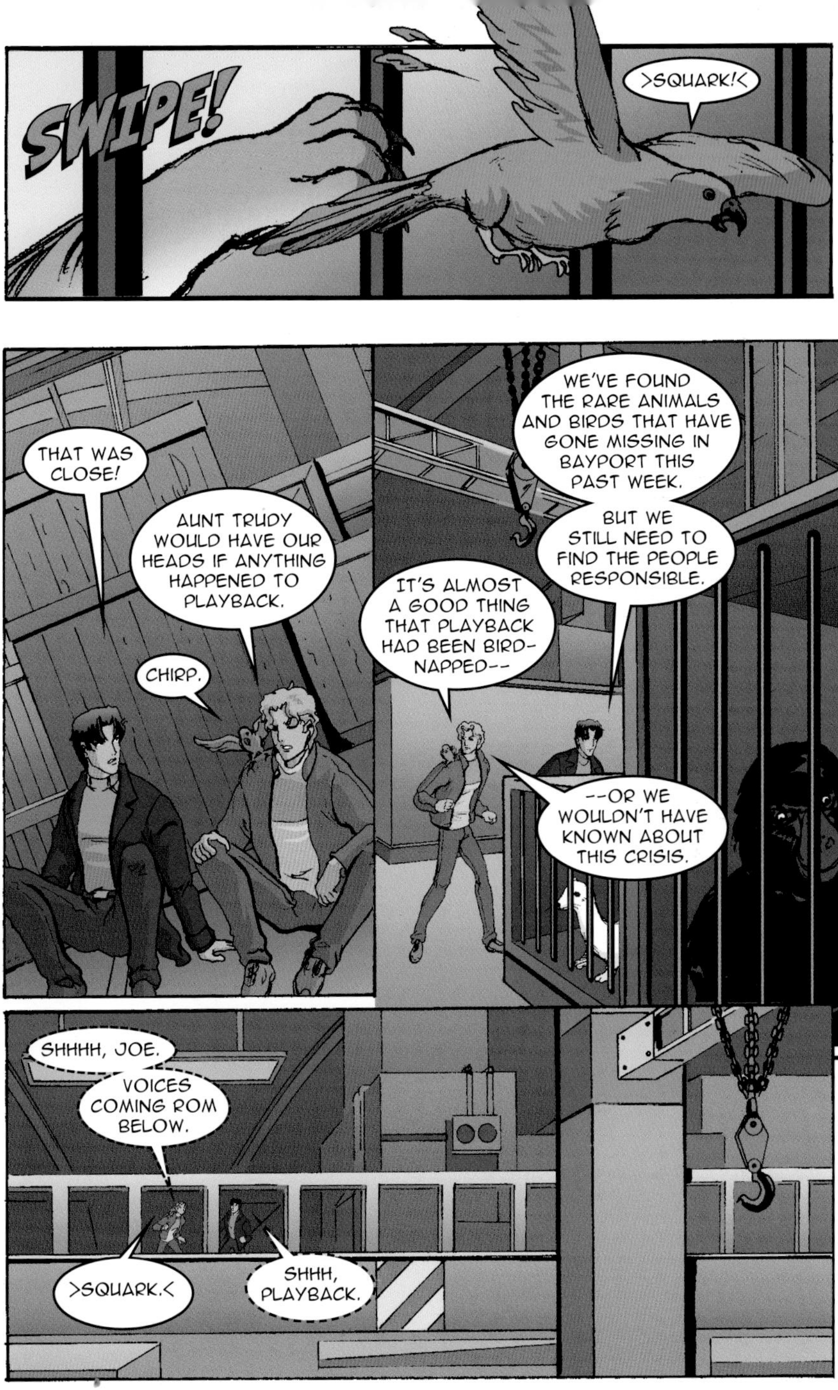
SWIPE!
>SQUARK!<
THAT WAS CLOSE!
AUNT TRUDY WOULD HAVE OUR HEADS IF ANYTHING HAPPENED TO PLAYBACK.
CHIRP.
WE'VE FOUND THE RARE ANIMALS AND BIRDS THAT HAVE GONE MISSING IN BAYPORT THIS PAST WEEK.
BUT WE STILL NEED TO FIND THE PEOPLE RESPONSIBLE.
IT'S ALMOST A GOOD THING THAT PLAYBACK HAD BEEN BIRD-NAPPED--
--OR WE WOULDN'T HAVE KNOWN ABOUT THIS CRISIS.
SHHHH, JOE.
VOICES COMING ROM BELOW.
>SQUARK.<
SHHH, PLAYBACK.

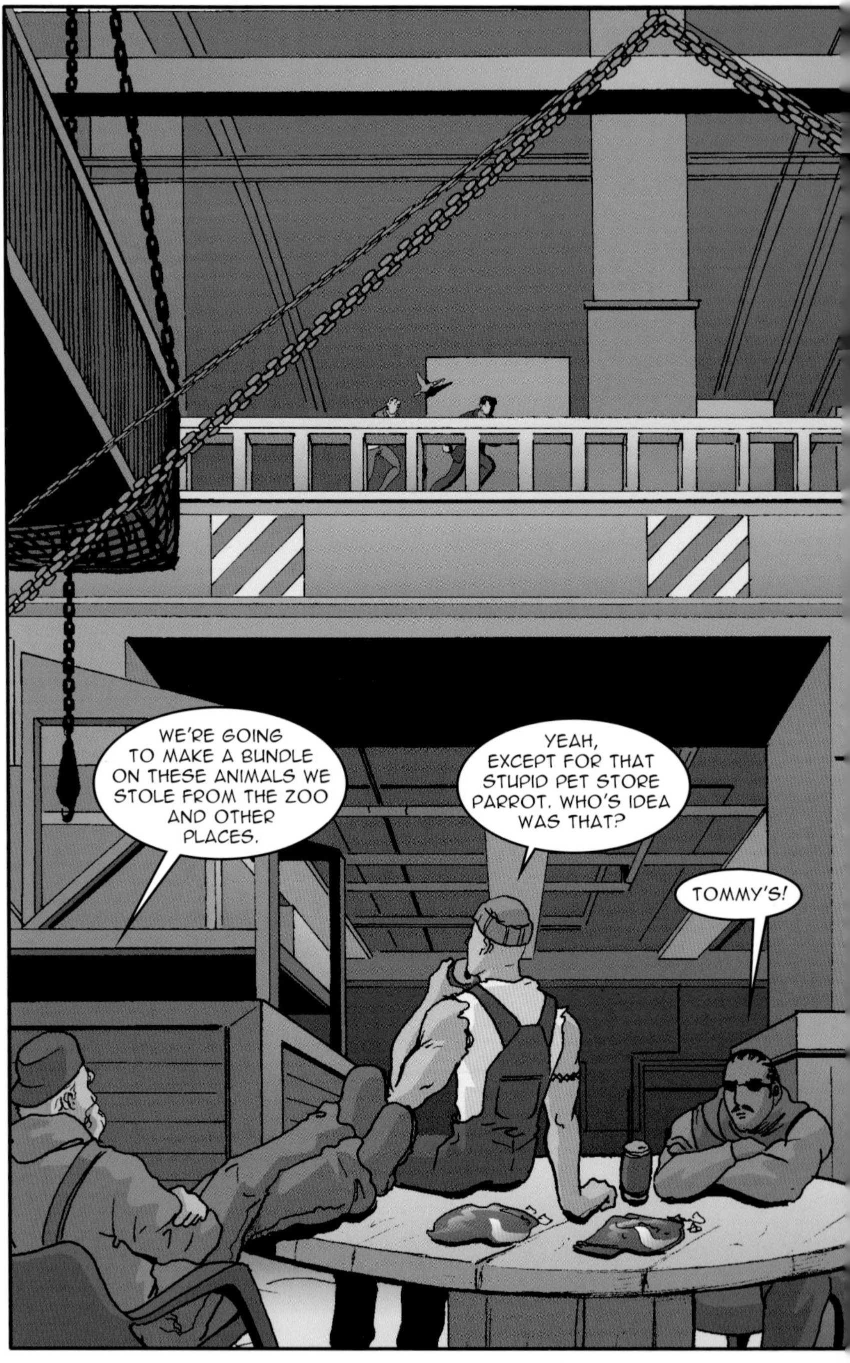
WE'RE GOING TO MAKE A BUNDLE ON THESE ANIMALS WE STOLE FROM THE ZOO AND OTHER PLACES.
YEAH, EXCEPT FOR THAT STUPID PET STORE PARROT. WHO'S IDEA WAS THAT?
TOMMY'S!

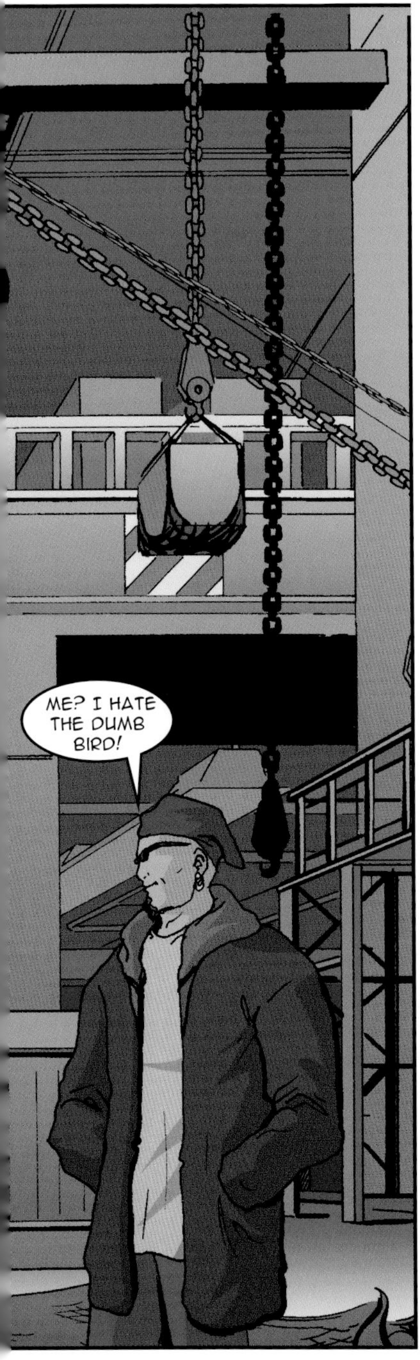
ME? I HATE THE DUMB BIRD!

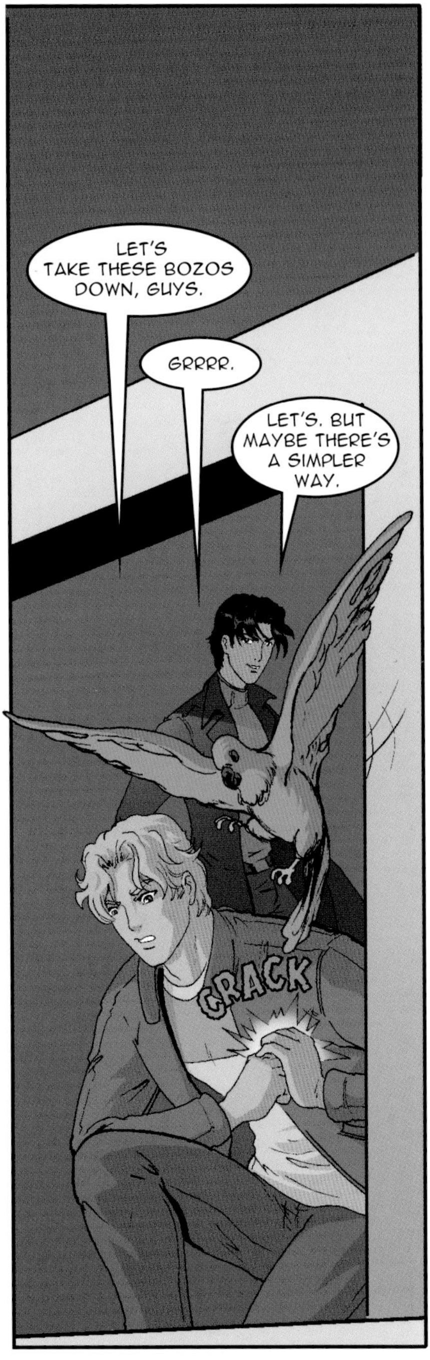
LET'S TAKE THESE BOZOS DOWN, GUYS.
GRRRR.
LET'S. BUT MAYBE THERE'S A SIMPLER WAY.
CRACK

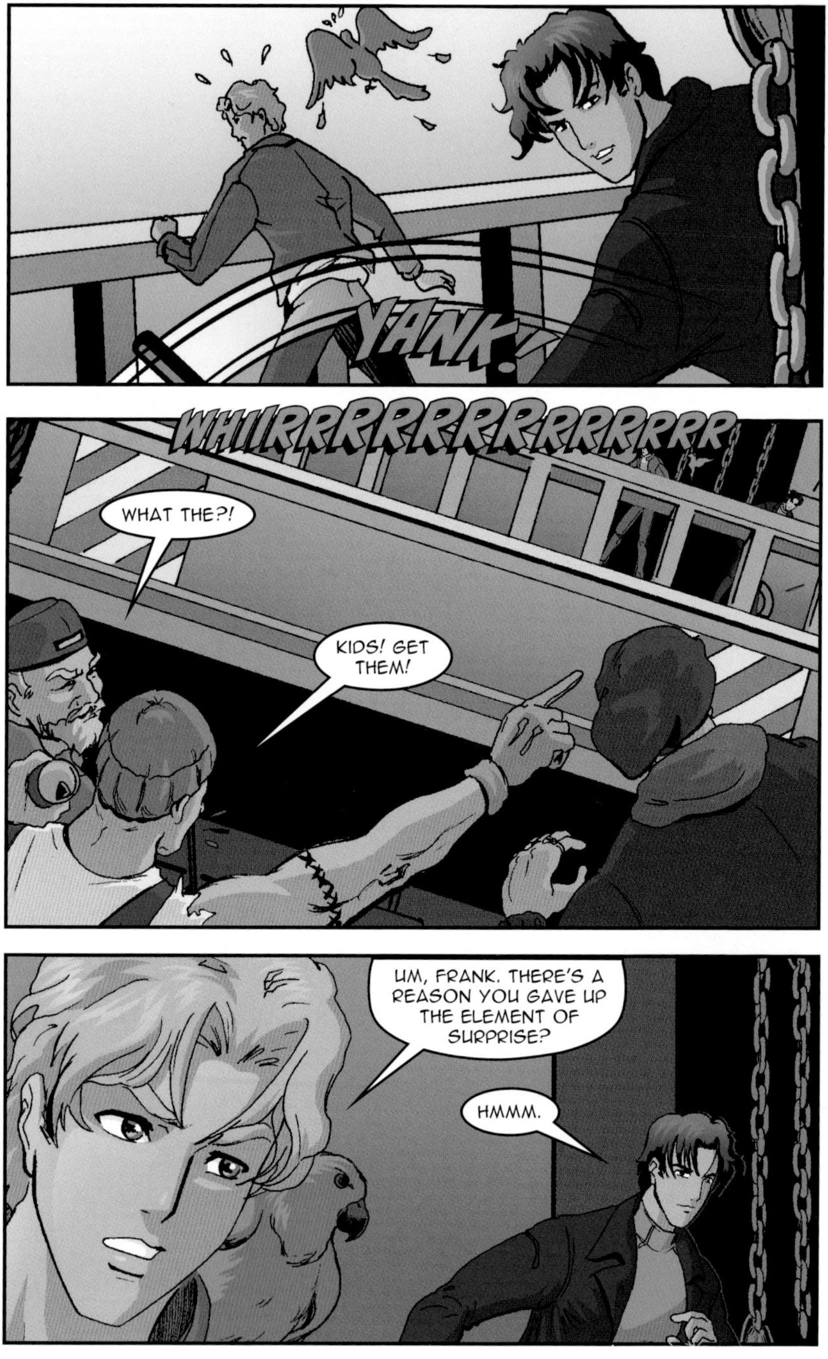
YANK!
WHIIRRRRRRRRRRRRRRR
WHAT THE?!
KIDS! GET THEM!
UM, FRANK. THERE'S A REASON YOU GAVE UP THE ELEMENT OF SURPRISE?
HMMM.

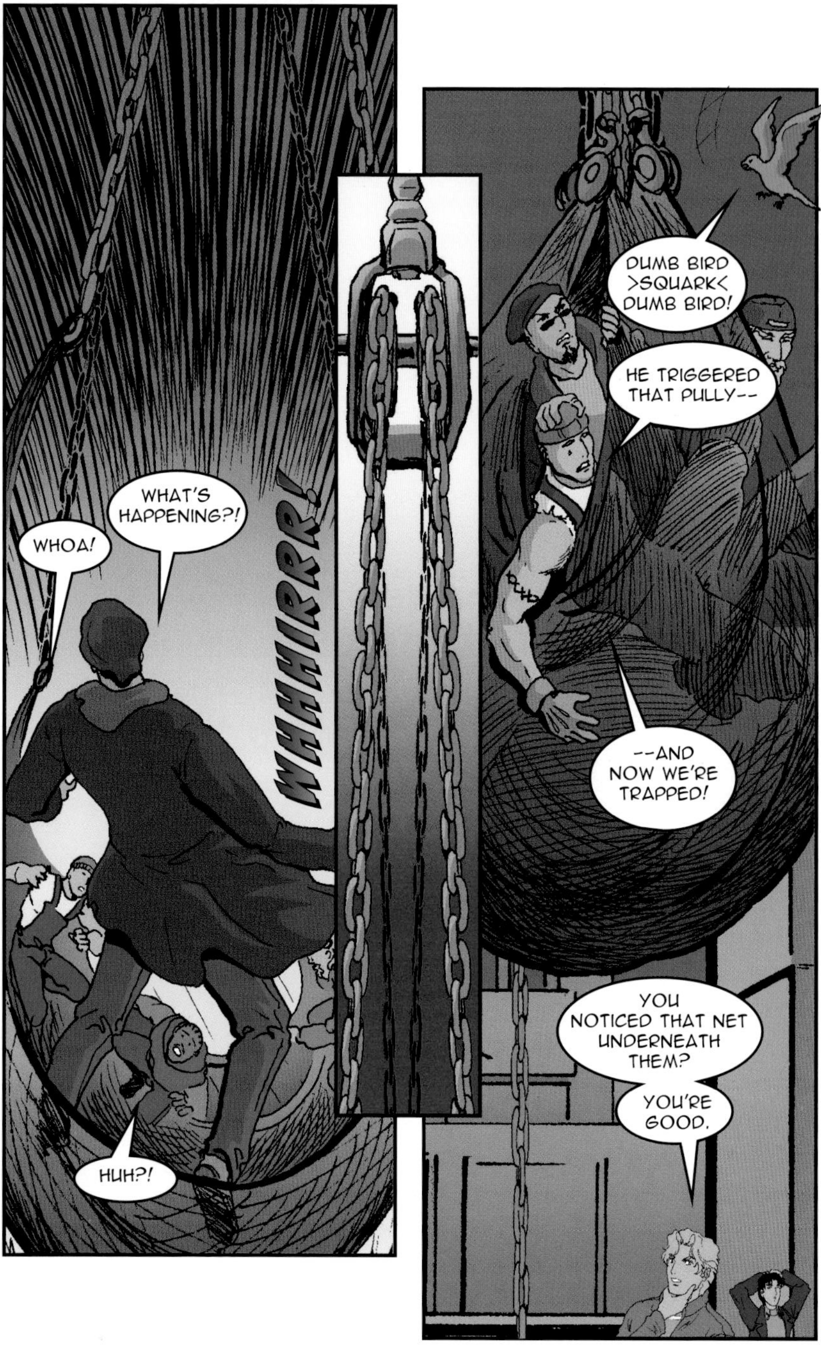
WHOA!
WHAT'S HAPPENING?!
WHHHIRRR!
HUH?!
DUMB BIRD >SQUARK< DUMB BIRD!
HE TRIGGERED THAT PULLY--
--AND NOW WE'RE TRAPPED!
YOU NOTICED THAT NET UNDERNEATH THEM?
YOU'RE GOOD.

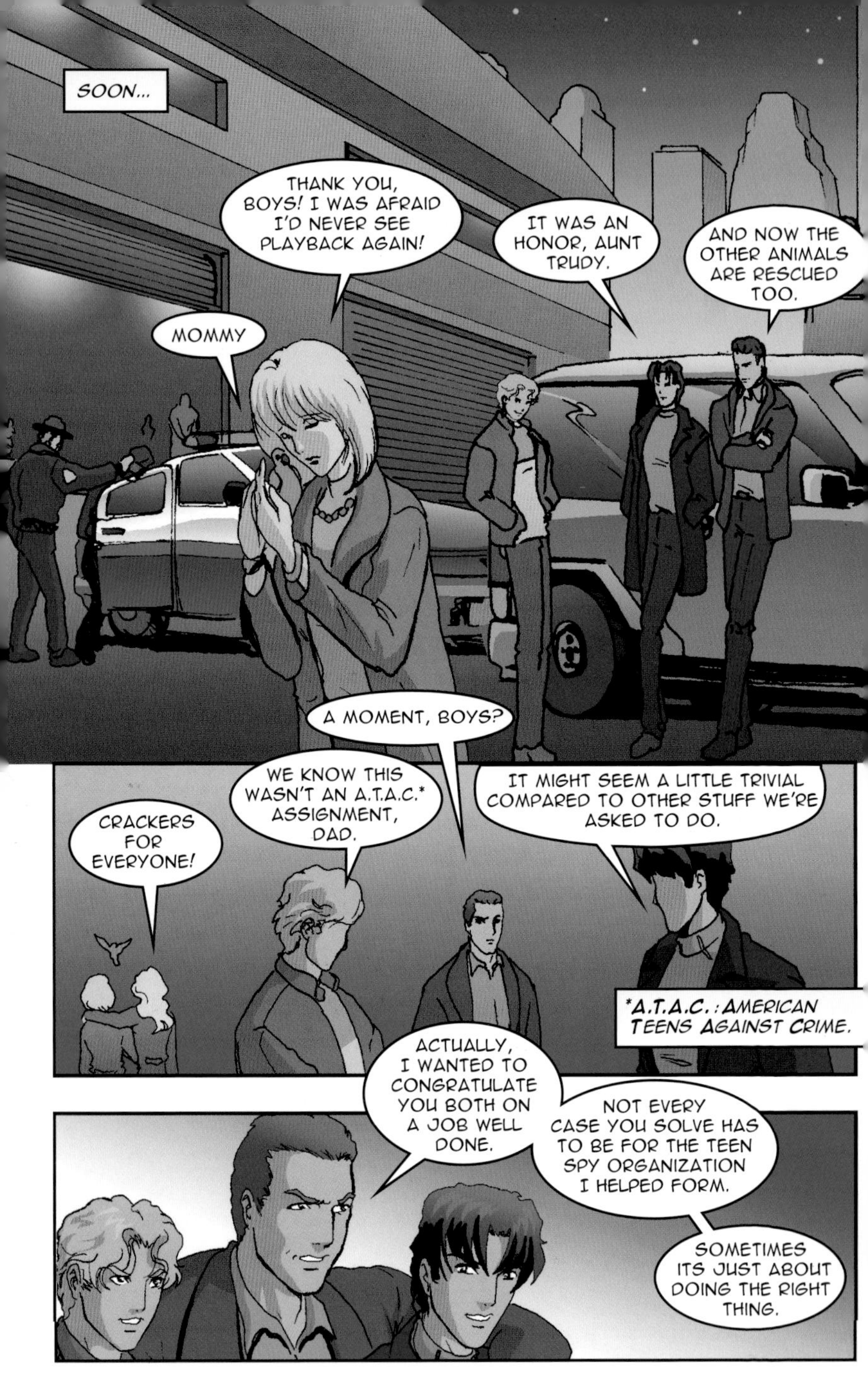
SOON...
THANK YOU, BOYS! I WAS AFRAID I'D NEVER SEE PLAYBACK AGAIN!
IT WAS AN HONOR, AUNT TRUDY.
AND NOW THE OTHER ANIMALS ARE RESCUED TOO.
MOMMY
A MOMENT, BOYS?
CRACKERS FOR EVERYONE!
WE KNOW THIS WASN'T AN A.T.A.C.* ASSIGNMENT, DAD.
IT MIGHT SEEM A LITTLE TRIVIAL COMPARED TO OTHER STUFF WE'RE ASKED TO DO.
*A.T.A.C. : AMERICAN TEENS AGAINST CRIME.
ACTUALLY, I WANTED TO CONGRATULATE YOU BOTH ON A JOB WELL DONE.
NOT EVERY CASE YOU SOLVE HAS TO BE FOR THE TEEN SPY ORGANIZATION I HELPED FORM.
SOMETIMES ITS JUST ABOUT DOING THE RIGHT THING.

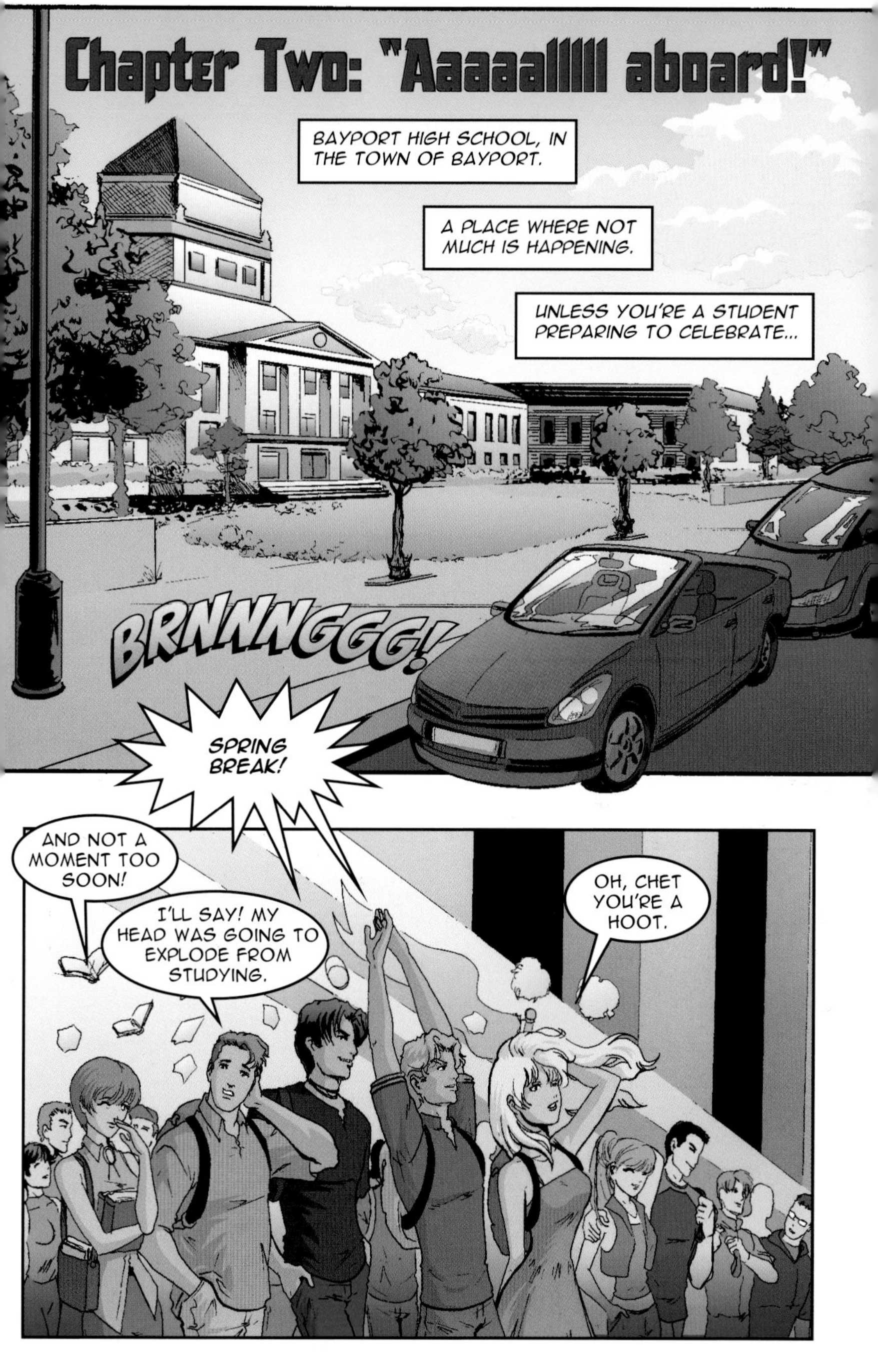
Chapter Two: "Aaaaalllll aboard!"
BAYPORT HIGH SCHOOL, IN THE TOWN OF BAYPORT.
A PLACE WHERE NOT MUCH IS HAPPENING.
UNLESS YOU'RE A STUDENT PREPARING TO CELEBRATE...
BRNNNGGG!
SPRING BREAK!
AND NOT A MOMENT TOO SOON!
I'LL SAY! MY HEAD WAS GOING TO EXPLODE FROM STUDYING.
OH, CHET YOU'RE A HOOT.

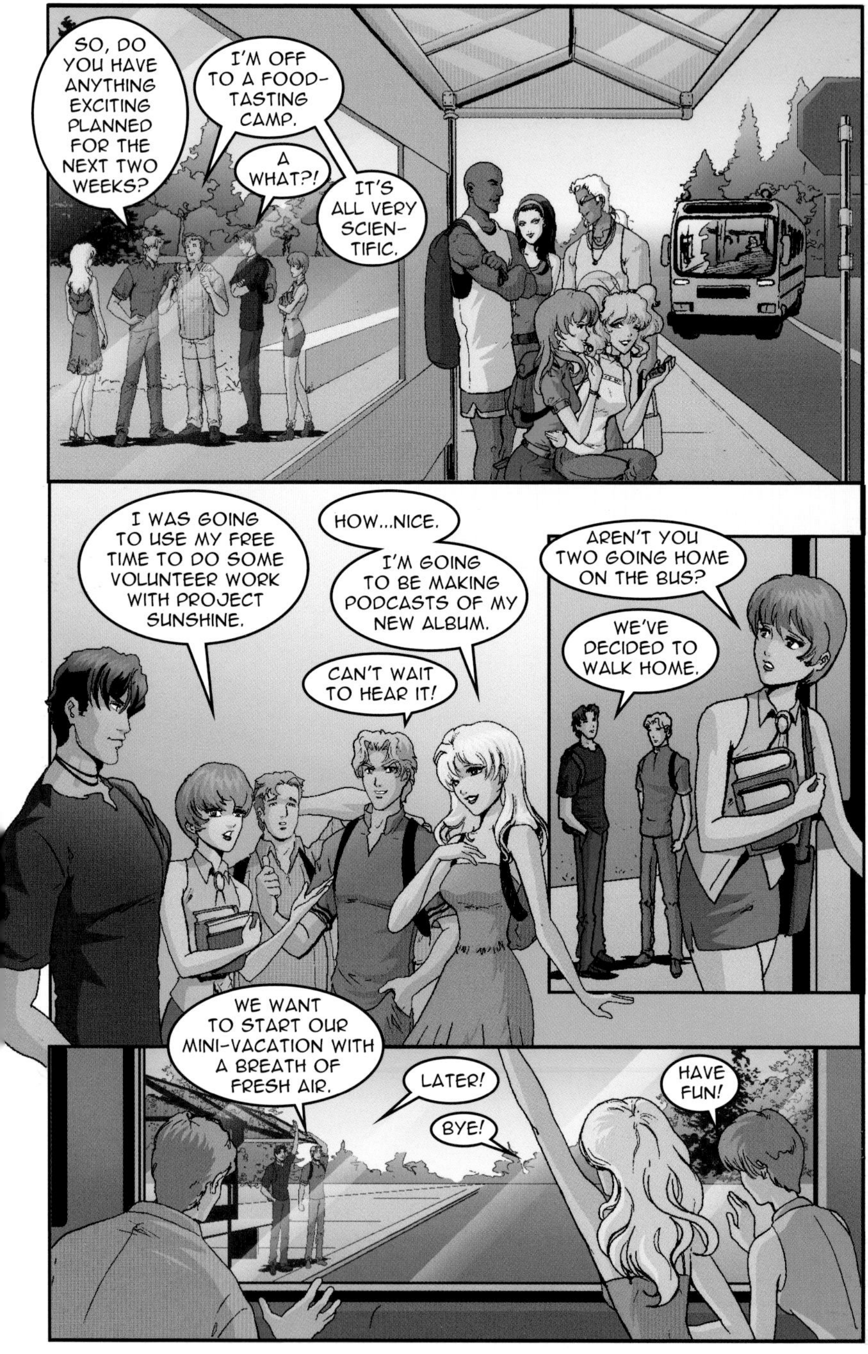
SO, DO YOU HAVE ANYTHING EXCITING PLANNED FOR THE NEXT TWO WEEKS?
I'M OFF TO A FOOD-TASTING CAMP.
A WHAT?!
IT'S ALL VERY SCIEN-TIFIC.
I WAS GOING TO USE MY FREE TIME TO DO SOME VOLUNTEER WORK WITH PROJECT SUNSHINE.
HOW...NICE.
I'M GOING TO BE MAKING PODCASTS OF MY NEW ALBUM.
CAN'T WAIT TO HEAR IT!
AREN'T YOU TWO GOING HOME ON THE BUS?
WE'VE DECIDED TO WALK HOME.
WE WANT TO START OUR MINI-VACATION WITH A BREATH OF FRESH AIR.
LATER!
BYE!
HAVE FUN!

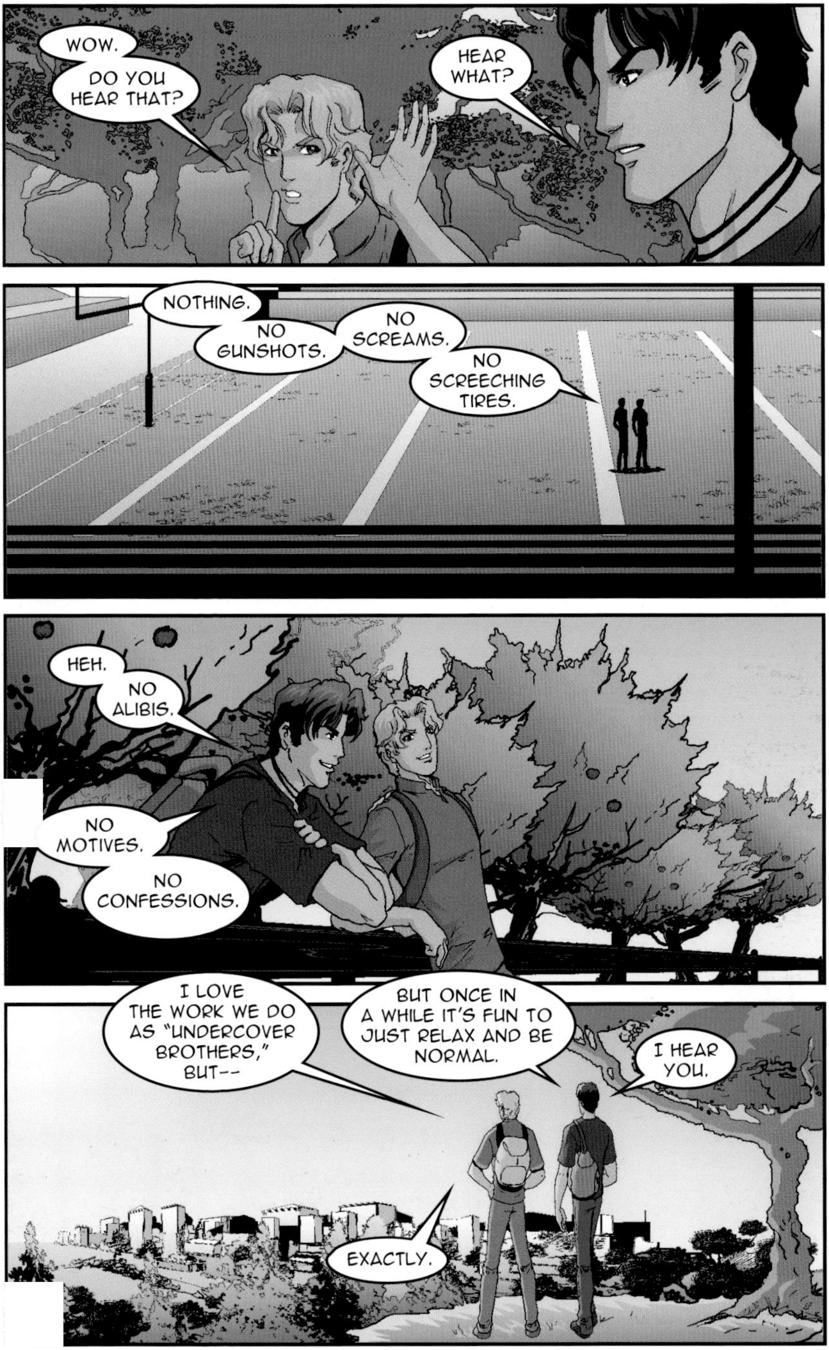
WOW.
DO YOU HEAR THAT?
HEAR WHAT?
NOTHING.
NO GUNSHOTS.
NO SCREAMS.
NO SCREECHING TIRES.
HEH.
NO ALIBIS.
NO MOTIVES.
NO CONFESSIONS.
I LOVE THE WORK WE DO AS "UNDERCOVER BROTHERS," BUT--
BUT ONCE IN A WHILE IT'S FUN TO JUST RELAX AND BE NORMAL.
I HEAR YOU.
EXACTLY.

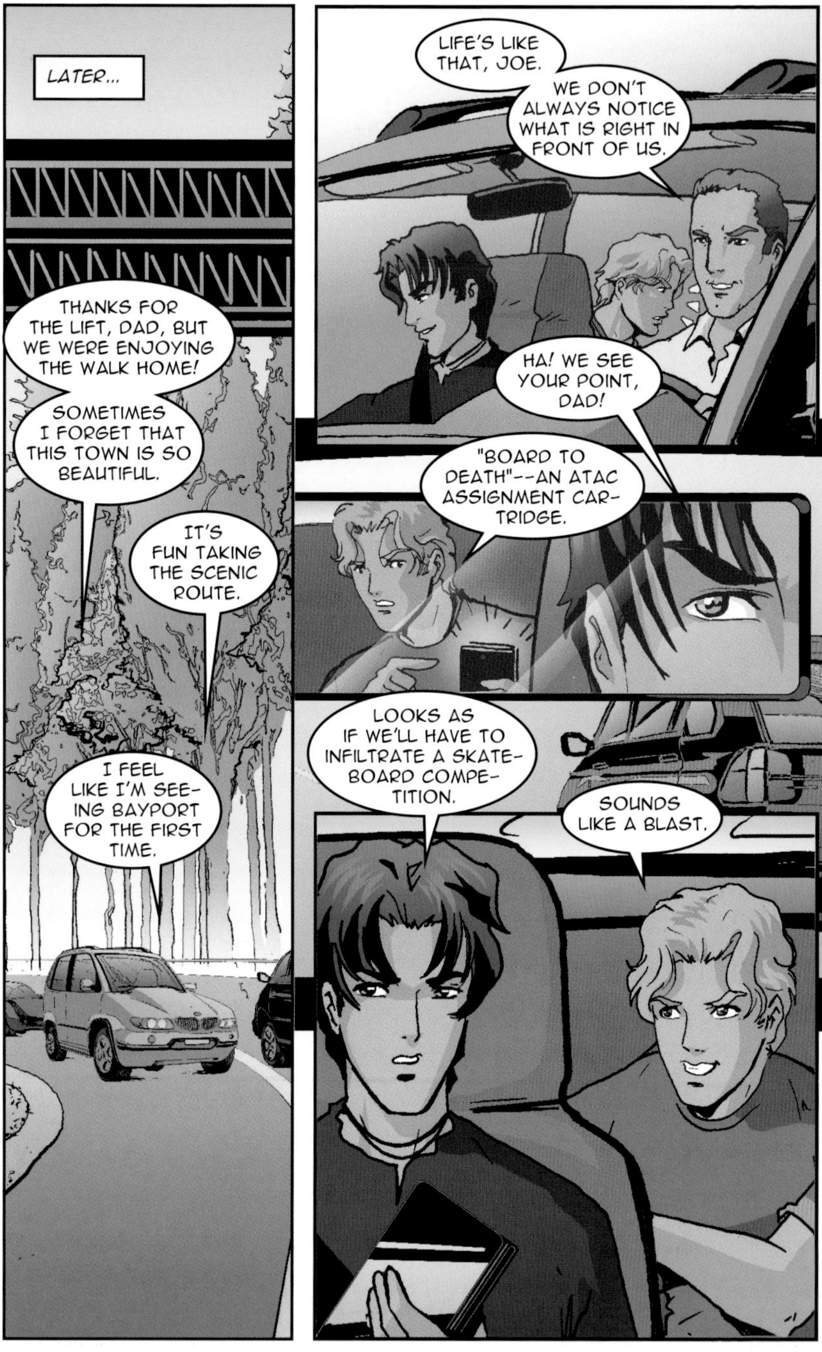
LATER...
THANKS FOR THE LIFT, DAD, BUT WE WERE ENJOYING THE WALK HOME!
SOMETIMES I FORGET THAT THIS TOWN IS SO BEAUTIFUL.
IT'S FUN TAKING THE SCENIC ROUTE.
I FEEL LIKE I'M SEE-ING BAYPORT FOR THE FIRST TIME.
LIFE'S LIKE THAT, JOE.
WE DON'T ALWAYS NOTICE WHAT IS RIGHT IN FRONT OF US.
HA! WE SEE YOUR POINT, DAD!
"BOARD TO DEATH"--AN ATAC ASSIGNMENT CAR-TRIDGE.
LOOKS AS IF WE'LL HAVE TO INFILTRATE A SKATE-BOARD COMPE-TITION.
SOUNDS LIKE A BLAST.

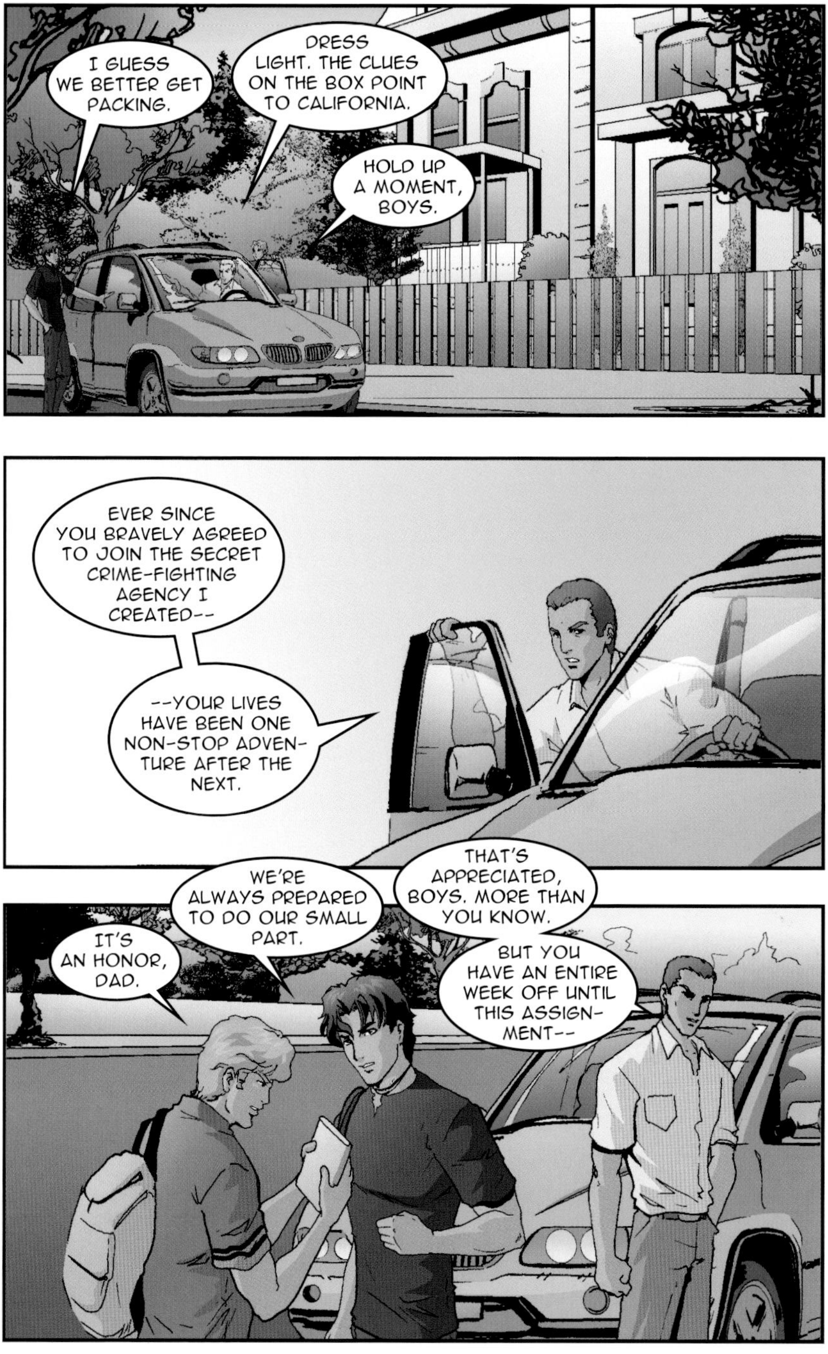
I GUESS WE BETTER GET PACKING.
DRESS LIGHT. THE CLUES ON THE BOX POINT TO CALIFORNIA.
HOLD UP A MOMENT, BOYS.
EVER SINCE YOU BRAVELY AGREED TO JOIN THE SECRET CRIME-FIGHTING AGENCY I CREATED--
--YOUR LIVES HAVE BEEN ONE NON-STOP ADVEN-TURE AFTER THE NEXT.
IT'S AN HONOR, DAD.
WE'RE ALWAYS PREPARED TO DO OUR SMALL PART.
THAT'S APPRECIATED, BOYS. MORE THAN YOU KNOW.
BUT YOU HAVE AN ENTIRE WEEK OFF UNTIL THIS ASSIGN-MENT--

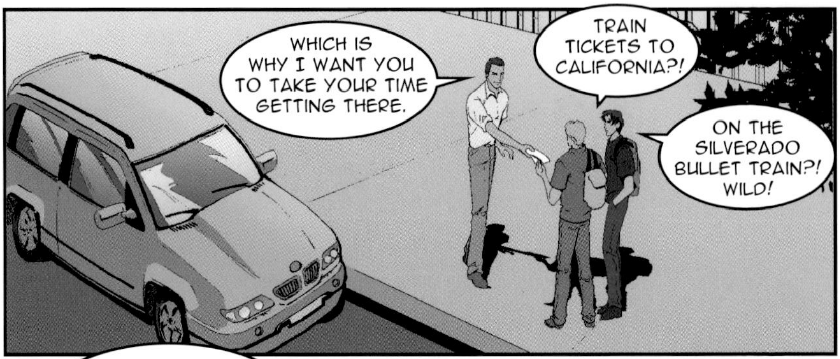
WHICH IS WHY I WANT YOU TO TAKE YOUR TIME GETTING THERE.
TRAIN TICKETS TO CALIFORNIA?!
ON THE SILVERADO BULLET TRAIN?! WILD!

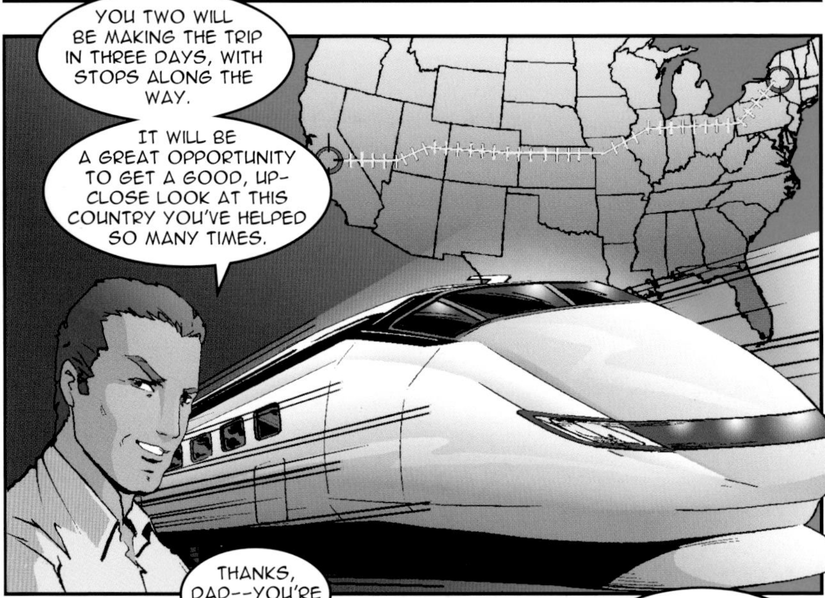
YOU TWO WILL BE MAKING THE TRIP IN THREE DAYS, WITH STOPS ALONG THE WAY.
IT WILL BE A GREAT OPPORTUNITY TO GET A GOOD, UP-CLOSE LOOK AT THIS COUNTRY YOU'VE HELPED SO MANY TIMES.

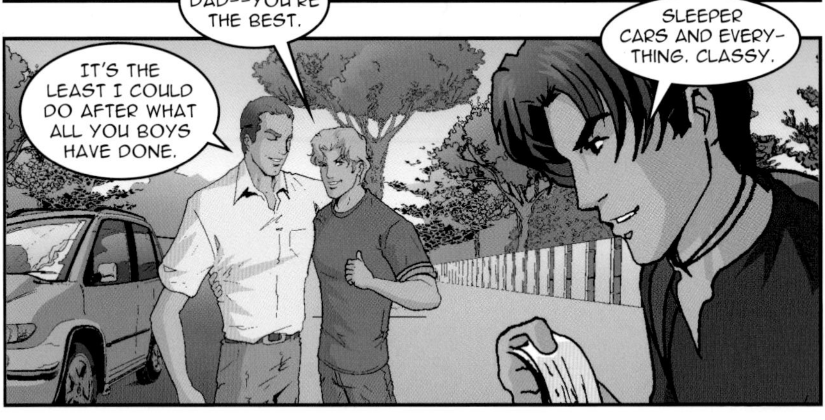
THANKS, DAD--YOU'RE THE BEST.
IT'S THE LEAST I COULD DO AFTER WHAT ALL YOU BOYS HAVE DONE.
SLEEPER CARS AND EVERY-THING. CLASSY.

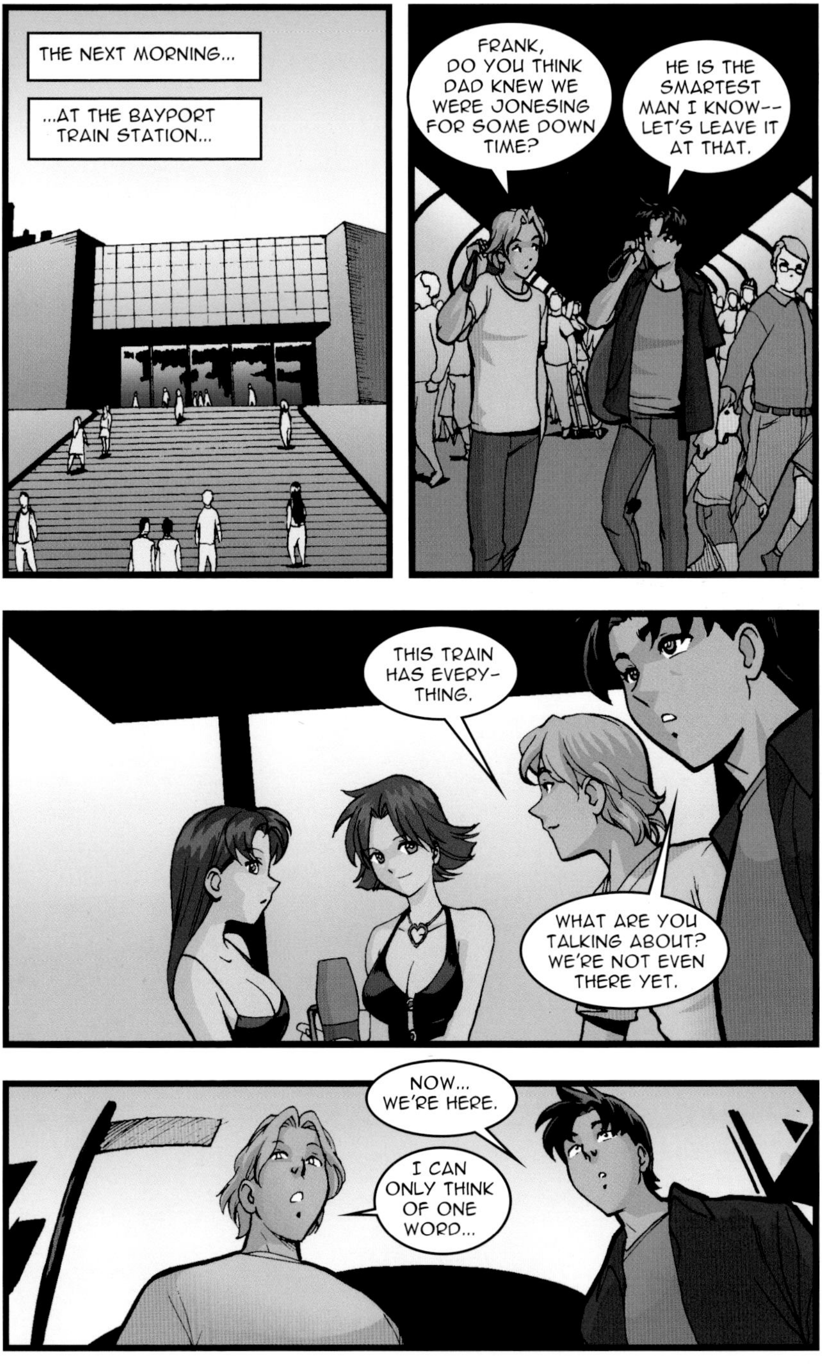
THE NEXT MORNING...
...AT THE BAYPORT TRAIN STATION...
FRANK, DO YOU THINK DAD KNEW WE WERE JONESING FOR SOME DOWN TIME?
HE IS THE SMARTEST MAN I KNOW--LET'S LEAVE IT AT THAT.
THIS TRAIN HAS EVERY-THING.
WHAT ARE YOU TALKING ABOUT? WE'RE NOT EVEN THERE YET.
NOW... WE'RE HERE.
I CAN ONLY THINK OF ONE WORD...

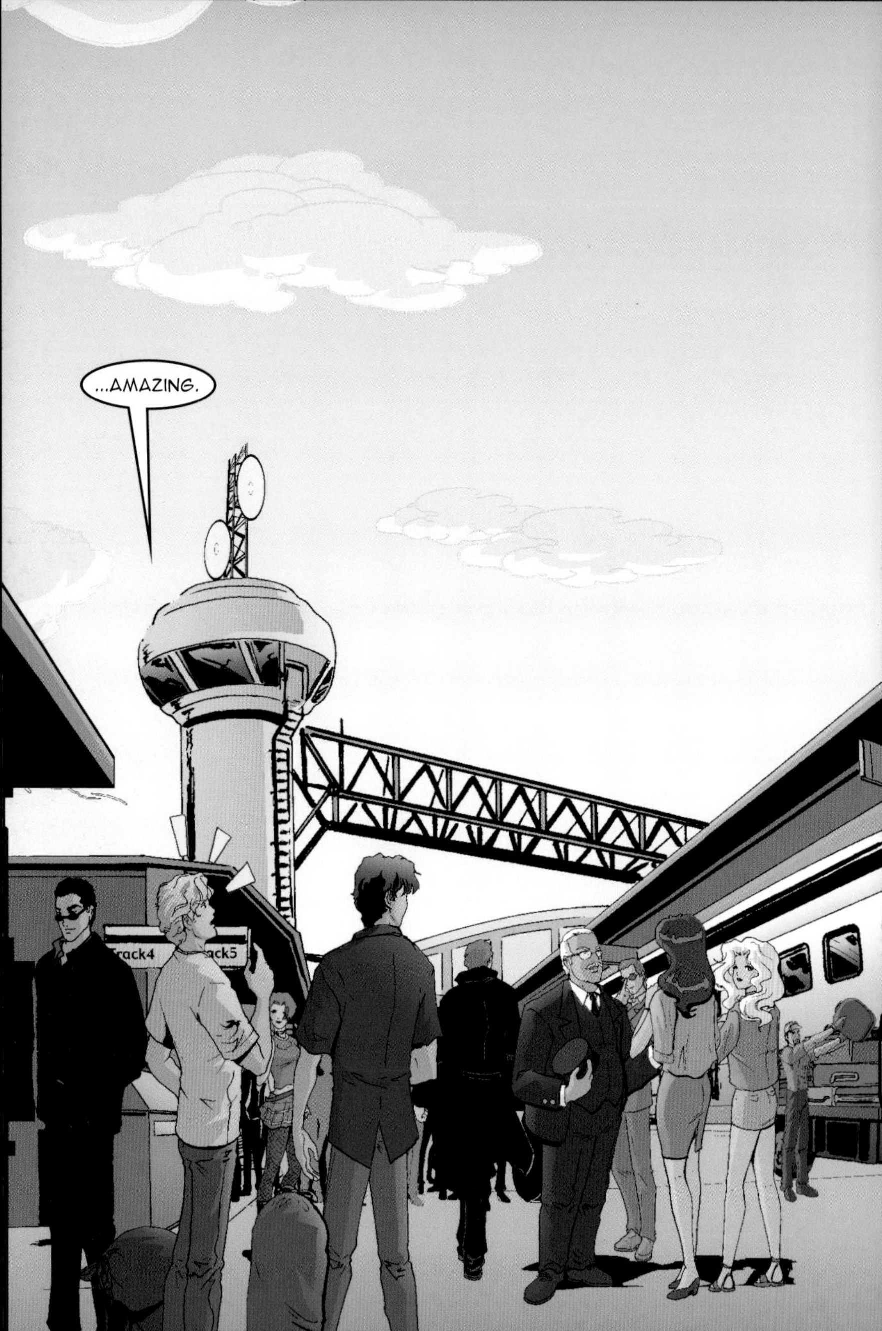
...AMAZING.
Track4
Track5

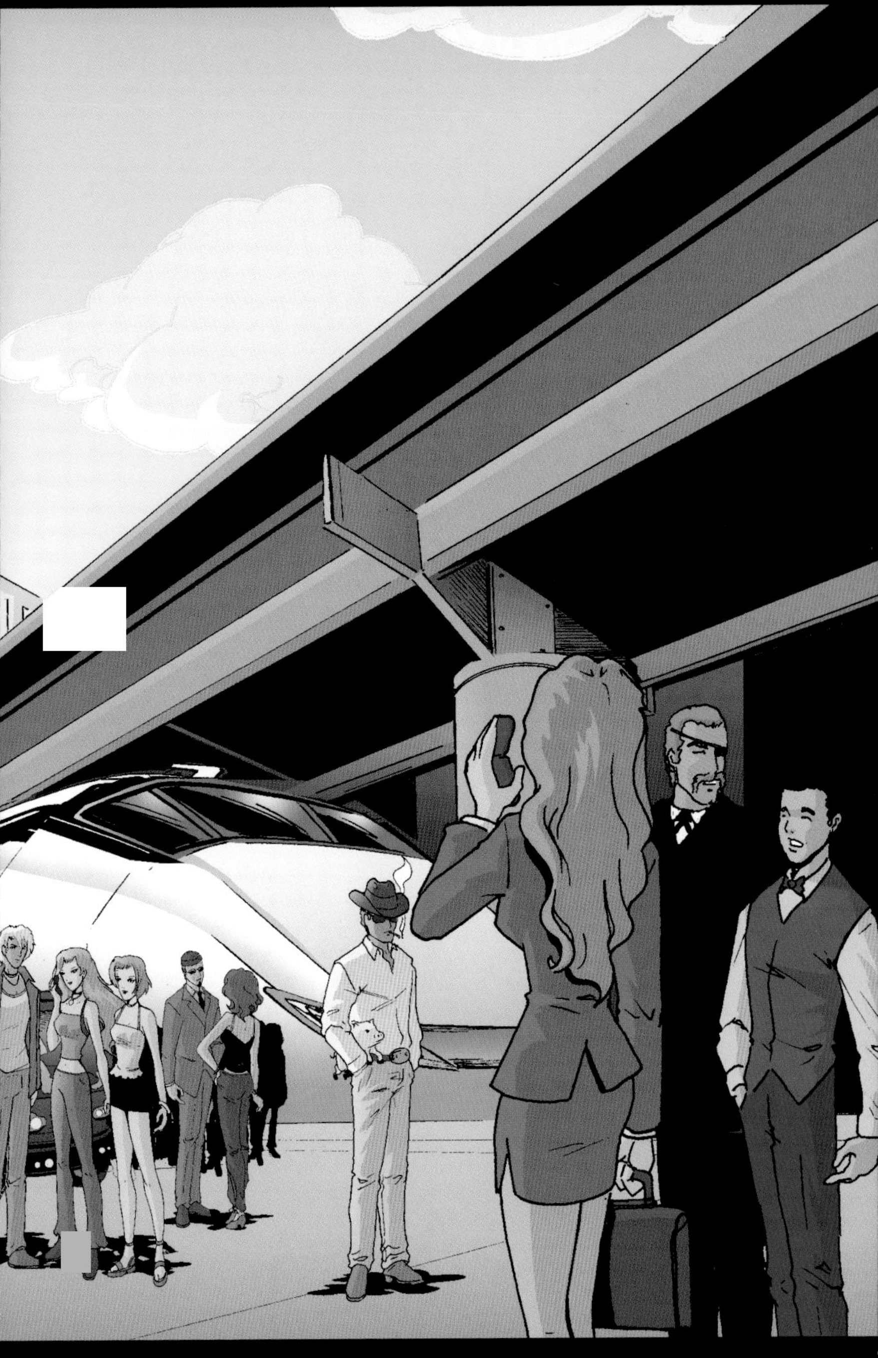

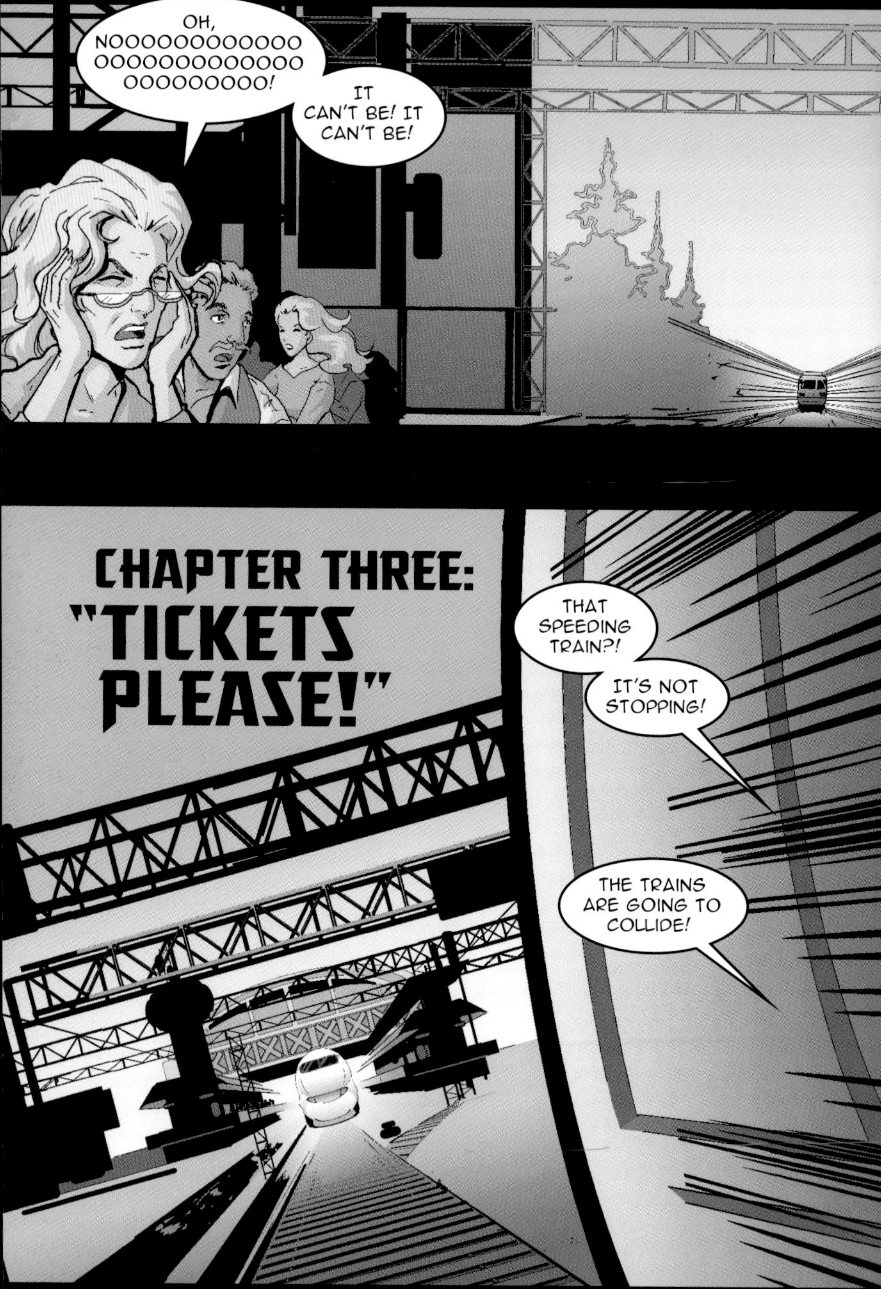

OH, NOOOOOOOOOOOOOOOOOOOOOOOOOOOOOOOOOO!
IT CAN'T BE! IT CAN'T BE!
CHAPTER THREE:
"TICKETS PLEASE!"
THAT SPEEDING TRAIN?!
IT'S NOT STOPPING!
THE TRAINS ARE GOING TO COLLIDE!

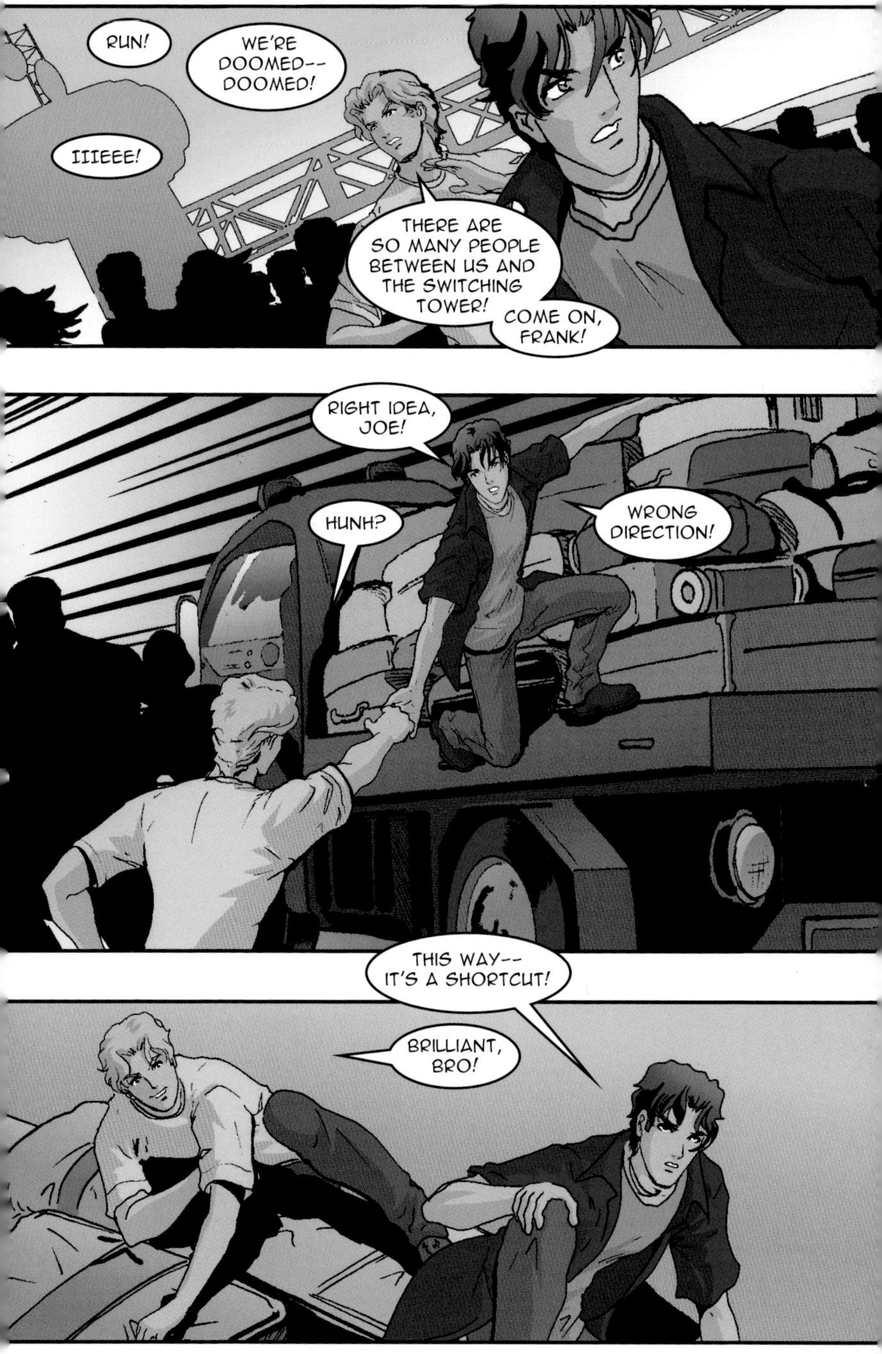
RUN!
WE'RE DOOMED-- DOOMED!
IIIEEE!
THERE ARE SO MANY PEOPLE BETWEEN US AND THE SWITCHING TOWER!
COME ON, FRANK!
RIGHT IDEA, JOE!
WRONG DIRECTION!
HUNH?
THIS WAY-- IT'S A SHORTCUT!
BRILLIANT, BRO!

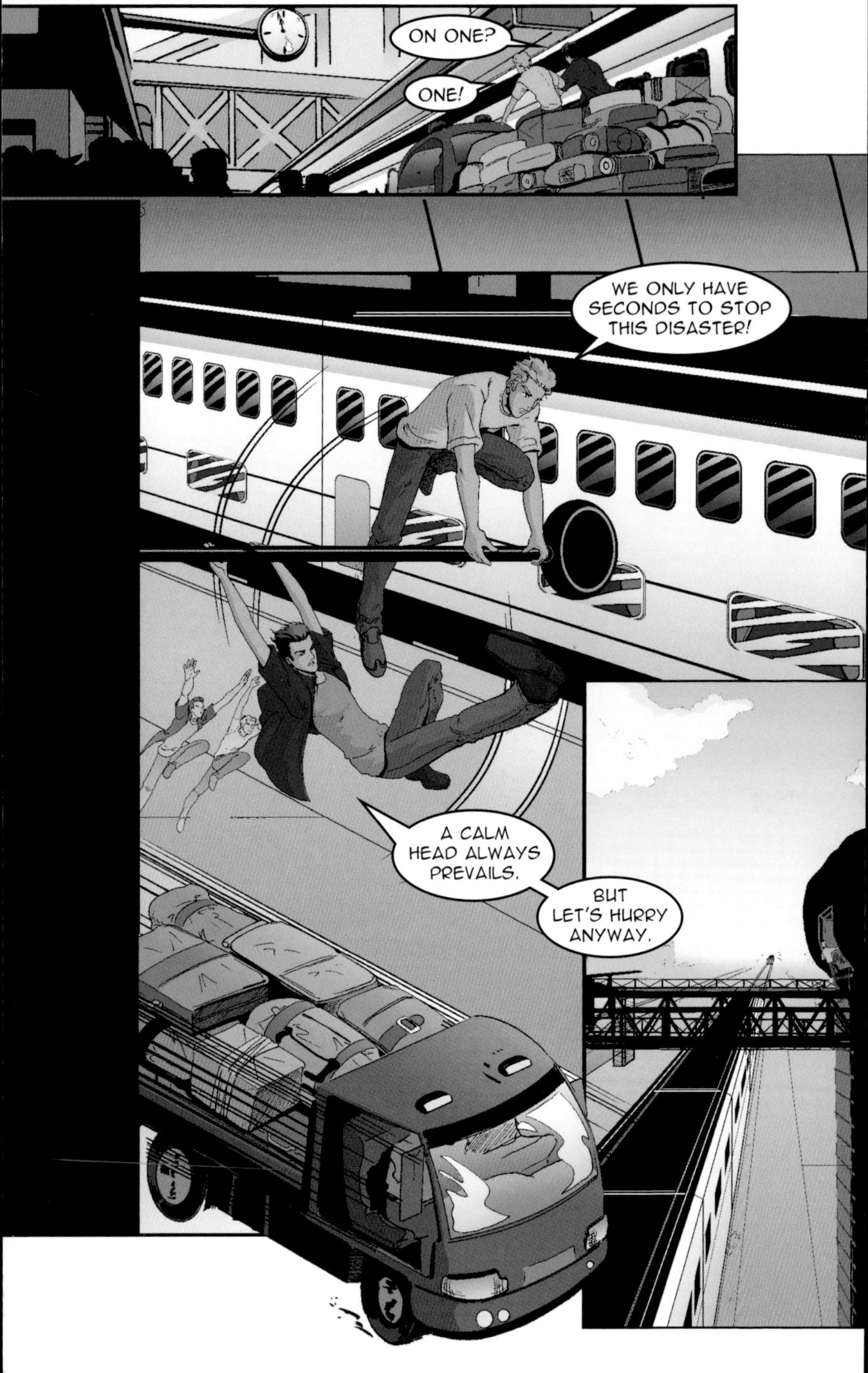
ON ONE?
ONE!
WE ONLY HAVE SECONDS TO STOP THIS DISASTER!
A CALM HEAD ALWAYS PREVAILS.
BUT LET'S HURRY ANYWAY.

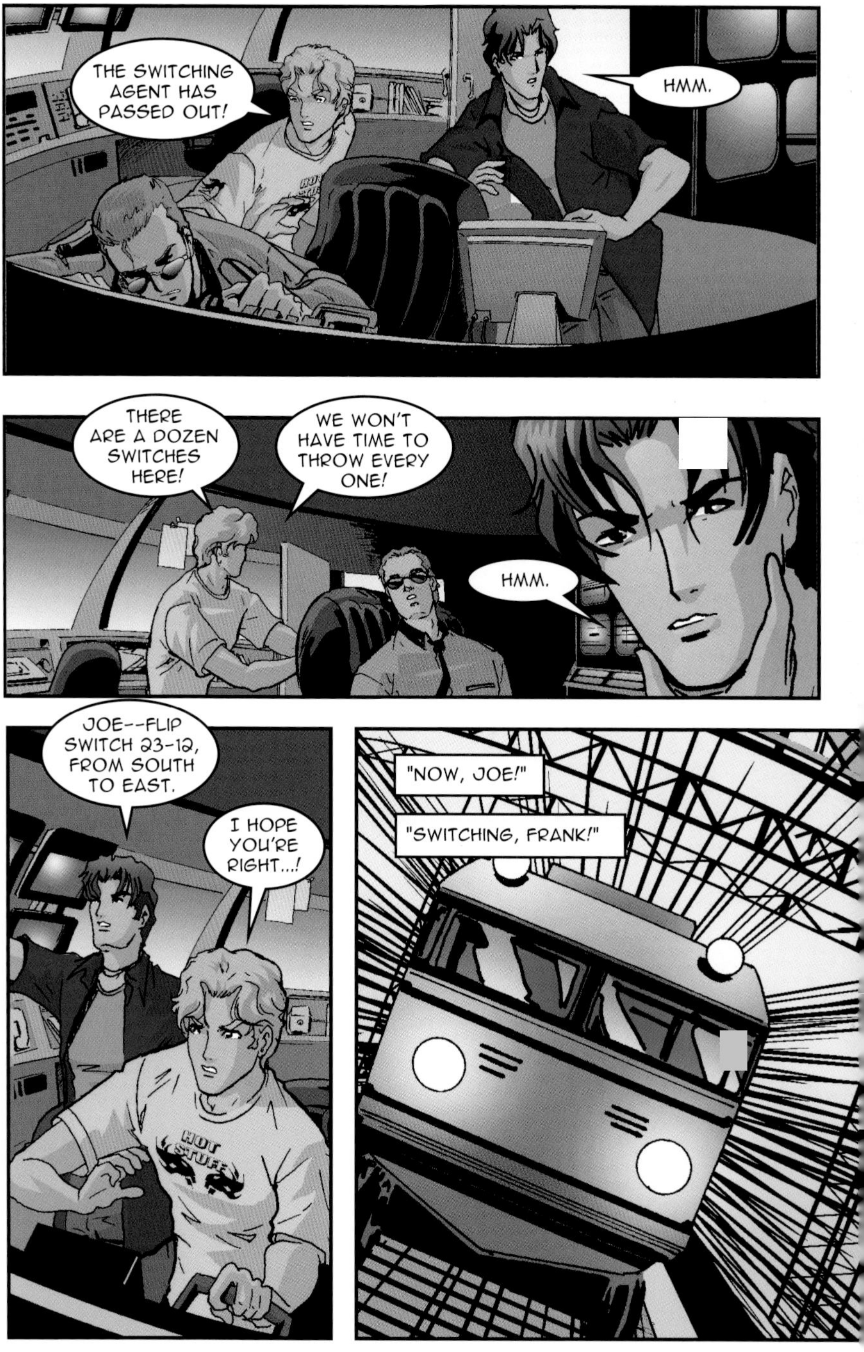
THE SWITCHING AGENT HAS PASSED OUT!
HMM.
THERE ARE A DOZEN SWITCHES HERE!
WE WON'T HAVE TIME TO THROW EVERY ONE!
HMM.
JOE--FLIP SWITCH 23-12, FROM SOUTH TO EAST.
I HOPE YOU'RE RIGHT...!
"NOW, JOE!"
"SWITCHING, FRANK!"

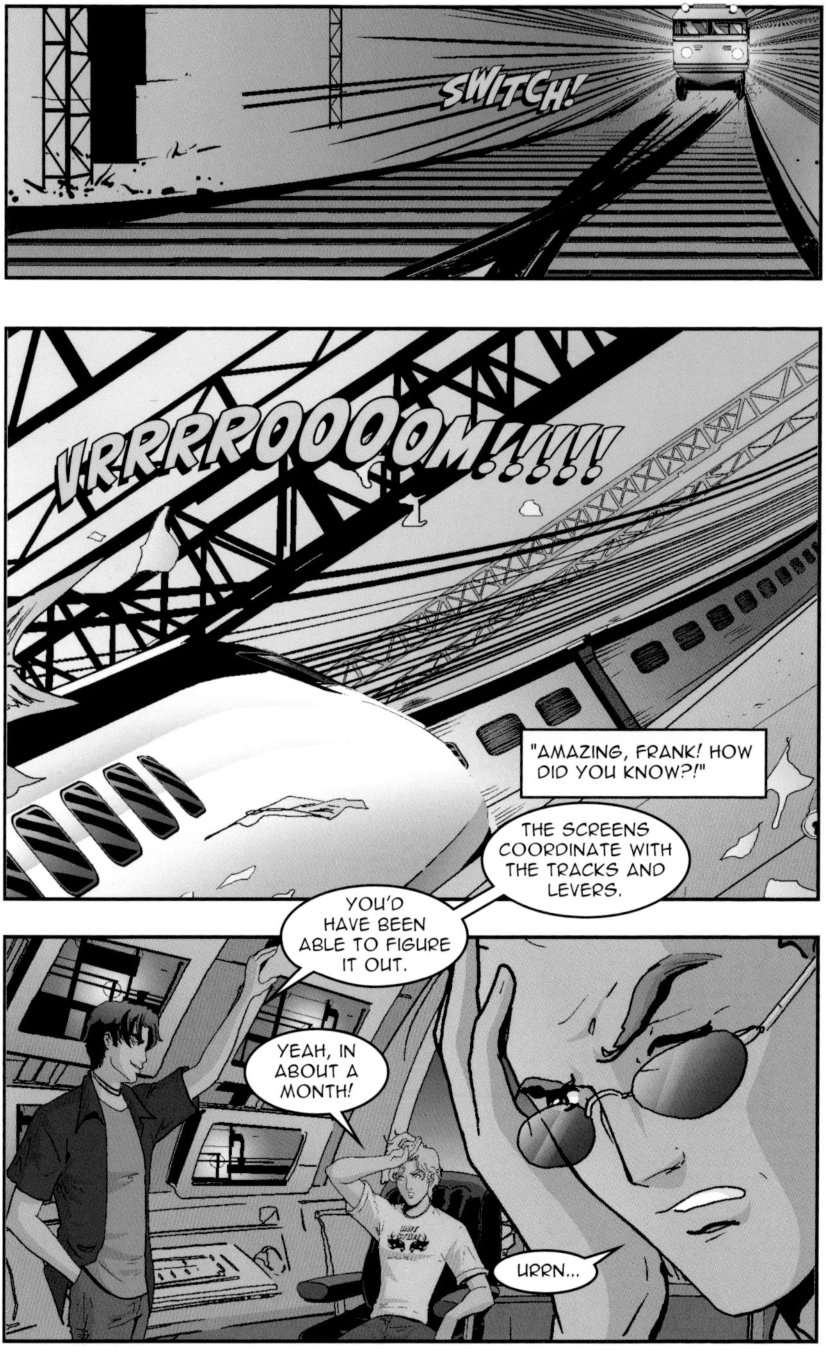
SWITCH!
VRRRROOOOOM!!!!!
"AMAZING, FRANK! HOW DID YOU KNOW?!"
THE SCREENS COORDINATE WITH THE TRACKS AND LEVERS.
YOU'D HAVE BEEN ABLE TO FIGURE IT OUT.
YEAH, IN ABOUT A MONTH!
URRN...

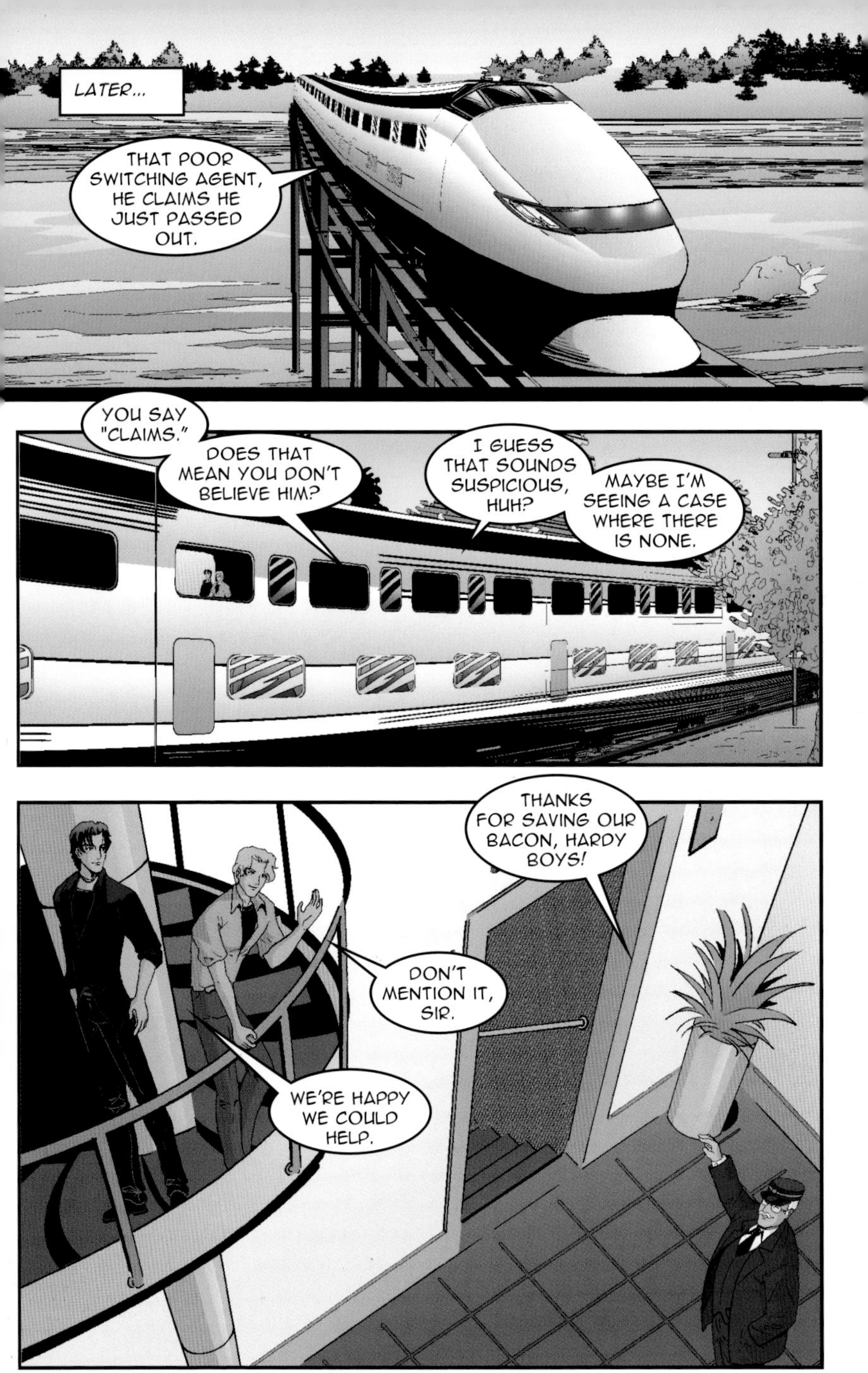
LATER...
THAT POOR SWITCHING AGENT, HE CLAIMS HE JUST PASSED OUT.
YOU SAY "CLAIMS."
DOES THAT MEAN YOU DON'T BELIEVE HIM?
I GUESS THAT SOUNDS SUSPICIOUS, HUH?
MAYBE I'M SEEING A CASE WHERE THERE IS NONE.
THANKS FOR SAVING OUR BACON, HARDY BOYS!
DON'T MENTION IT, SIR.
WE'RE HAPPY WE COULD HELP.

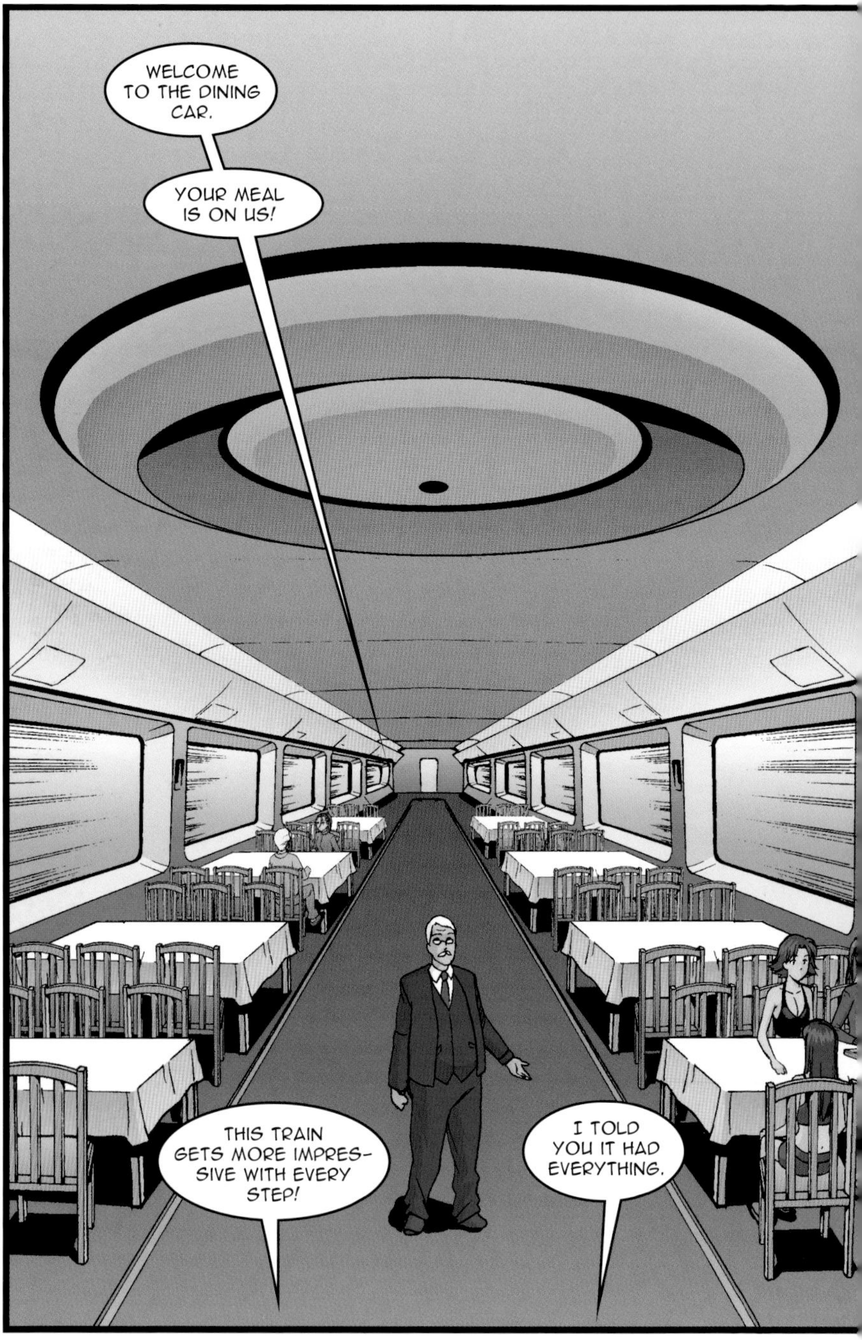
WELCOME TO THE DINING CAR.
YOUR MEAL IS ON US!
THIS TRAIN GETS MORE IMPRES-SIVE WITH EVERY STEP!
I TOLD YOU IT HAD EVERYTHING.

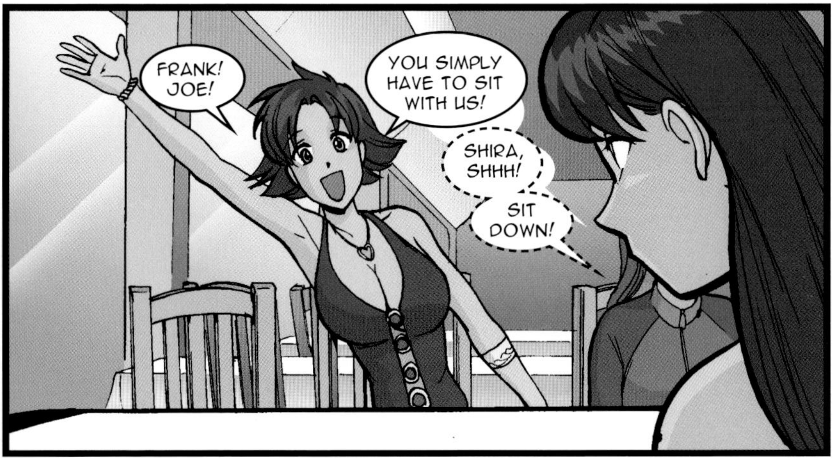
FRANK! JOE!
YOU SIMPLY HAVE TO SIT WITH US!
SHIRA, SHHH!
SIT DOWN!

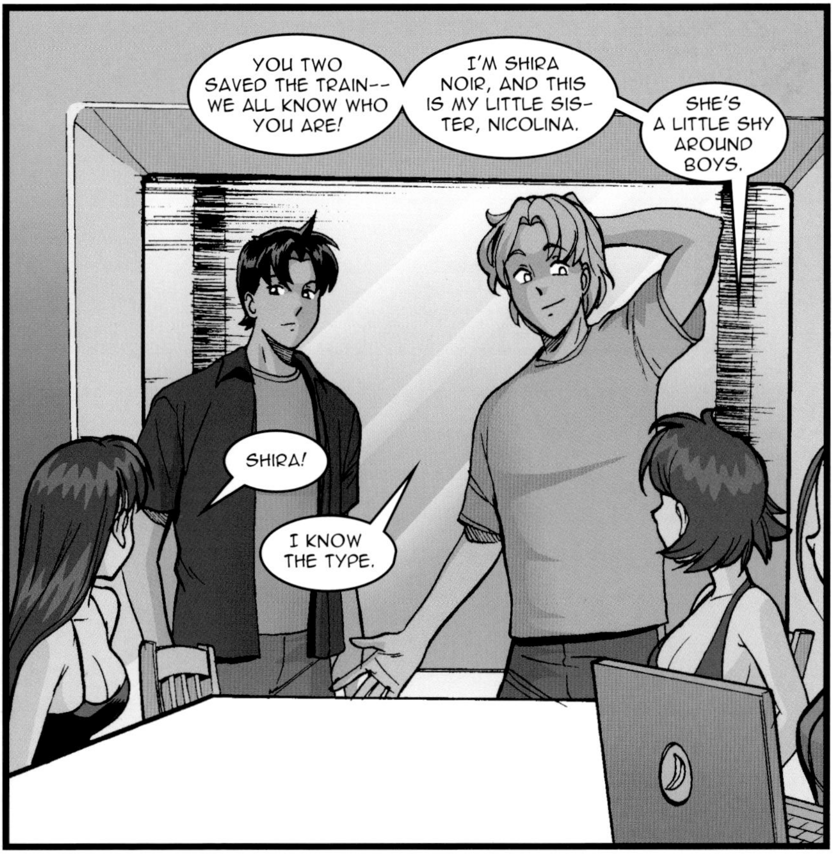
YOU TWO SAVED THE TRAIN-- WE ALL KNOW WHO YOU ARE!
I'M SHIRA NOIR, AND THIS IS MY LITTLE SIS-TER, NICOLINA.
SHE'S A LITTLE SHY AROUND BOYS.
SHIRA!
I KNOW THE TYPE.

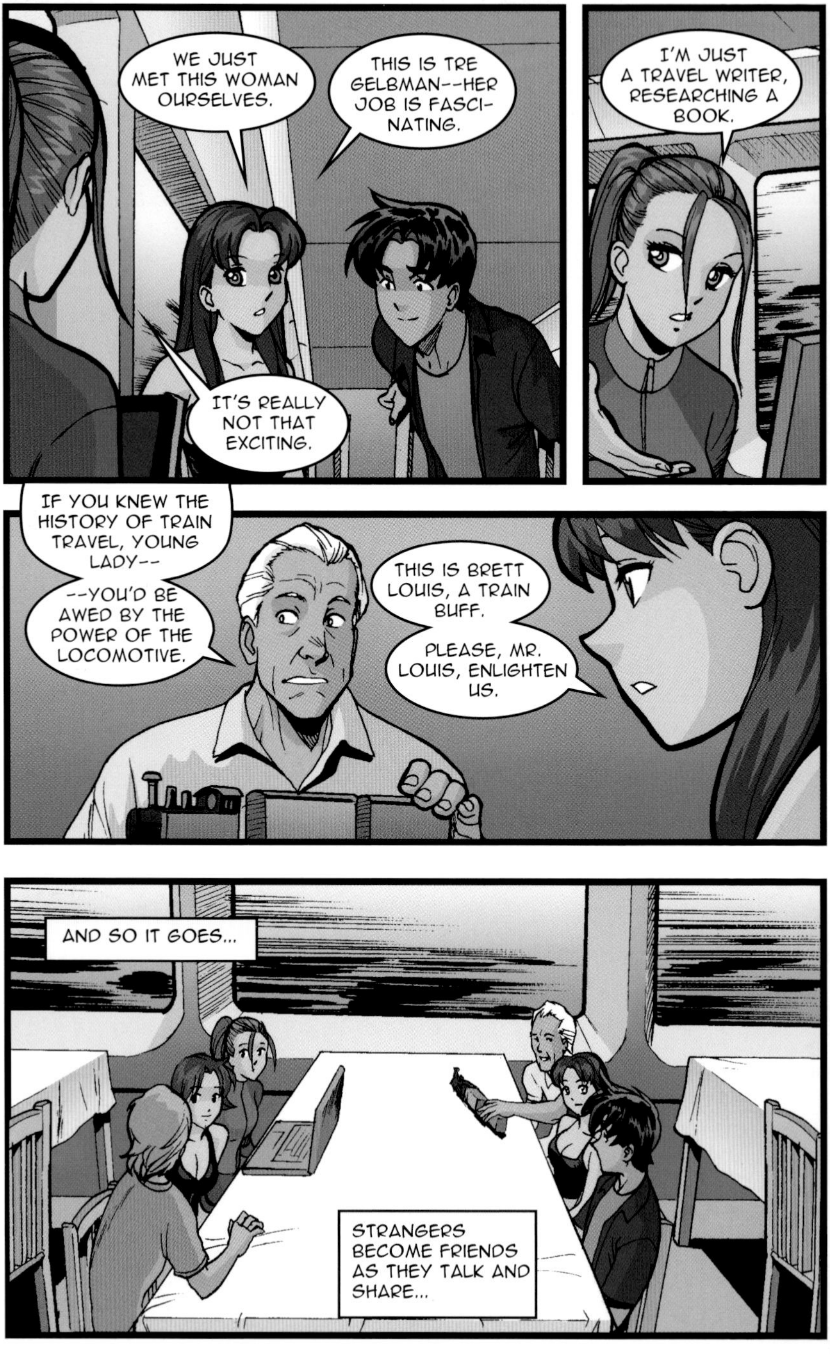
WE JUST MET THIS WOMAN OURSELVES.
THIS IS TRE GELBMAN--HER JOB IS FASCI-NATING.
IT'S REALLY NOT THAT EXCITING.
I'M JUST A TRAVEL WRITER, RESEARCHING A BOOK.
IF YOU KNEW THE HISTORY OF TRAIN TRAVEL, YOUNG LADY--
--YOU'D BE AWED BY THE POWER OF THE LOCOMOTIVE.
THIS IS BRETT LOUIS, A TRAIN BUFF.
PLEASE, MR. LOUIS, ENLIGHTEN US.
AND SO IT GOES...
STRANGERS BECOME FRIENDS AS THEY TALK AND SHARE...

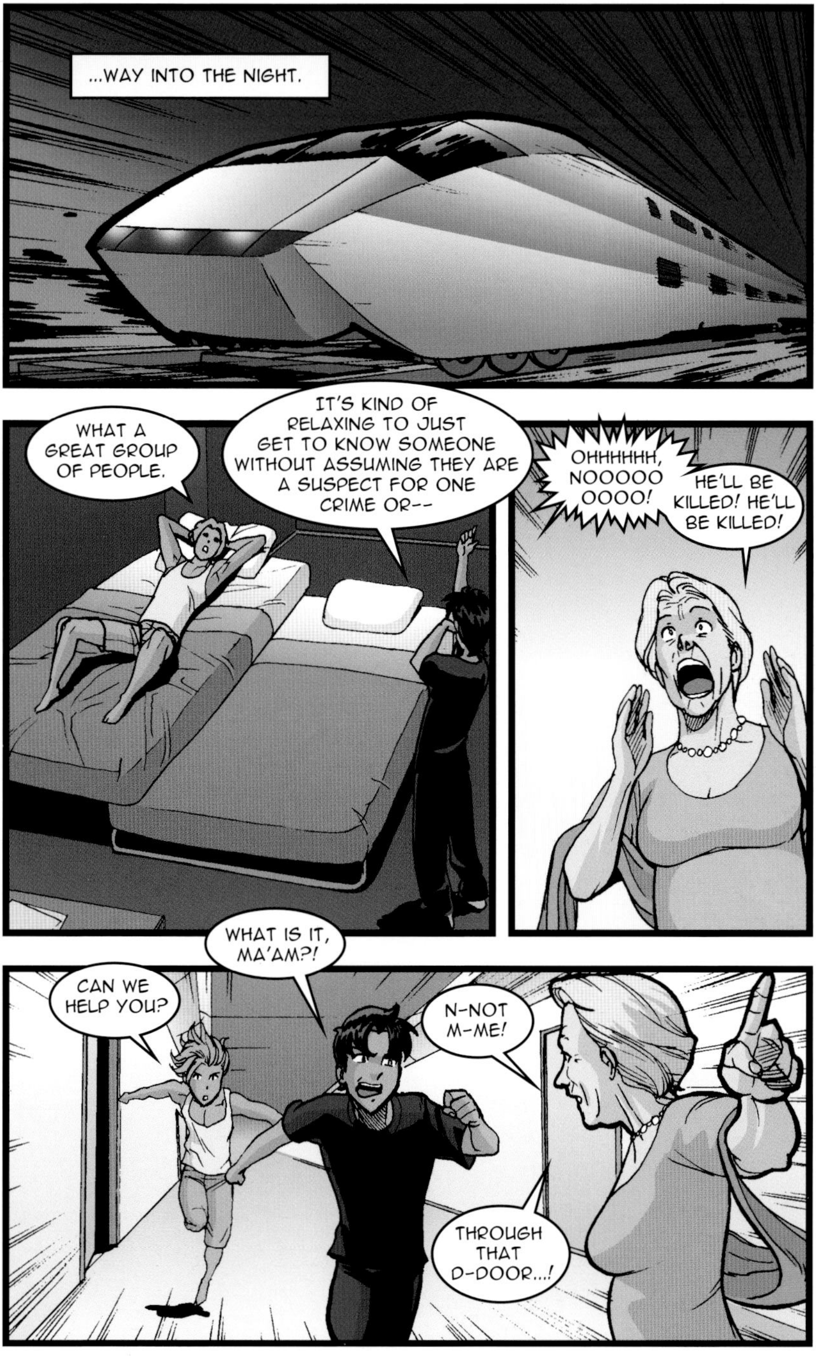
...WAY INTO THE NIGHT.
WHAT A GREAT GROUP OF PEOPLE.
IT'S KIND OF RELAXING TO JUST GET TO KNOW SOMEONE WITHOUT ASSUMING THEY ARE A SUSPECT FOR ONE CRIME OR--
OHHHHHH, NOOOOO OOOO!
HE'LL BE KILLED! HE'LL BE KILLED!
CAN WE HELP YOU?
WHAT IS IT, MA'AM?!
N-NOT M-ME!
THROUGH THAT D-DOOR...!

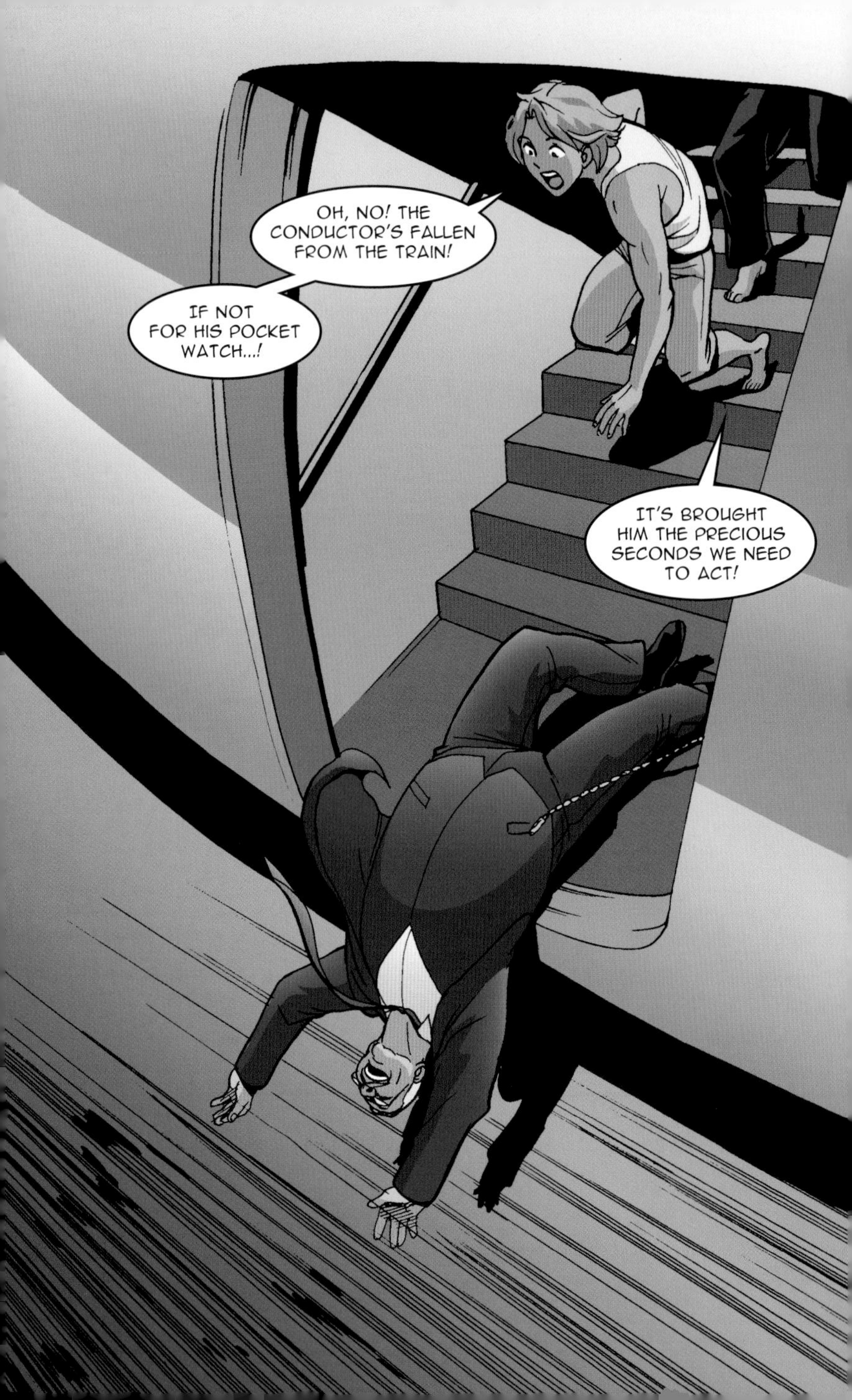
OH, NO! THE CONDUCTOR'S FALLEN FROM THE TRAIN!
IF NOT FOR HIS POCKET WATCH...!
IT'S BROUGHT HIM THE PRECIOUS SECONDS WE NEED TO ACT!

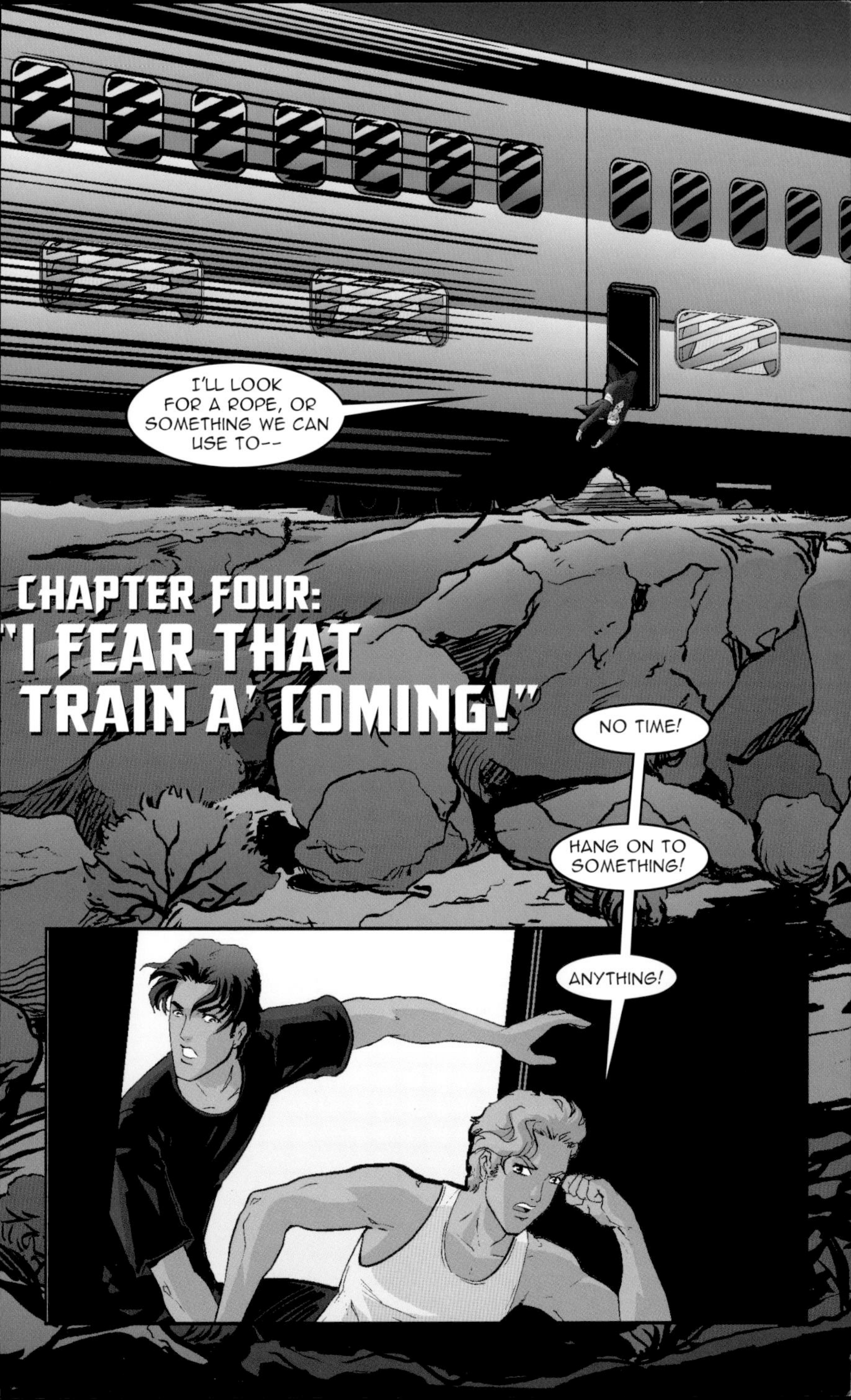
I'LL LOOK FOR A ROPE, OR SOMETHING WE CAN USE TO--
CHAPTER FOUR:
"I FEAR THAT TRAIN A' COMING!"
NO TIME!
HANG ON TO SOMETHING!
ANYTHING!

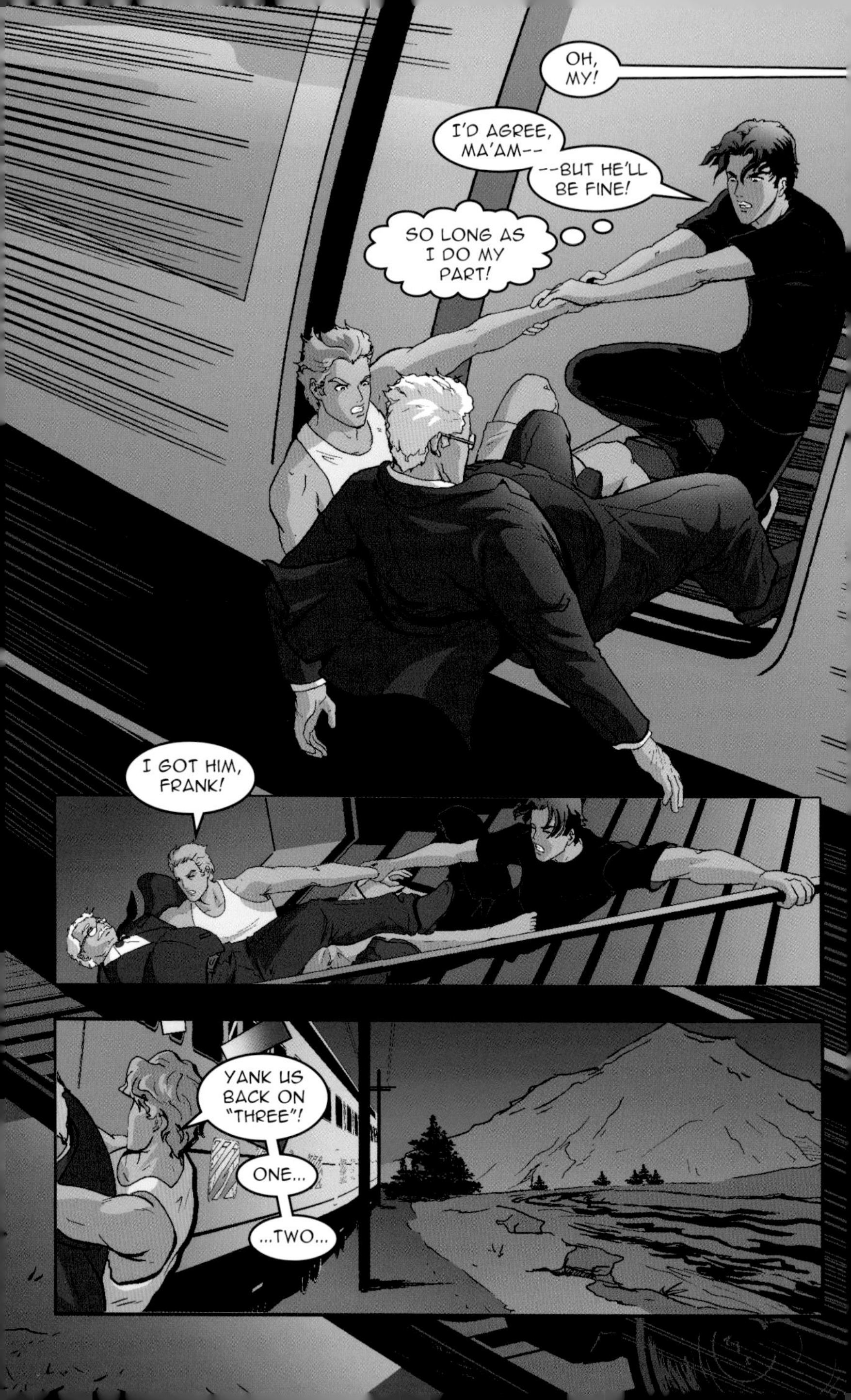
OH, MY!
I'D AGREE, MA'AM--
--BUT HE'LL BE FINE!
SO LONG AS I DO MY PART!
I GOT HIM, FRANK!
YANK US BACK ON "THREE"!
ONE...
...TWO...

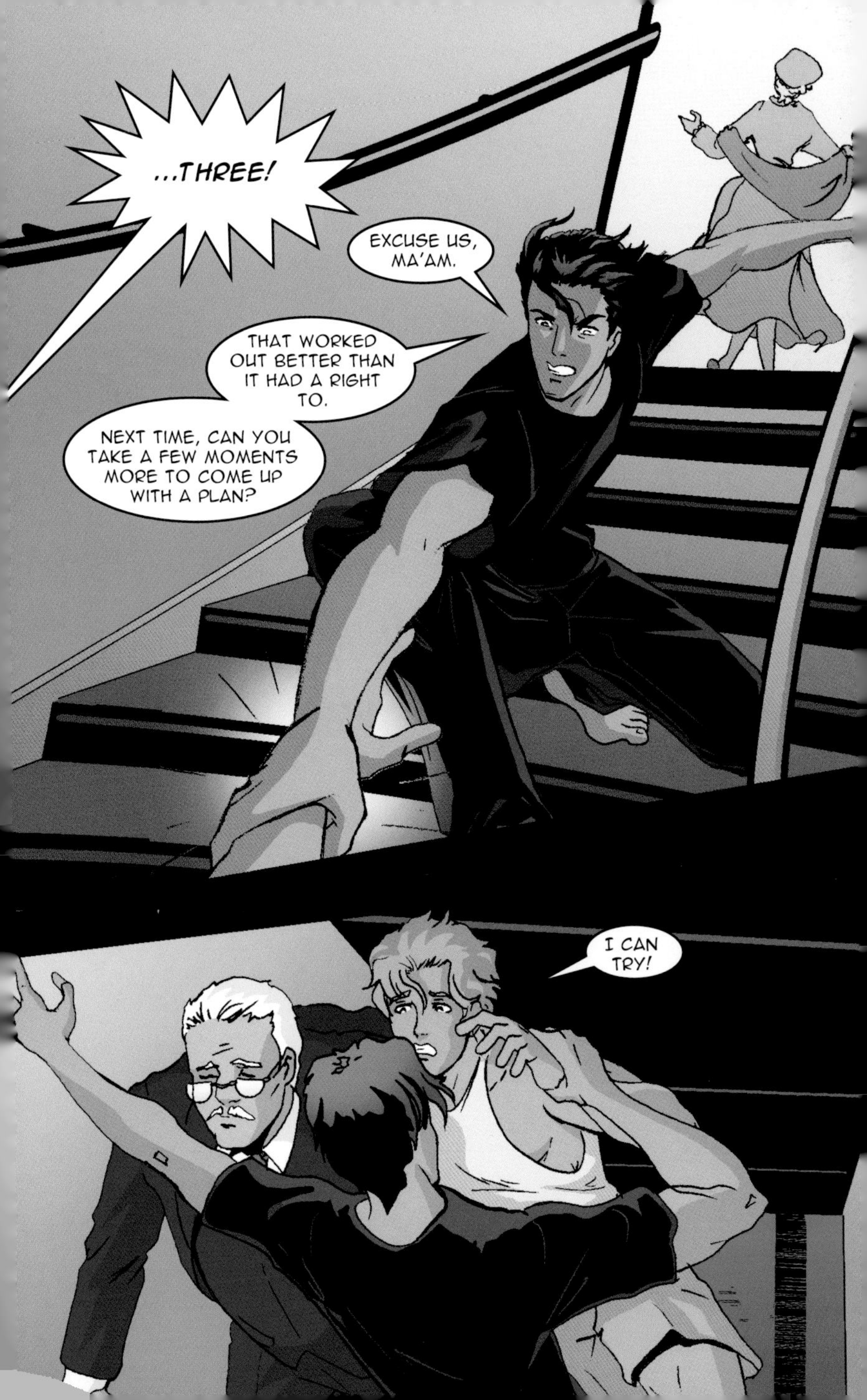
...THREE!
EXCUSE US, MA'AM.
THAT WORKED OUT BETTER THAN IT HAD A RIGHT TO.
NEXT TIME, CAN YOU TAKE A FEW MOMENTS MORE TO COME UP WITH A PLAN?
I CAN TRY!

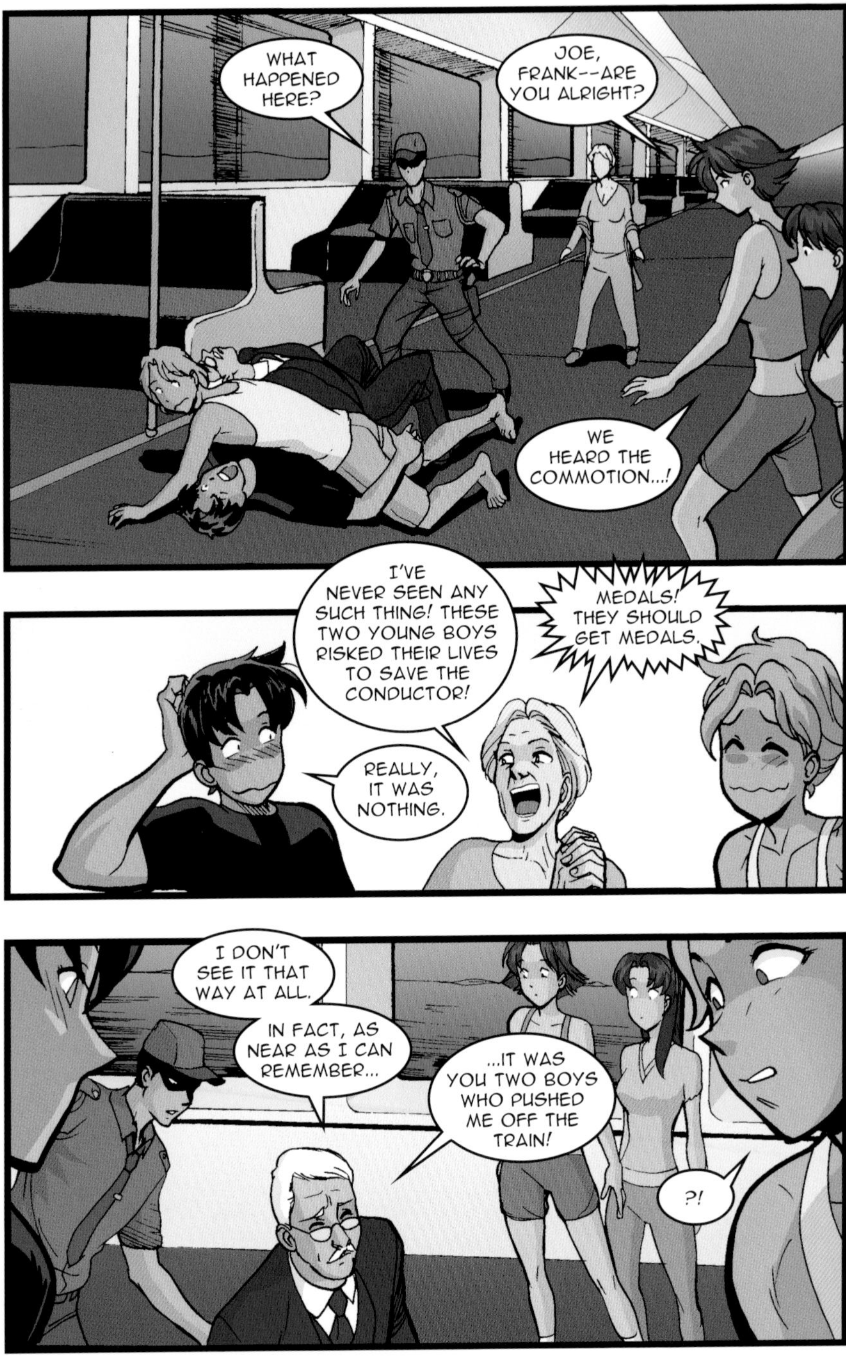
WHAT HAPPENED HERE?
JOE, FRANK--ARE YOU ALRIGHT?
WE HEARD THE COMMOTION...!
I'VE NEVER SEEN ANY SUCH THING! THESE TWO YOUNG BOYS RISKED THEIR LIVES TO SAVE THE CONDUCTOR!
MEDALS! THEY SHOULD GET MEDALS.
REALLY, IT WAS NOTHING.
I DON'T SEE IT THAT WAY AT ALL.
IN FACT, AS NEAR AS I CAN REMEMBER...
...IT WAS YOU TWO BOYS WHO PUSHED ME OFF THE TRAIN!
?!

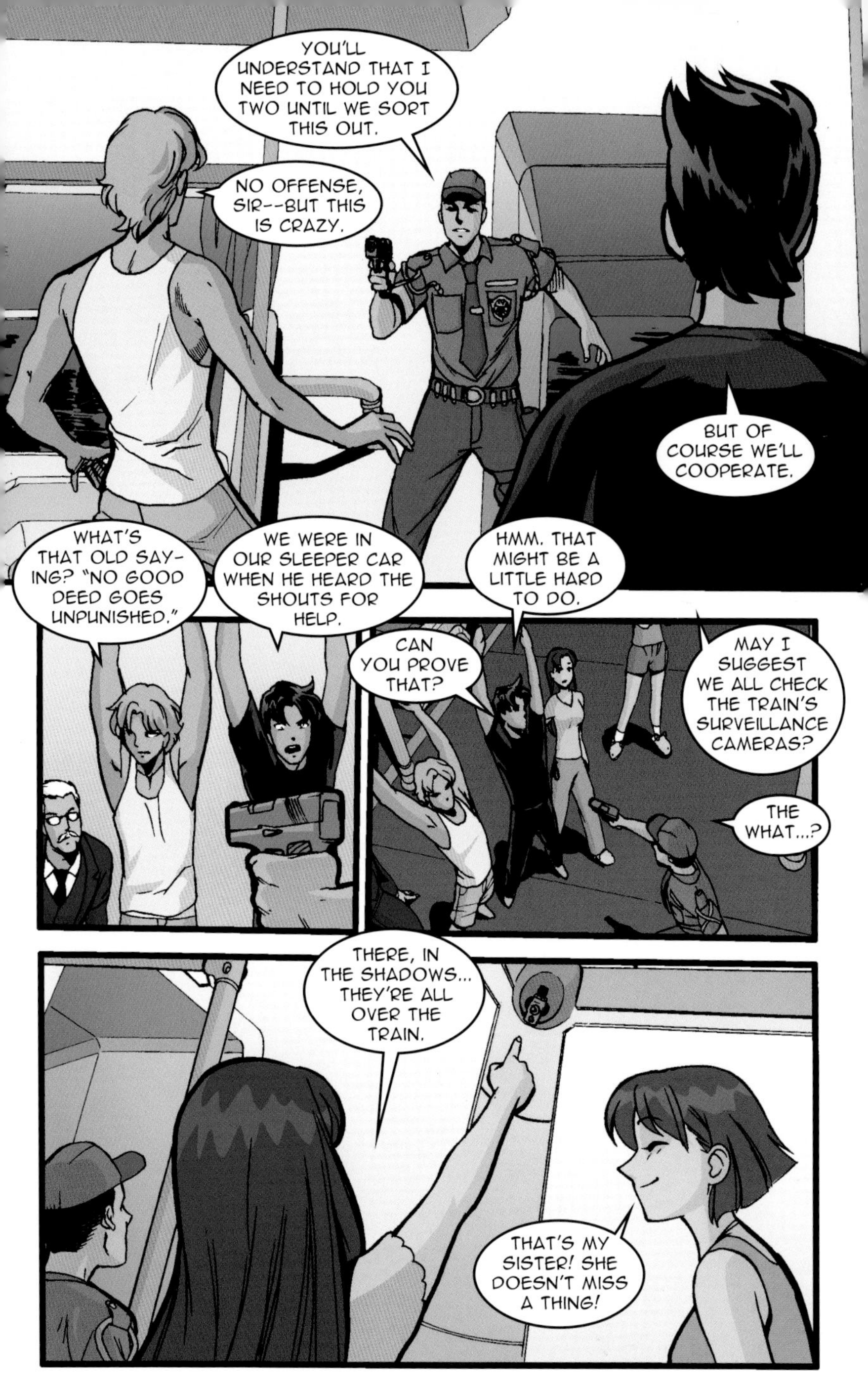
YOU'LL UNDERSTAND THAT I NEED TO HOLD YOU TWO UNTIL WE SORT THIS OUT.
NO OFFENSE, SIR--BUT THIS IS CRAZY.
BUT OF COURSE WE'LL COOPERATE.
WHAT'S THAT OLD SAY-ING? "NO GOOD DEED GOES UNPUNISHED."
WE WERE IN OUR SLEEPER CAR WHEN HE HEARD THE SHOUTS FOR HELP.
HMM. THAT MIGHT BE A LITTLE HARD TO DO.
CAN YOU PROVE THAT?
MAY I SUGGEST WE ALL CHECK THE TRAIN'S SURVEILLANCE CAMERAS?
THE WHAT...?
THERE, IN THE SHADOWS... THEY'RE ALL OVER THE TRAIN.
THAT'S MY SISTER! SHE DOESN'T MISS A THING!

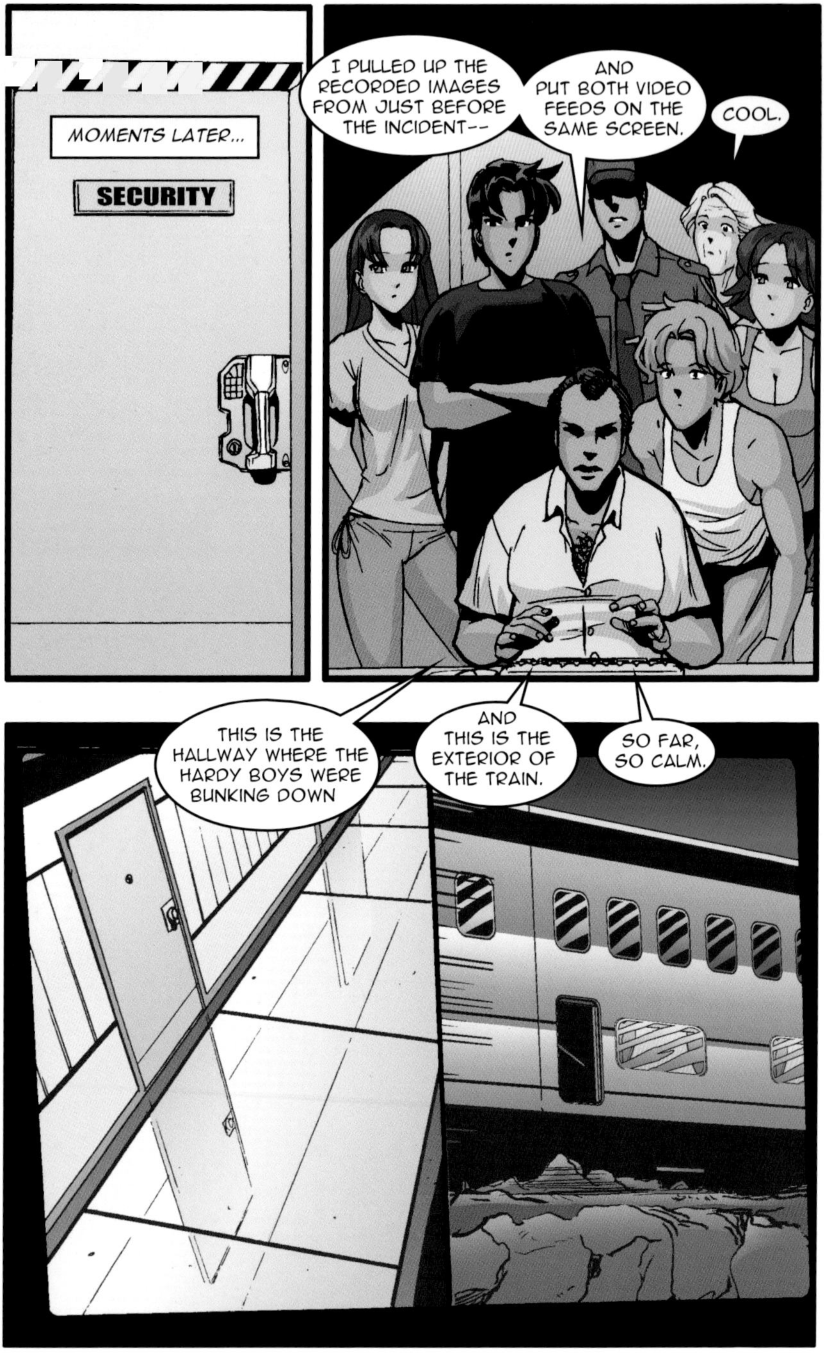
MOMENTS LATER...
SECURITY
I PULLED UP THE RECORDED IMAGES FROM JUST BEFORE THE INCIDENT--
AND PUT BOTH VIDEO FEEDS ON THE SAME SCREEN.
COOL.
THIS IS THE HALLWAY WHERE THE HARDY BOYS WERE BUNKING DOWN
AND THIS IS THE EXTERIOR OF THE TRAIN.
SO FAR, SO CALM.

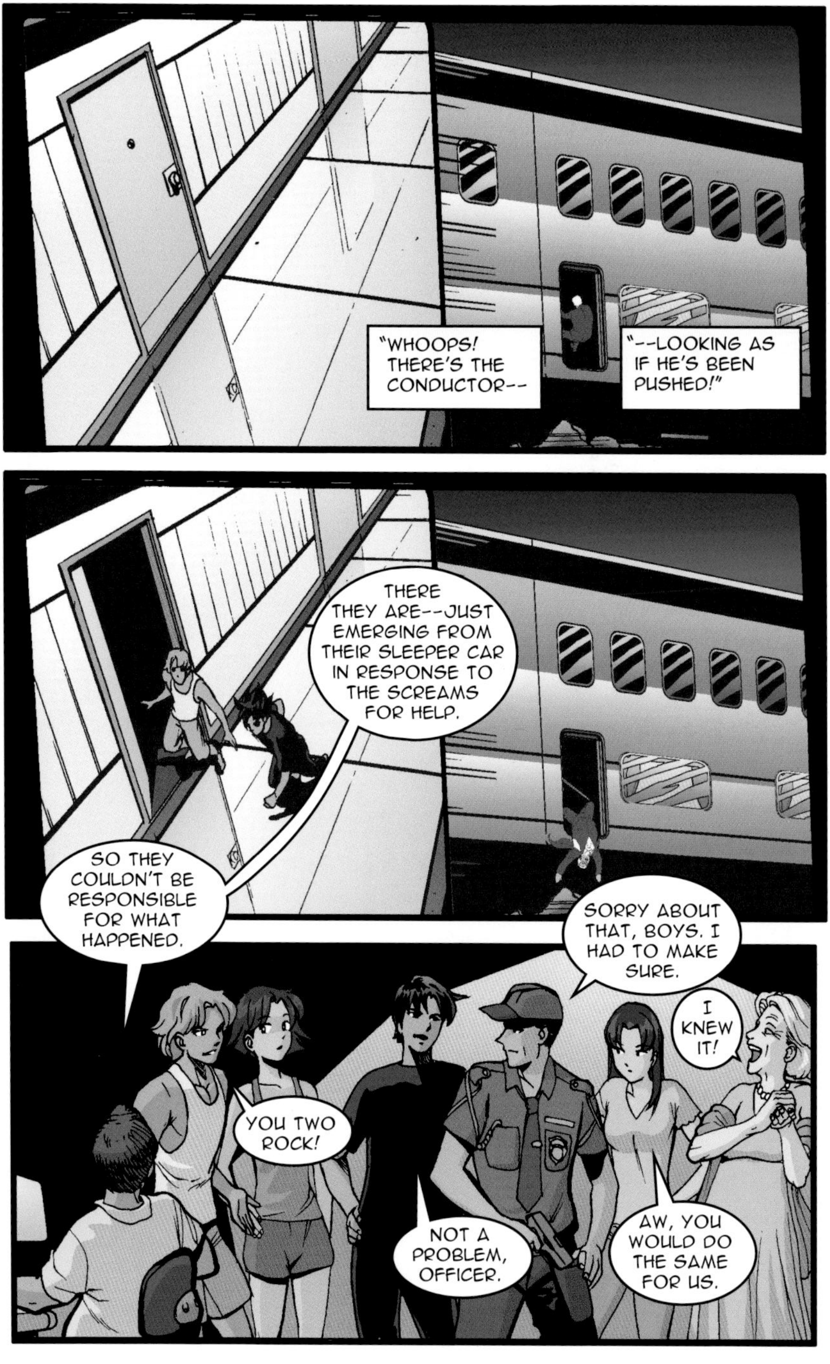
"WHOOPS! THERE'S THE CONDUCTOR--
"--LOOKING AS IF HE'S BEEN PUSHED!"
THERE THEY ARE--JUST EMERGING FROM THEIR SLEEPER CAR IN RESPONSE TO THE SCREAMS FOR HELP.
SO THEY COULDN'T BE RESPONSIBLE FOR WHAT HAPPENED.
SORRY ABOUT THAT, BOYS. I HAD TO MAKE SURE.
I KNEW IT!
YOU TWO ROCK!
NOT A PROBLEM, OFFICER.
AW, YOU WOULD DO THE SAME FOR US.

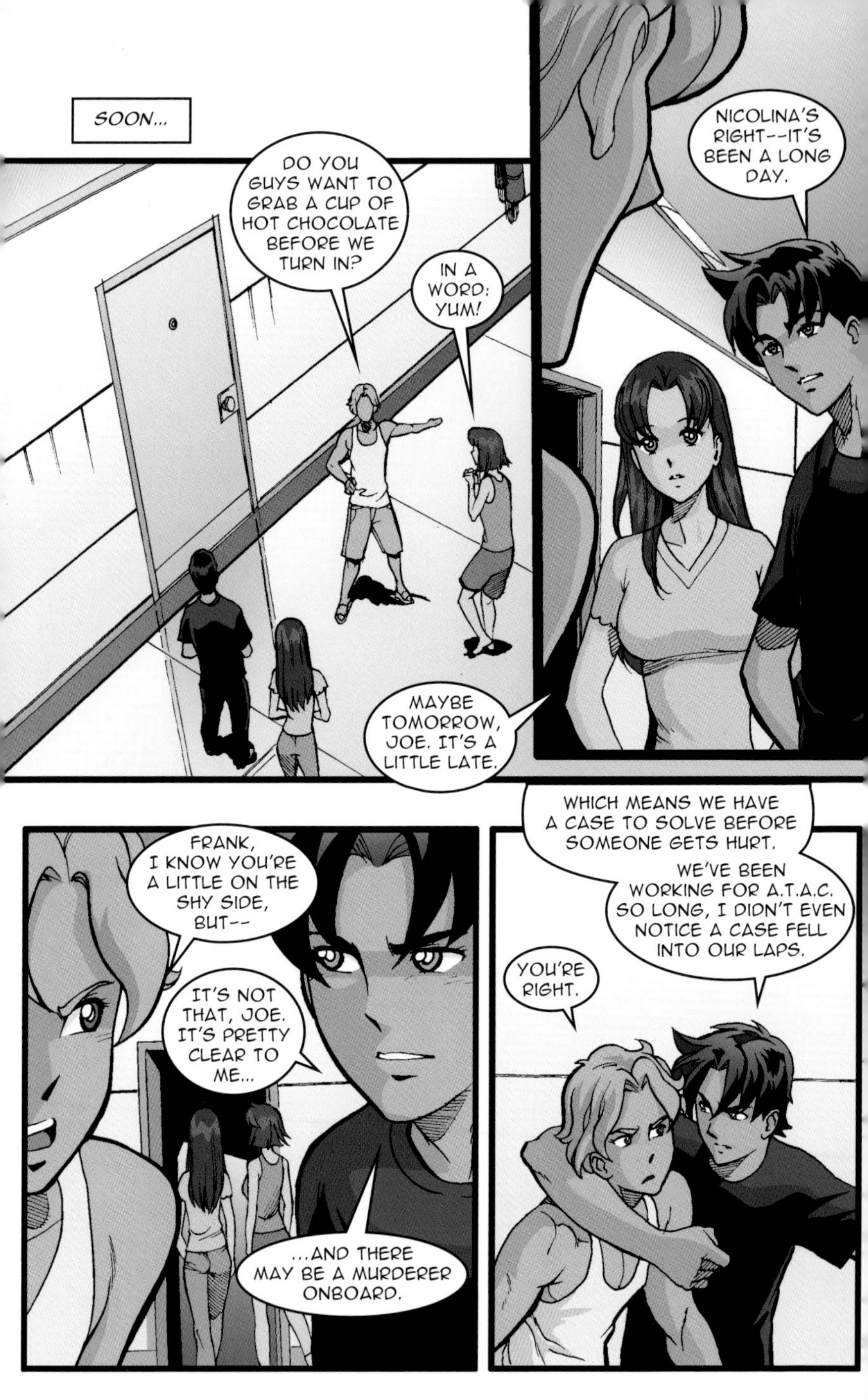
SOON...
DO YOU GUYS WANT TO GRAB A CUP OF HOT CHOCOLATE BEFORE WE TURN IN?
IN A WORD: YUM!
MAYBE TOMORROW, JOE. IT'S A LITTLE LATE.
NICOLINA'S RIGHT--IT'S BEEN A LONG DAY.
FRANK, I KNOW YOU'RE A LITTLE ON THE SHY SIDE, BUT--
IT'S NOT THAT, JOE. IT'S PRETTY CLEAR TO ME...
...AND THERE MAY BE A MURDERER ONBOARD.
YOU'RE RIGHT.
WHICH MEANS WE HAVE A CASE TO SOLVE BEFORE SOMEONE GETS HURT.
WE'VE BEEN WORKING FOR A.T.A.C. SO LONG, I DIDN'T EVEN NOTICE A CASE FELL INTO OUR LAPS.

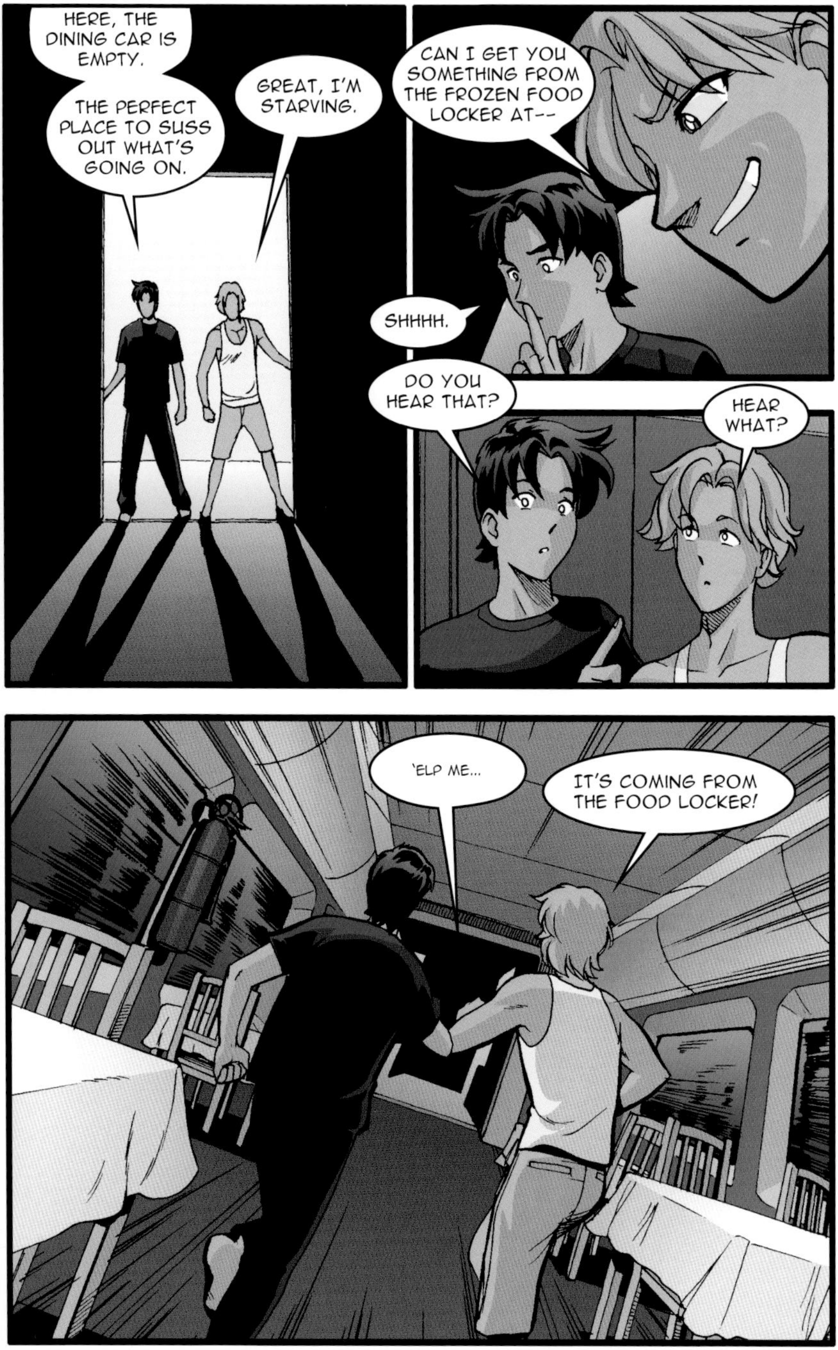
HERE, THE DINING CAR IS EMPTY.
THE PERFECT PLACE TO SUSS OUT WHAT'S GOING ON.
GREAT, I'M STARVING.
CAN I GET YOU SOMETHING FROM THE FROZEN FOOD LOCKER AT--
SHHHH.
DO YOU HEAR THAT?
HEAR WHAT?
'ELP ME...
IT'S COMING FROM THE FOOD LOCKER!

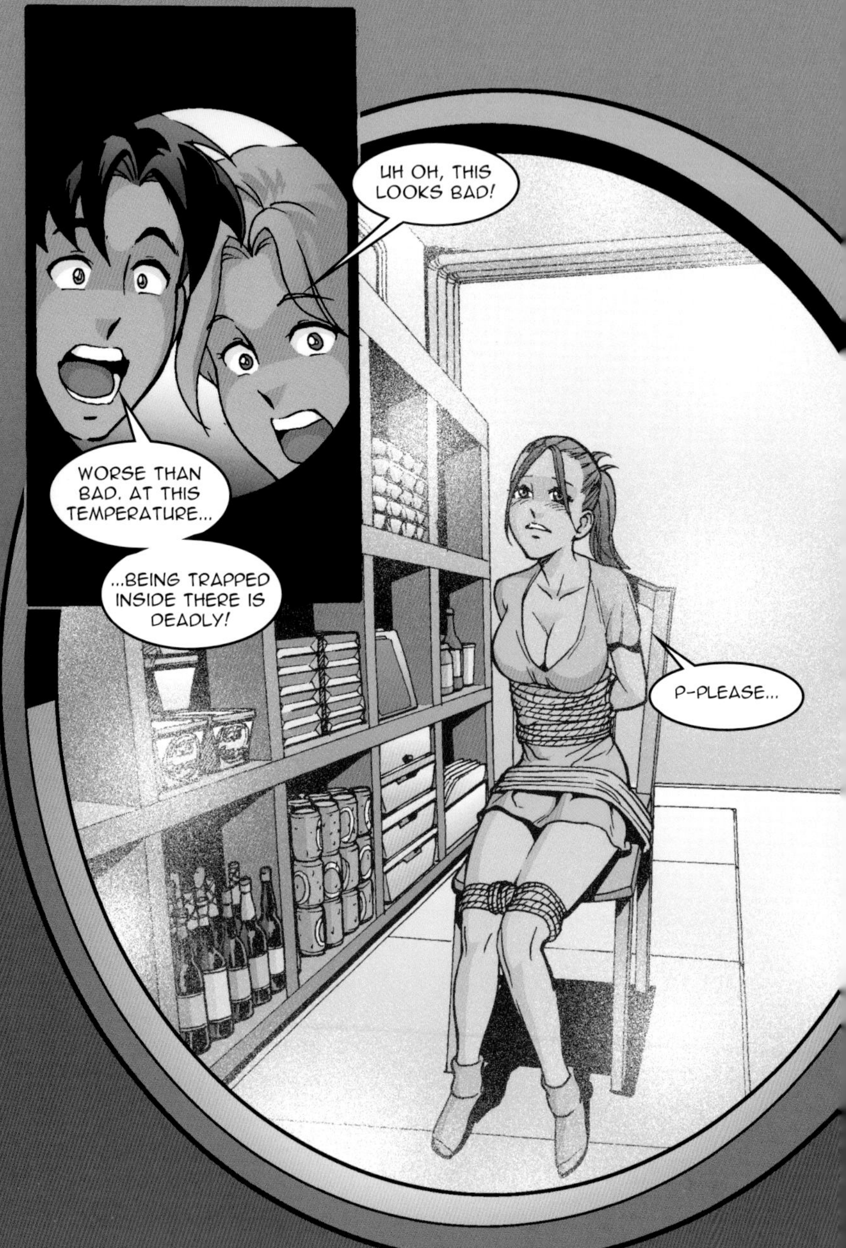
UH OH, THIS LOOKS BAD!
WORSE THAN BAD. AT THIS TEMPERATURE...
...BEING TRAPPED INSIDE THERE IS DEADLY!
P-PLEASE...

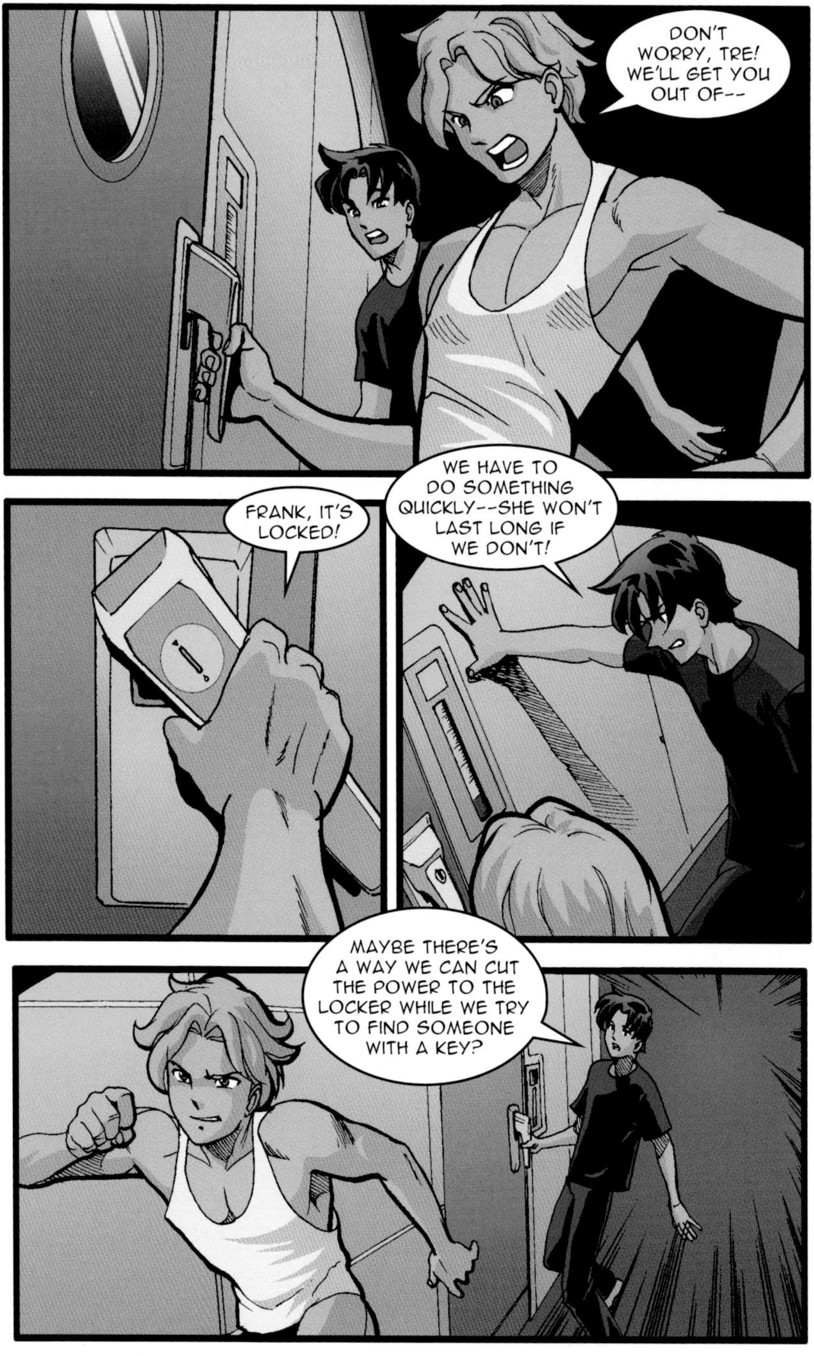
DON'T WORRY, TRE! WE'LL GET YOU OUT OF--
FRANK, IT'S LOCKED!
WE HAVE TO DO SOMETHING QUICKLY--SHE WON'T LAST LONG IF WE DON'T!
MAYBE THERE'S A WAY WE CAN CUT THE POWER TO THE LOCKER WHILE WE TRY TO FIND SOMEONE WITH A KEY?

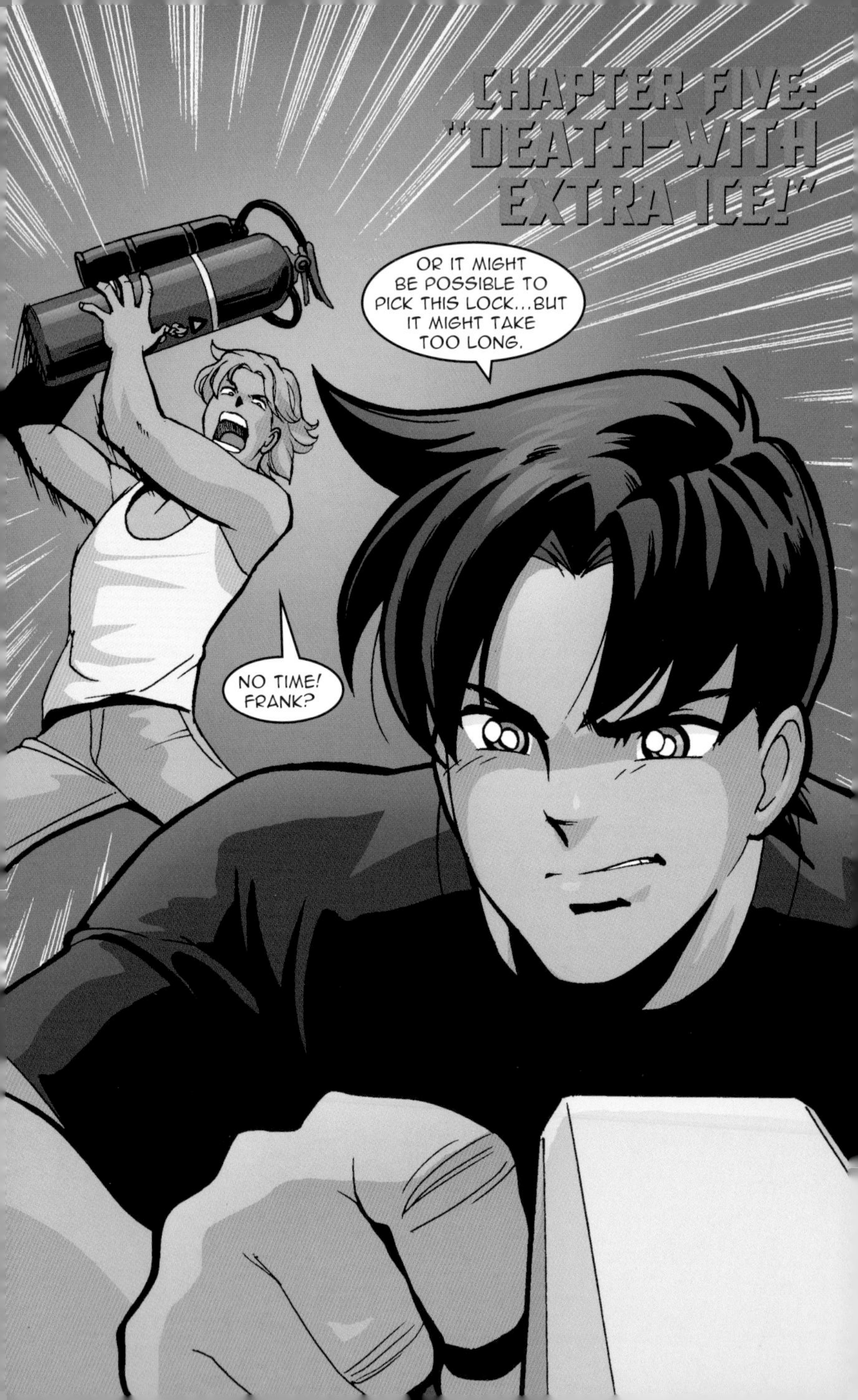
CHAPTER FIVE:
"DEATH-WITH EXTRA ICE!"
OR IT MIGHT BE POSSIBLE TO PICK THIS LOCK...BUT IT MIGHT TAKE TOO LONG.
NO TIME! FRANK?

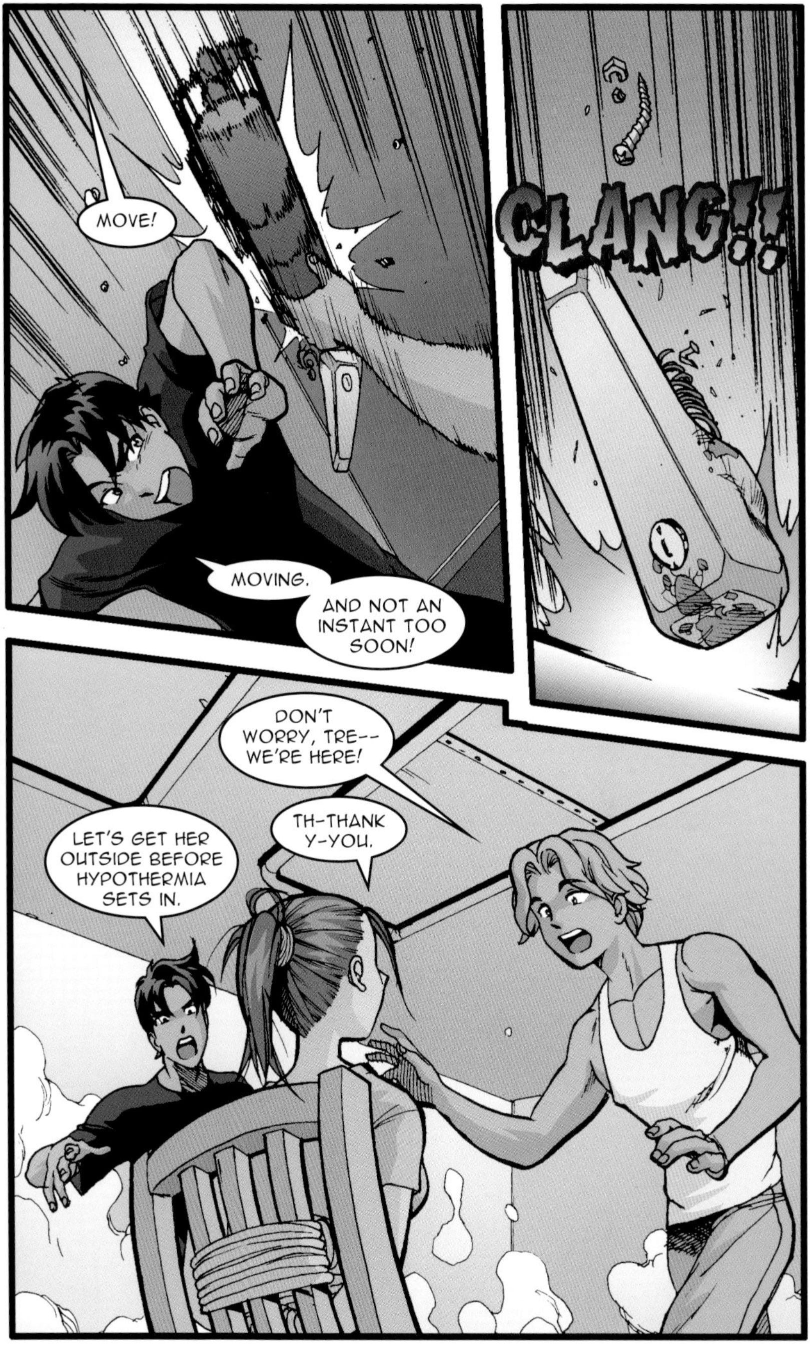
MOVE!
MOVING.
AND NOT AN INSTANT TOO SOON!
CLANG!!
DON'T WORRY, TRE-- WE'RE HERE!
TH-THANK Y-YOU.
LET'S GET HER OUTSIDE BEFORE HYPOTHERMIA SETS IN.

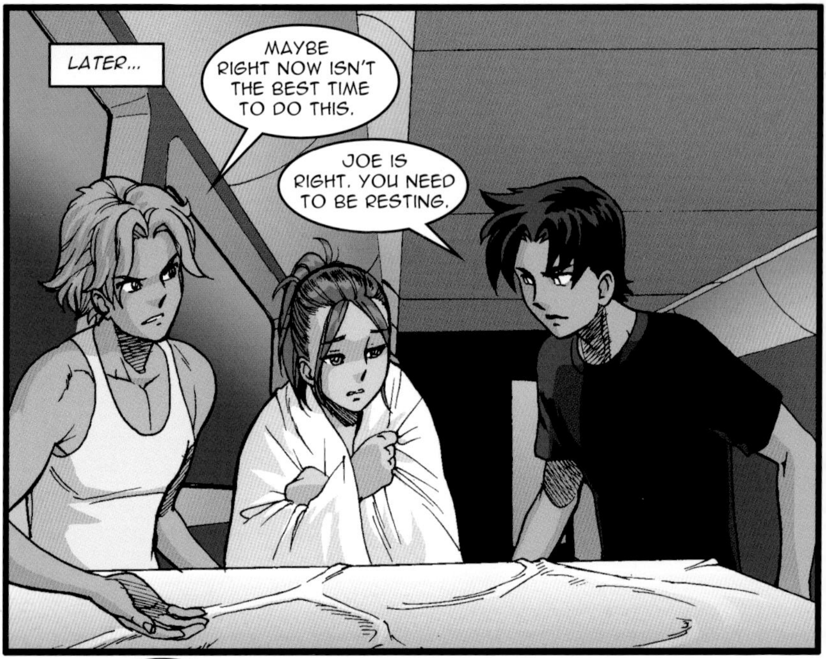
LATER...
MAYBE RIGHT NOW ISN'T THE BEST TIME TO DO THIS.
JOE IS RIGHT. YOU NEED TO BE RESTING.

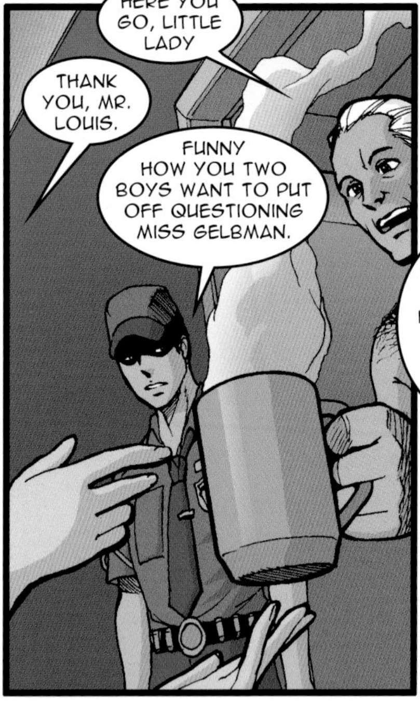
HERE YOU GO, LITTLE LADY
THANK YOU, MR. LOUIS.
FUNNY HOW YOU TWO BOYS WANT TO PUT OFF QUESTIONING MISS GELBMAN.

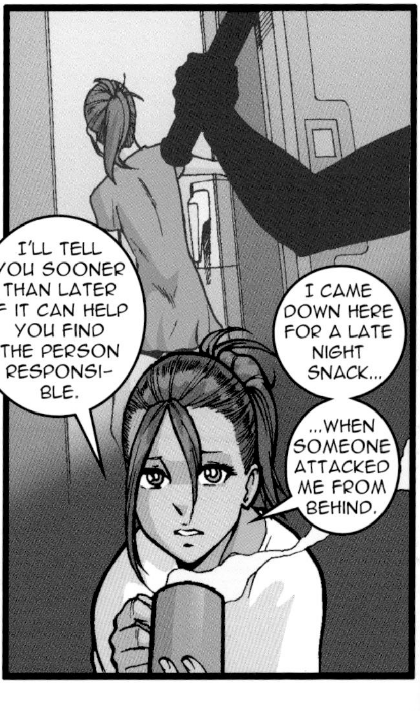
I'LL TELL YOU SOONER THAN LATER IF IT CAN HELP YOU FIND THE PERSON RESPONSI- BLE.
I CAME DOWN HERE FOR A LATE NIGHT SNACK...
...WHEN SOMEONE ATTACKED ME FROM BEHIND.

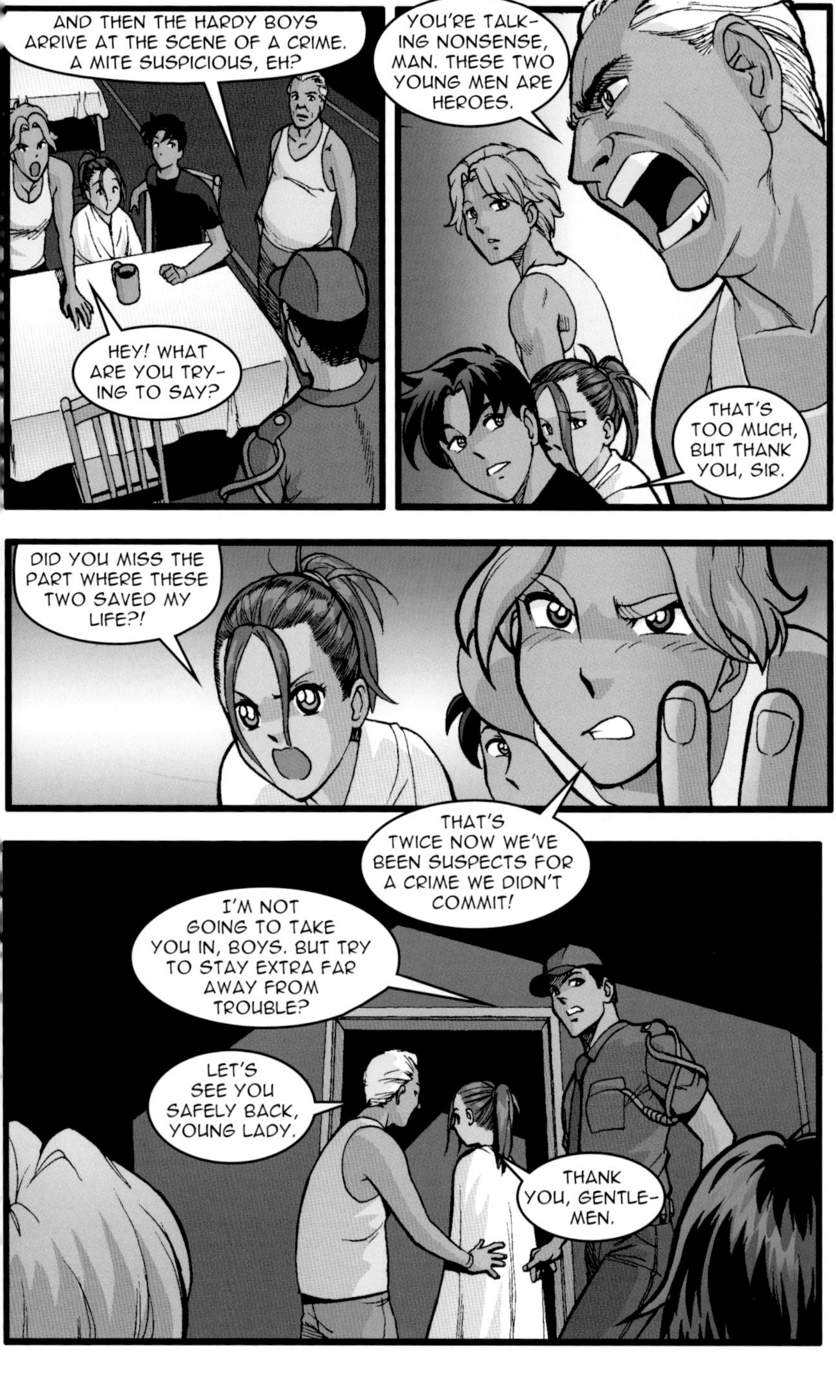

AND THEN THE HARDY BOYS ARRIVE AT THE SCENE OF A CRIME. A MITE SUSPICIOUS, EH?
HEY! WHAT ARE YOU TRYING TO SAY?
YOU'RE TALKING NONSENSE, MAN. THESE TWO YOUNG MEN ARE HEROES.
THAT'S TOO MUCH, BUT THANK YOU, SIR.
DID YOU MISS THE PART WHERE THESE TWO SAVED MY LIFE?!
THAT'S TWICE NOW WE'VE BEEN SUSPECTS FOR A CRIME WE DIDN'T COMMIT!
I'M NOT GOING TO TAKE YOU IN, BOYS. BUT TRY TO STAY EXTRA FAR AWAY FROM TROUBLE?
LET'S SEE YOU SAFELY BACK, YOUNG LADY.
THANK YOU, GENTLEMEN.

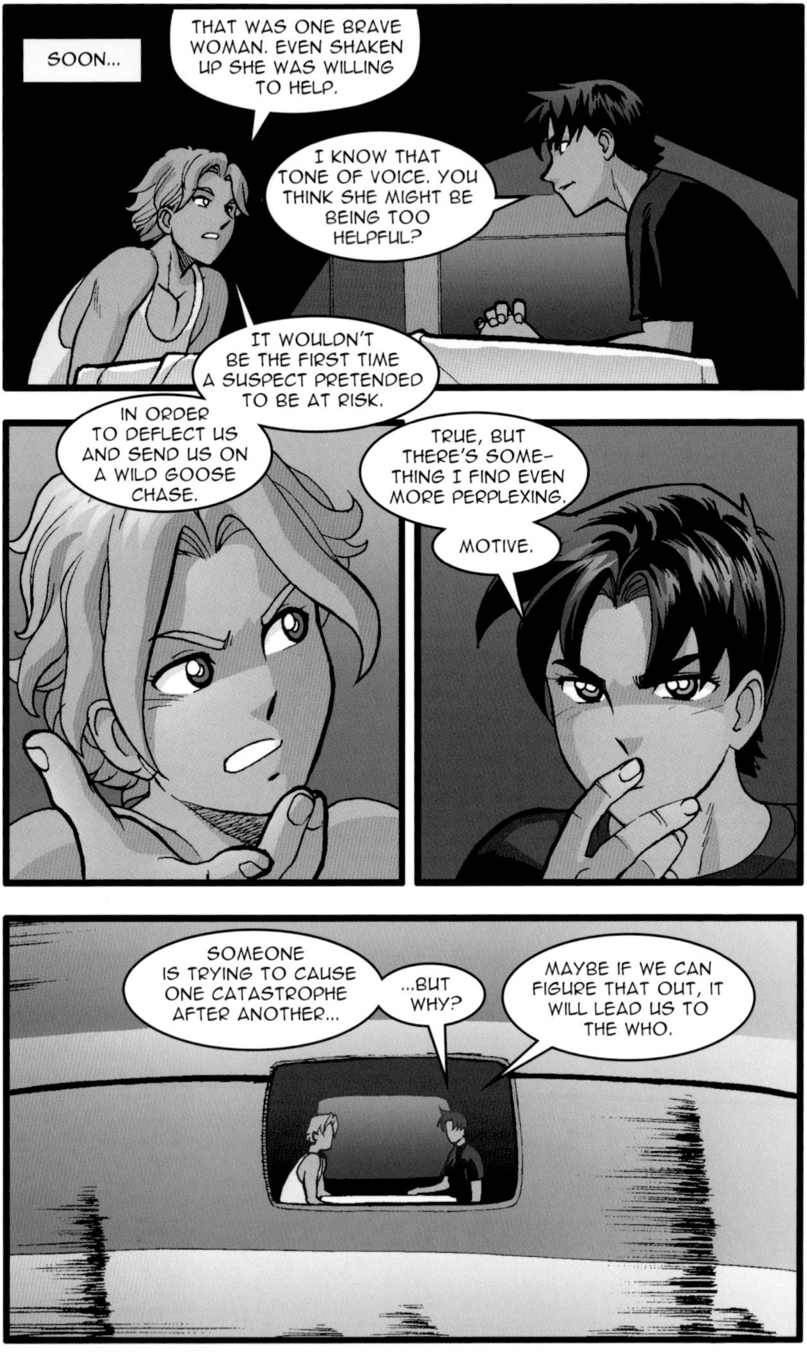
SOON...
THAT WAS ONE BRAVE WOMAN. EVEN SHAKEN UP SHE WAS WILLING TO HELP.
I KNOW THAT TONE OF VOICE. YOU THINK SHE MIGHT BE BEING TOO HELPFUL?
IT WOULDN'T BE THE FIRST TIME A SUSPECT PRETENDED TO BE AT RISK.
IN ORDER TO DEFLECT US AND SEND US ON A WILD GOOSE CHASE.
TRUE, BUT THERE'S SOME-THING I FIND EVEN MORE PERPLEXING.
MOTIVE.
SOMEONE IS TRYING TO CAUSE ONE CATASTROPHE AFTER ANOTHER...
...BUT WHY?
MAYBE IF WE CAN FIGURE THAT OUT, IT WILL LEAD US TO THE WHO.

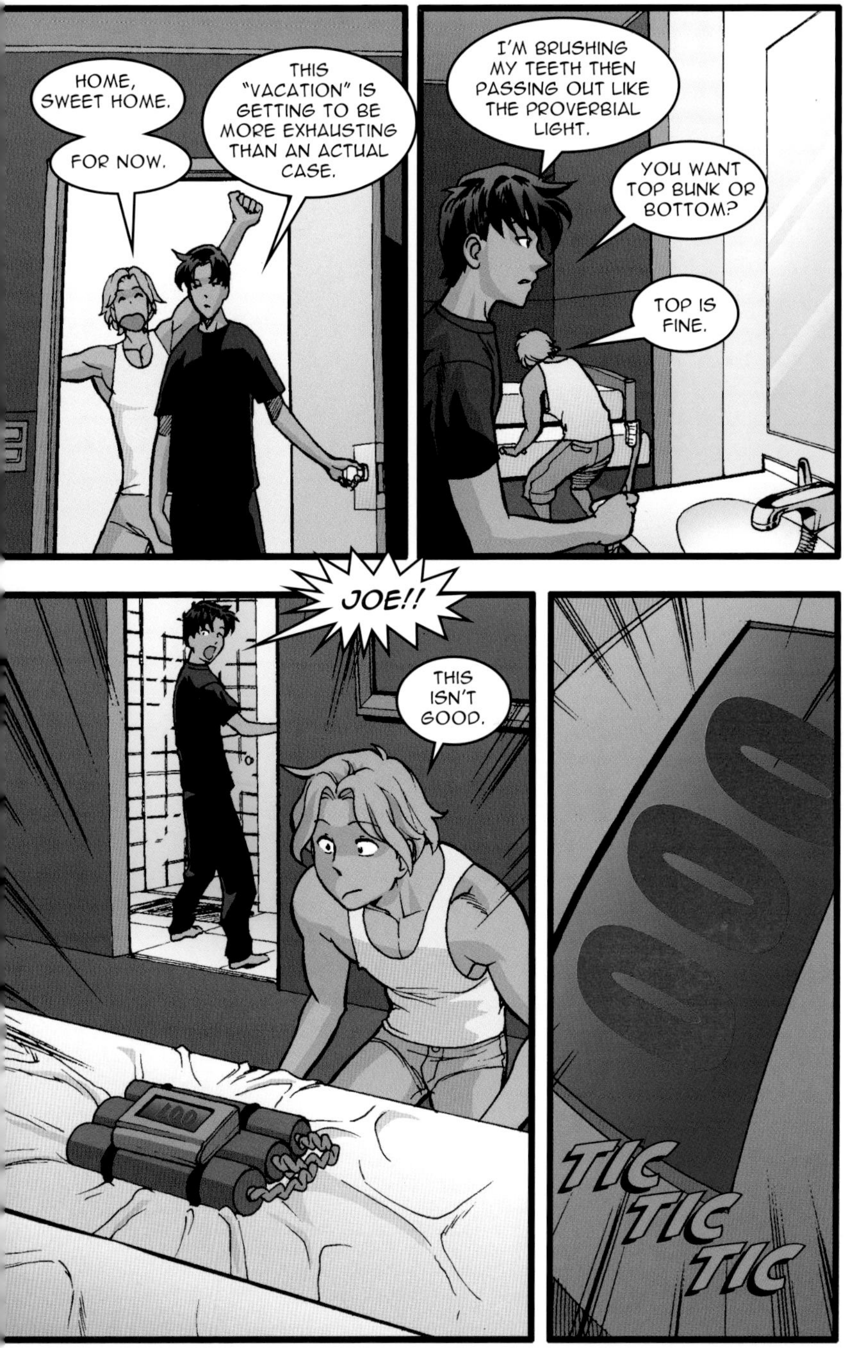
HOME, SWEET HOME.
FOR NOW.
THIS "VACATION" IS GETTING TO BE MORE EXHAUSTING THAN AN ACTUAL CASE.
I'M BRUSHING MY TEETH THEN PASSING OUT LIKE THE PROVERBIAL LIGHT.
YOU WANT TOP BUNK OR BOTTOM?
TOP IS FINE.
JOE!!
THIS ISN'T GOOD.
TIC
TIC
TIC

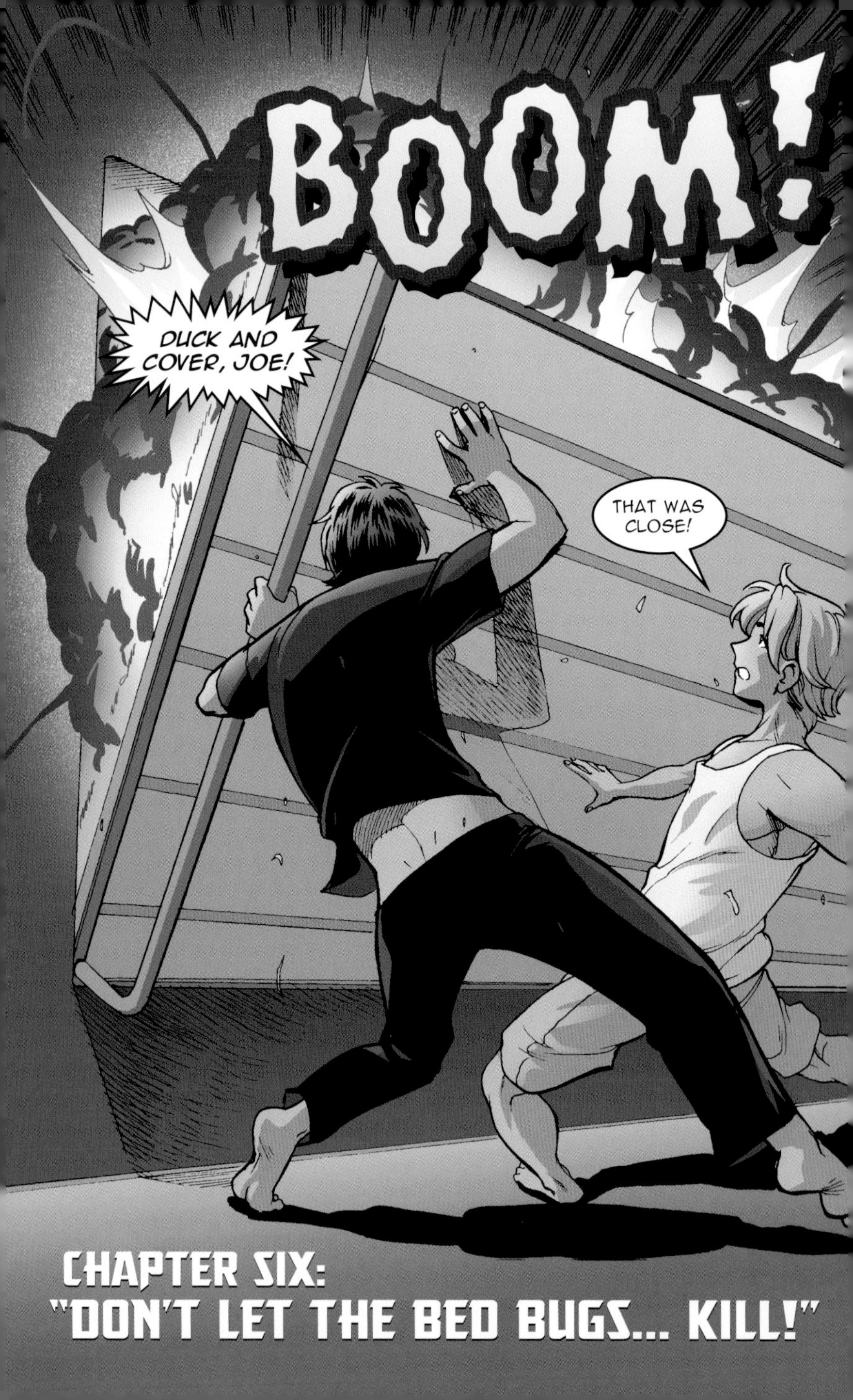
BOOM!
DUCK AND COVER, JOE!
THAT WAS CLOSE!

CHAPTER SIX: "DON'T LET THE BED BUGS... KILL!"

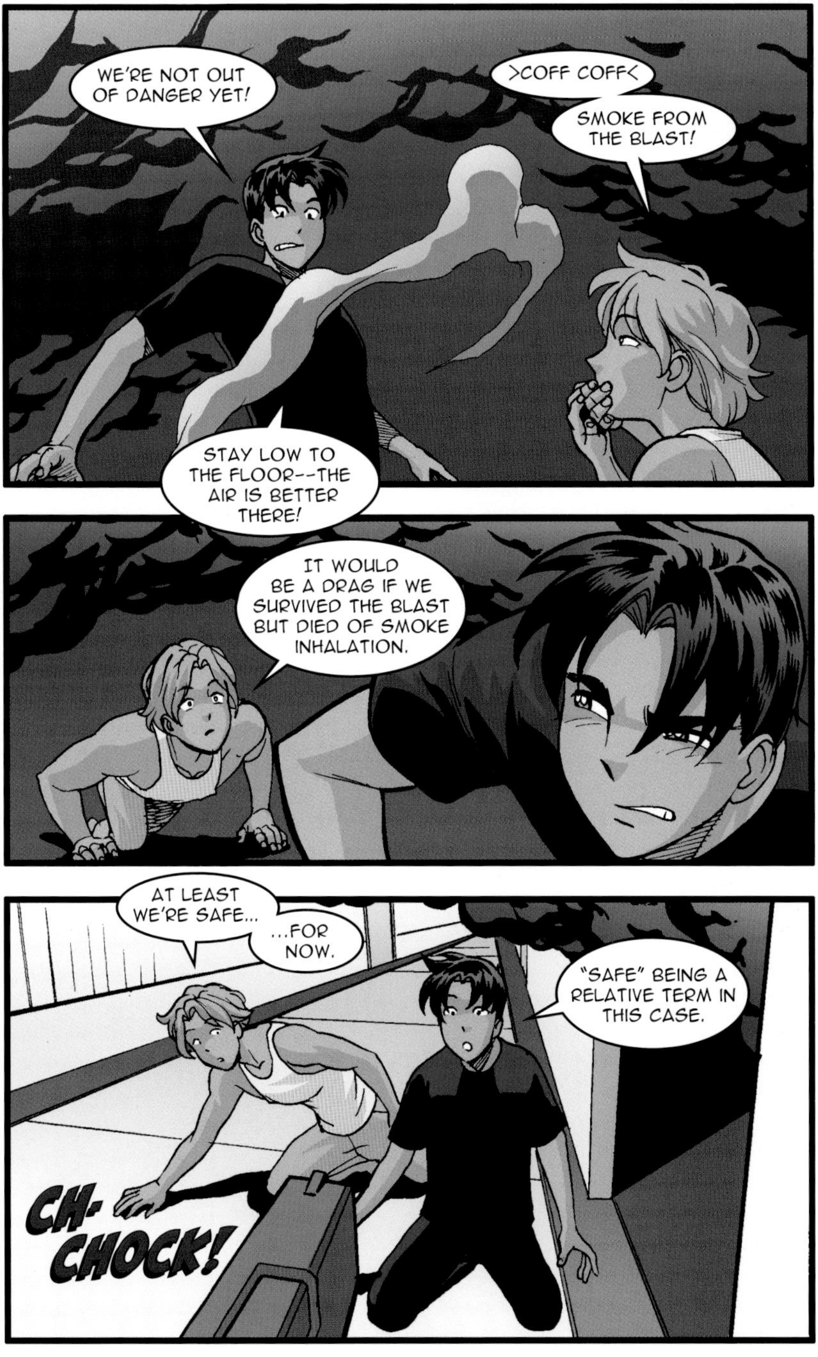
WE'RE NOT OUT OF DANGER YET!
>COFF COFF<
SMOKE FROM THE BLAST!
STAY LOW TO THE FLOOR--THE AIR IS BETTER THERE!
IT WOULD BE A DRAG IF WE SURVIVED THE BLAST BUT DIED OF SMOKE INHALATION.
AT LEAST WE'RE SAFE...
...FOR NOW.
"SAFE" BEING A RELATIVE TERM IN THIS CASE.
CH-CHOCK!

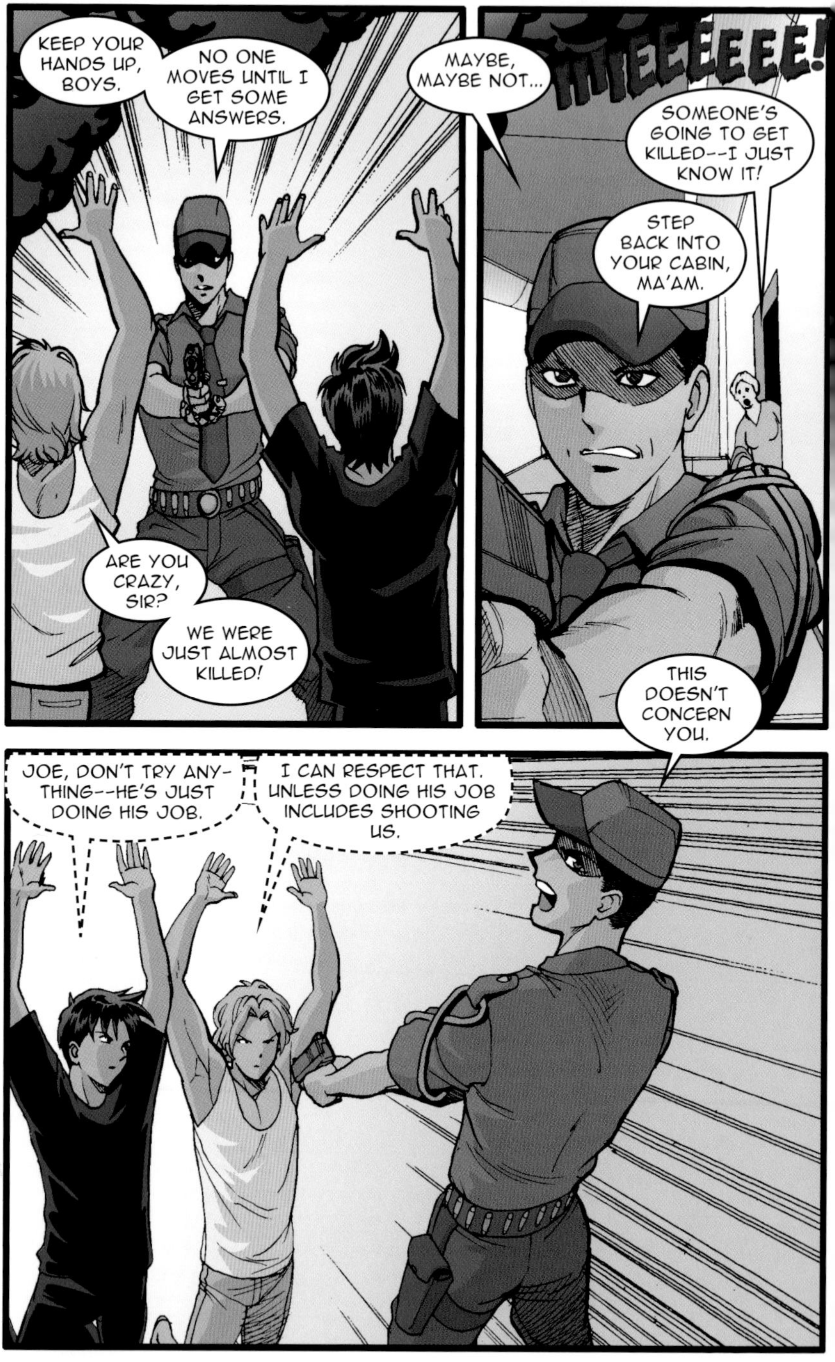
KEEP YOUR HANDS UP, BOYS.
NO ONE MOVES UNTIL I GET SOME ANSWERS.
ARE YOU CRAZY, SIR?
WE WERE JUST ALMOST KILLED!
MAYBE, MAYBE NOT...
IIIIEEEEEEE!
SOMEONE'S GOING TO GET KILLED--I JUST KNOW IT!
STEP BACK INTO YOUR CABIN, MA'AM.
THIS DOESN'T CONCERN YOU.
JOE, DON'T TRY ANY-THING--HE'S JUST DOING HIS JOB.
I CAN RESPECT THAT. UNLESS DOING HIS JOB INCLUDES SHOOTING US.

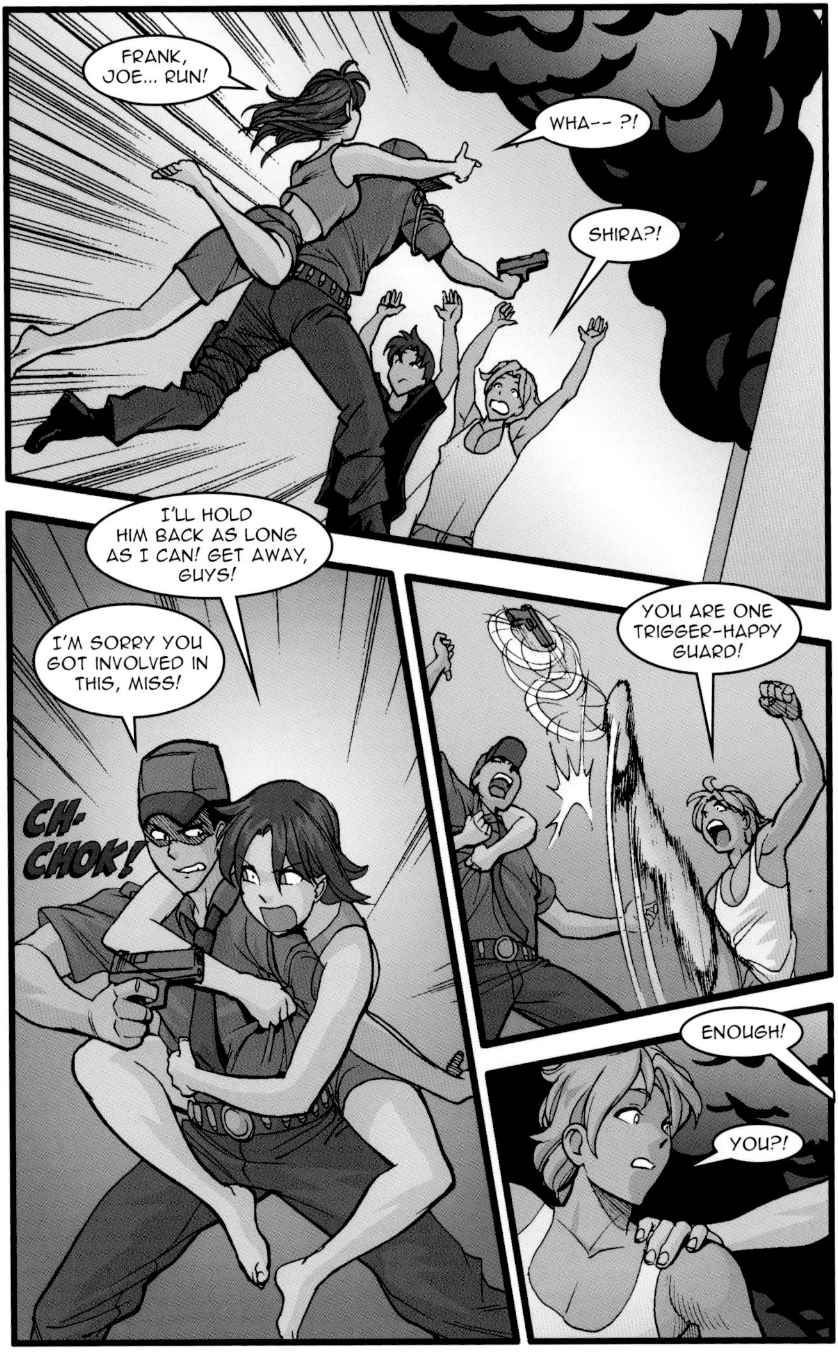
FRANK, JOE... RUN!
WHA-- ?!
SHIRA?!
I'LL HOLD HIM BACK AS LONG AS I CAN! GET AWAY, GUYS!
I'M SORRY YOU GOT INVOLVED IN THIS, MISS!
CH-CHOK!
YOU ARE ONE TRIGGER-HAPPY GUARD!
ENOUGH!
YOU?!

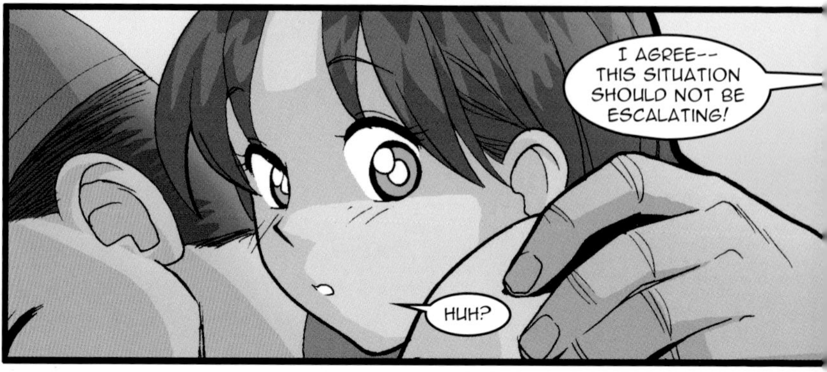
I AGREE-- THIS SITUATION SHOULD NOT BE ESCALATING!
HUH?

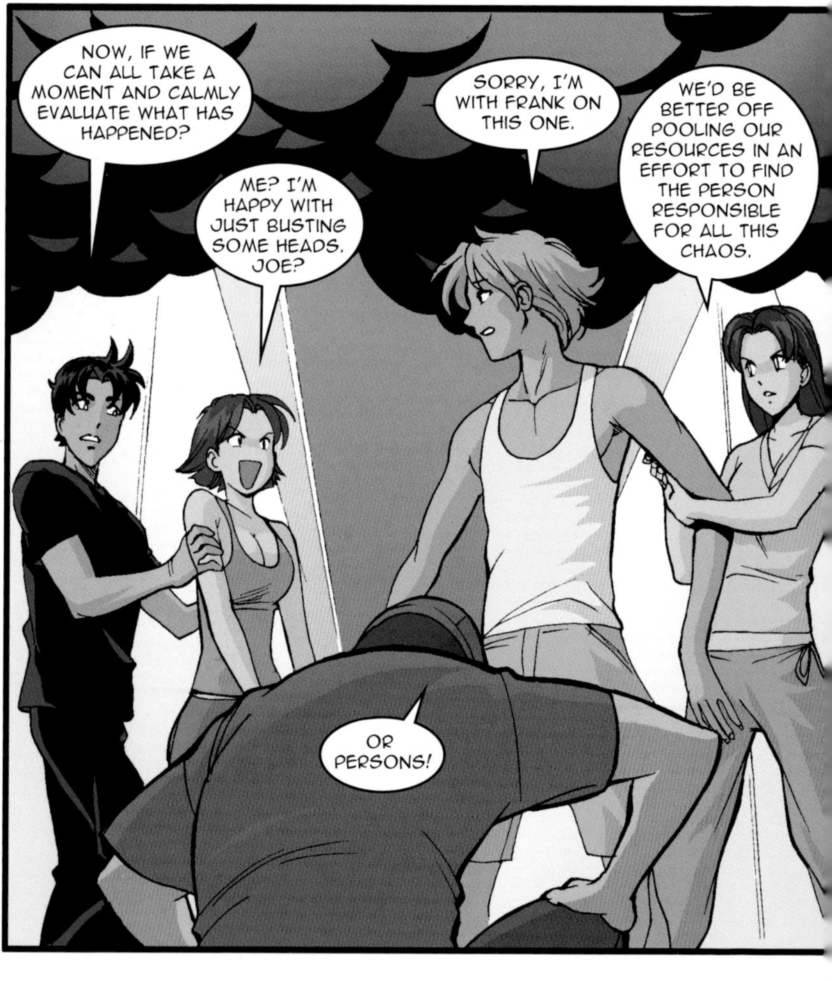
NOW, IF WE CAN ALL TAKE A MOMENT AND CALMLY EVALUATE WHAT HAS HAPPENED?
ME? I'M HAPPY WITH JUST BUSTING SOME HEADS. JOE?
SORRY, I'M WITH FRANK ON THIS ONE.
WE'D BE BETTER OFF POOLING OUR RESOURCES IN AN EFFORT TO FIND THE PERSON RESPONSIBLE FOR ALL THIS CHAOS.
OR PERSONS!

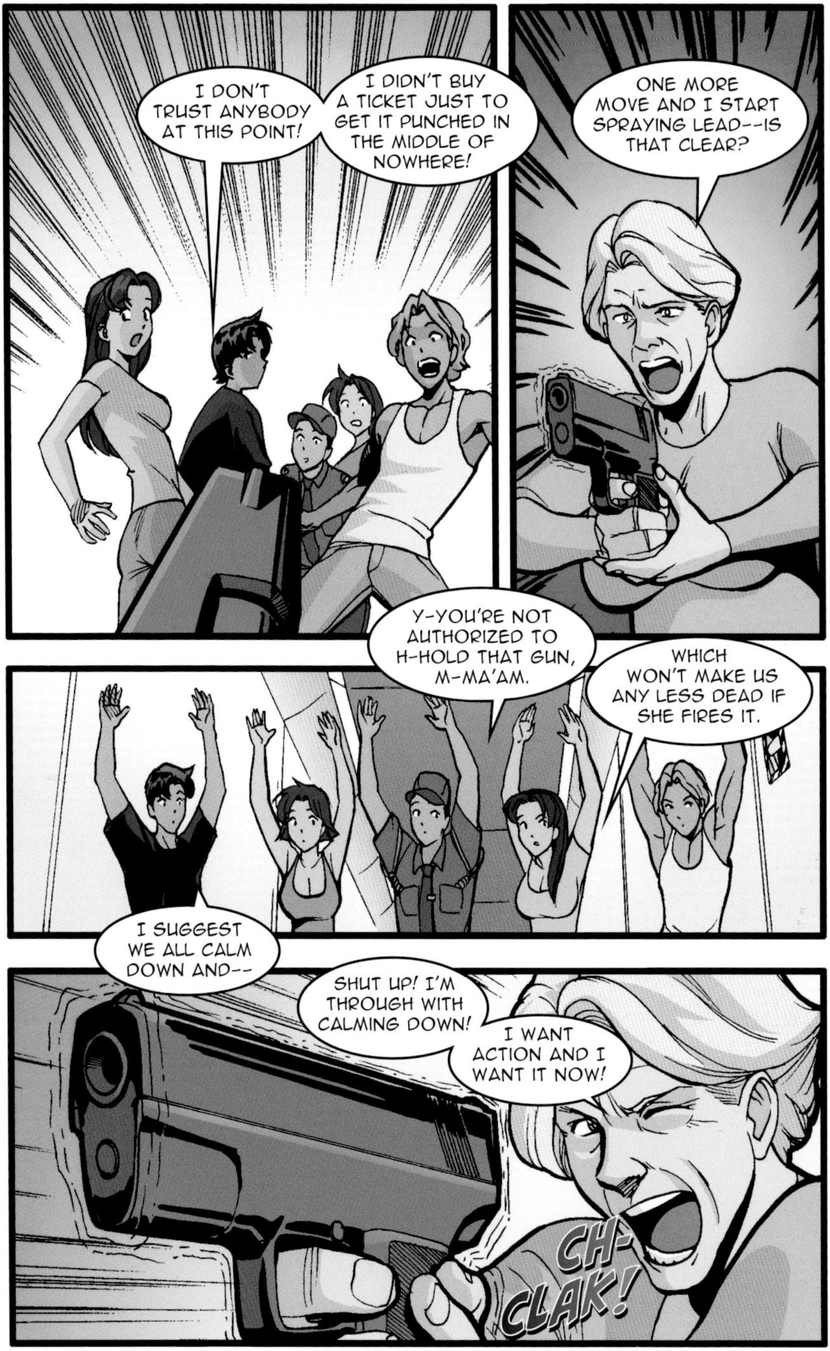
I DON'T TRUST ANYBODY AT THIS POINT!
I DIDN'T BUY A TICKET JUST TO GET IT PUNCHED IN THE MIDDLE OF NOWHERE!
ONE MORE MOVE AND I START SPRAYING LEAD--IS THAT CLEAR?
Y-YOU'RE NOT AUTHORIZED TO H-HOLD THAT GUN, M-MA'AM.
WHICH WON'T MAKE US ANY LESS DEAD IF SHE FIRES IT.
I SUGGEST WE ALL CALM DOWN AND--
SHUT UP! I'M THROUGH WITH CALMING DOWN!
I WANT ACTION AND I WANT IT NOW!
CH-CLAK!

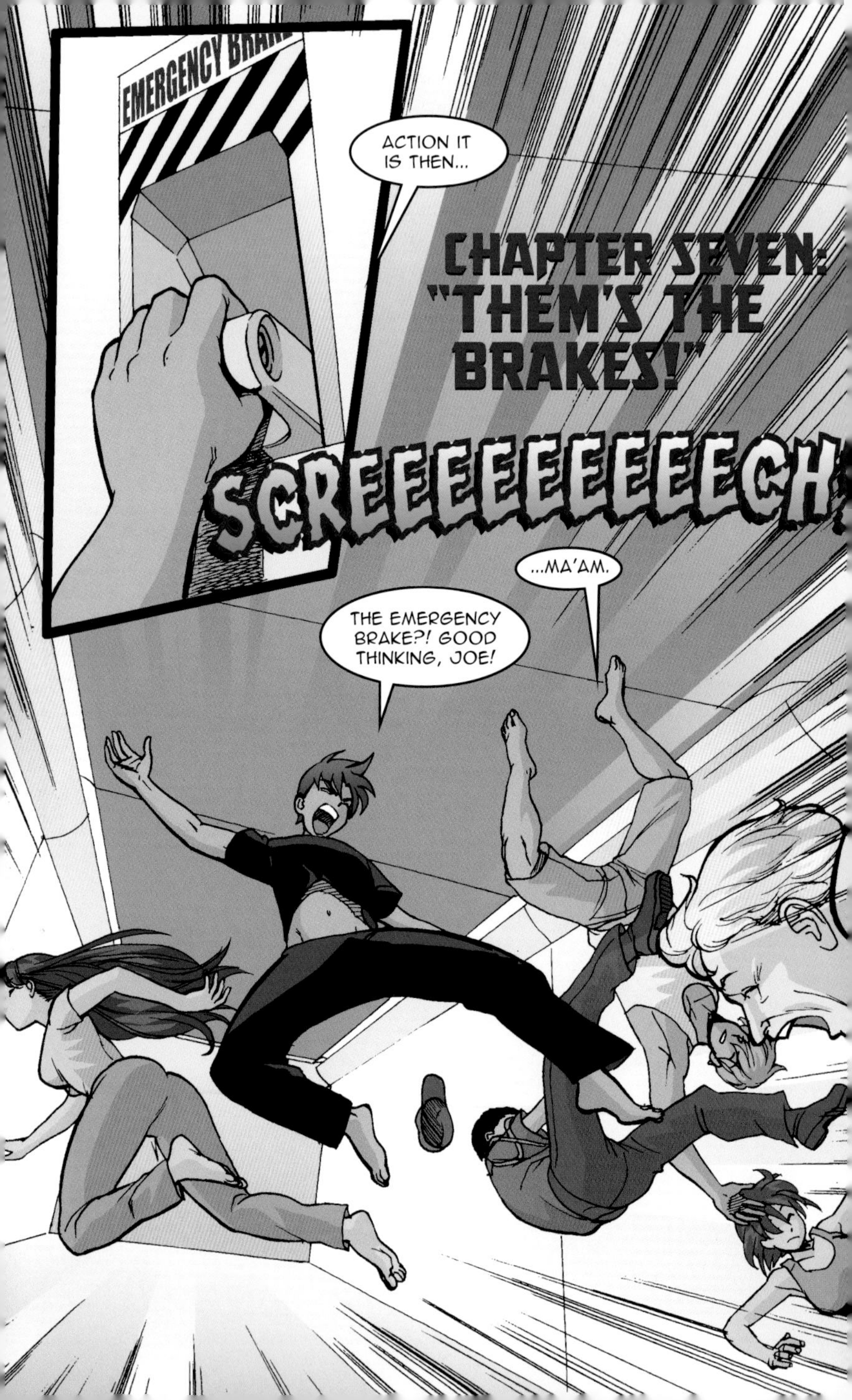
EMERGENCY BRAKE
ACTION IT IS THEN...
CHAPTER SEVEN: "THEM'S THE BRAKES!"
SCREEEEEEEEEEECH
THE EMERGENCY BRAKE?! GOOD THINKING, JOE!
...MA'AM.

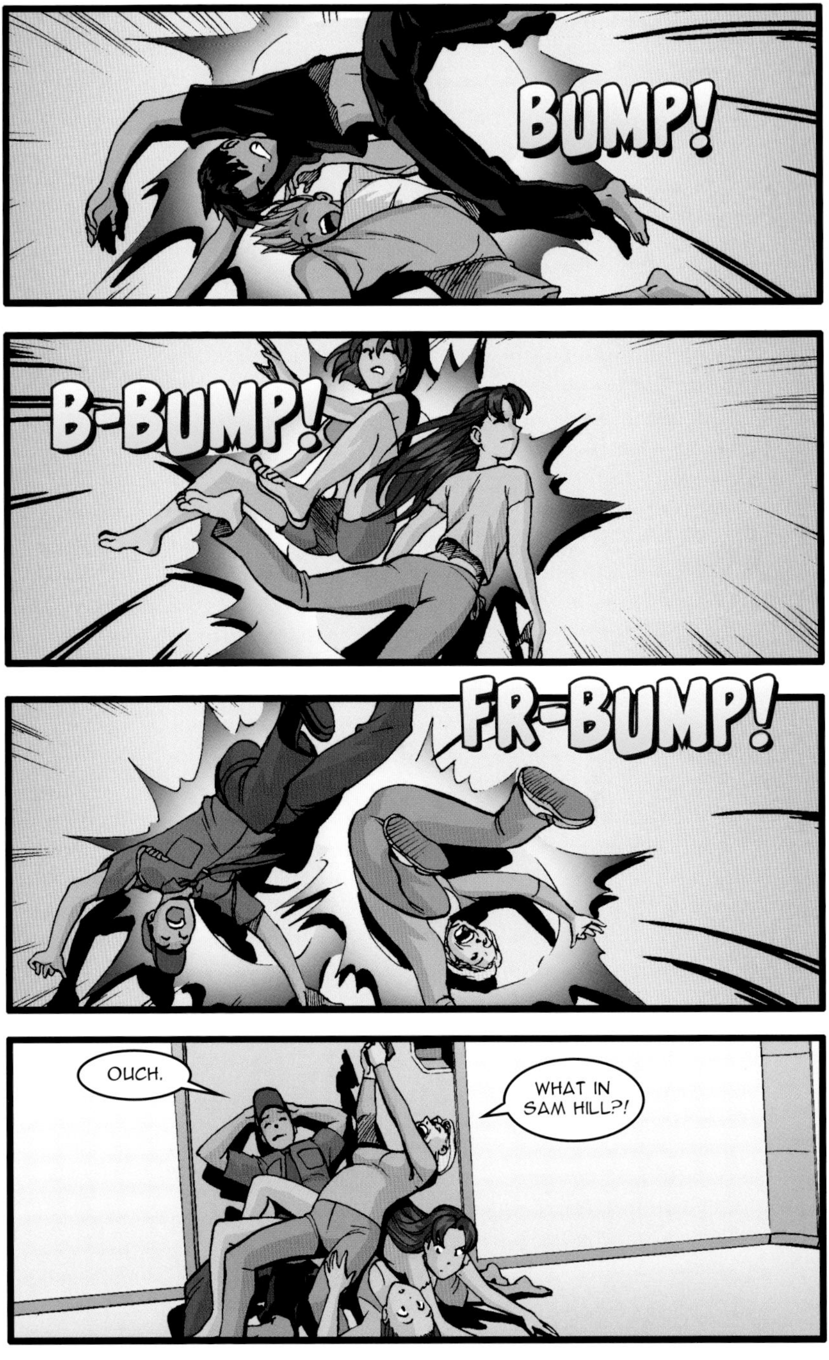
BUMP!
B-BUMP!
FR-BUMP!
OUCH.
WHAT IN SAM HILL?!

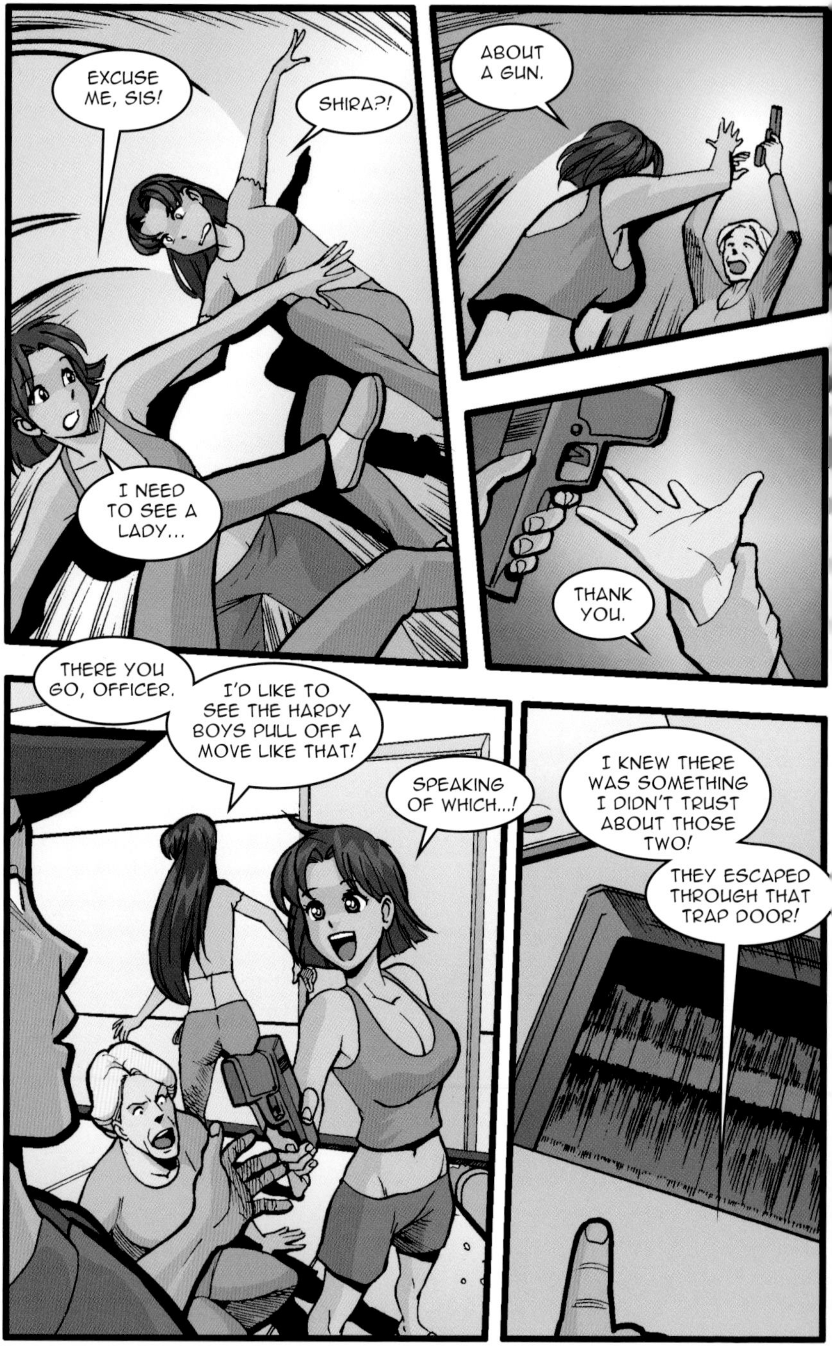
EXCUSE ME, SIS!
SHIRA?!
I NEED TO SEE A LADY...
ABOUT A GUN.
THANK YOU.
THERE YOU GO, OFFICER.
I'D LIKE TO SEE THE HARDY BOYS PULL OFF A MOVE LIKE THAT!
SPEAKING OF WHICH...!
I KNEW THERE WAS SOMETHING I DIDN'T TRUST ABOUT THOSE TWO!
THEY ESCAPED THROUGH THAT TRAP DOOR!

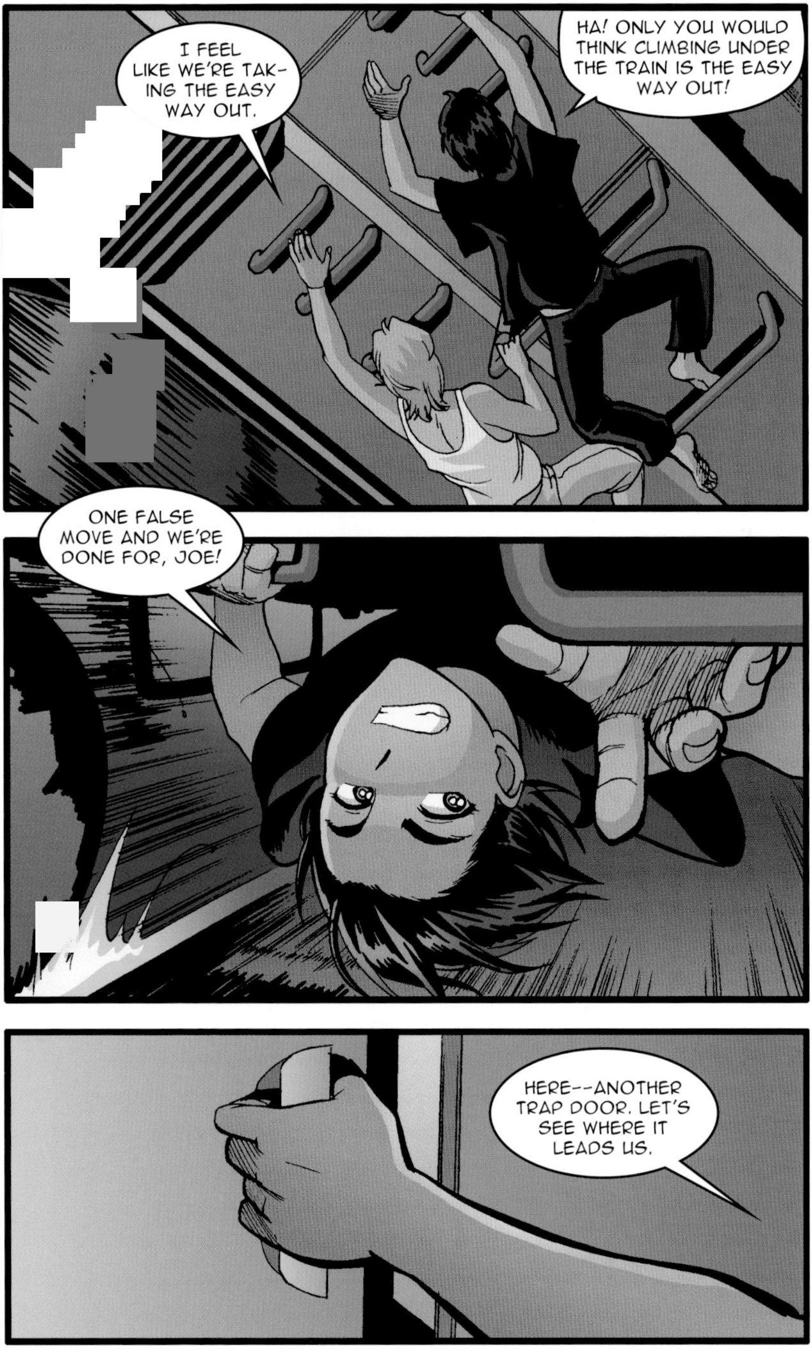
I FEEL LIKE WE'RE TAKING THE EASY WAY OUT.
HA! ONLY YOU WOULD THINK CLIMBING UNDER THE TRAIN IS THE EASY WAY OUT!
ONE FALSE MOVE AND WE'RE DONE FOR, JOE!
HERE--ANOTHER TRAP DOOR. LET'S SEE WHERE IT LEADS US.

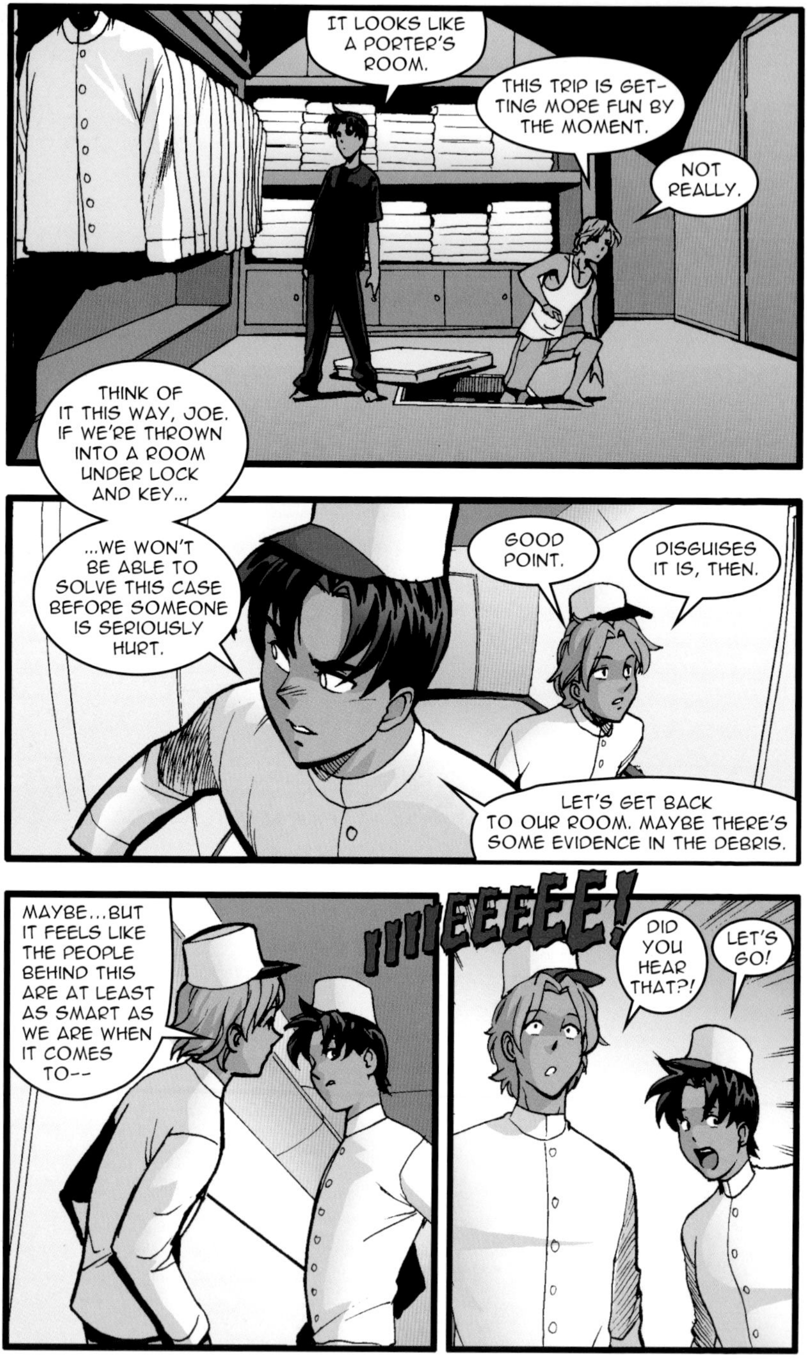
IT LOOKS LIKE A PORTER'S ROOM.
THIS TRIP IS GETTING MORE FUN BY THE MOMENT.
NOT REALLY.
THINK OF IT THIS WAY, JOE. IF WE'RE THROWN INTO A ROOM UNDER LOCK AND KEY...
...WE WON'T BE ABLE TO SOLVE THIS CASE BEFORE SOMEONE IS SERIOUSLY HURT.
GOOD POINT.
DISGUISES IT IS, THEN.
LET'S GET BACK TO OUR ROOM. MAYBE THERE'S SOME EVIDENCE IN THE DEBRIS.
MAYBE...BUT IT FEELS LIKE THE PEOPLE BEHIND THIS ARE AT LEAST AS SMART AS WE ARE WHEN IT COMES TO--
IIIIEEEEEE!
DID YOU HEAR THAT?!
LET'S GO!

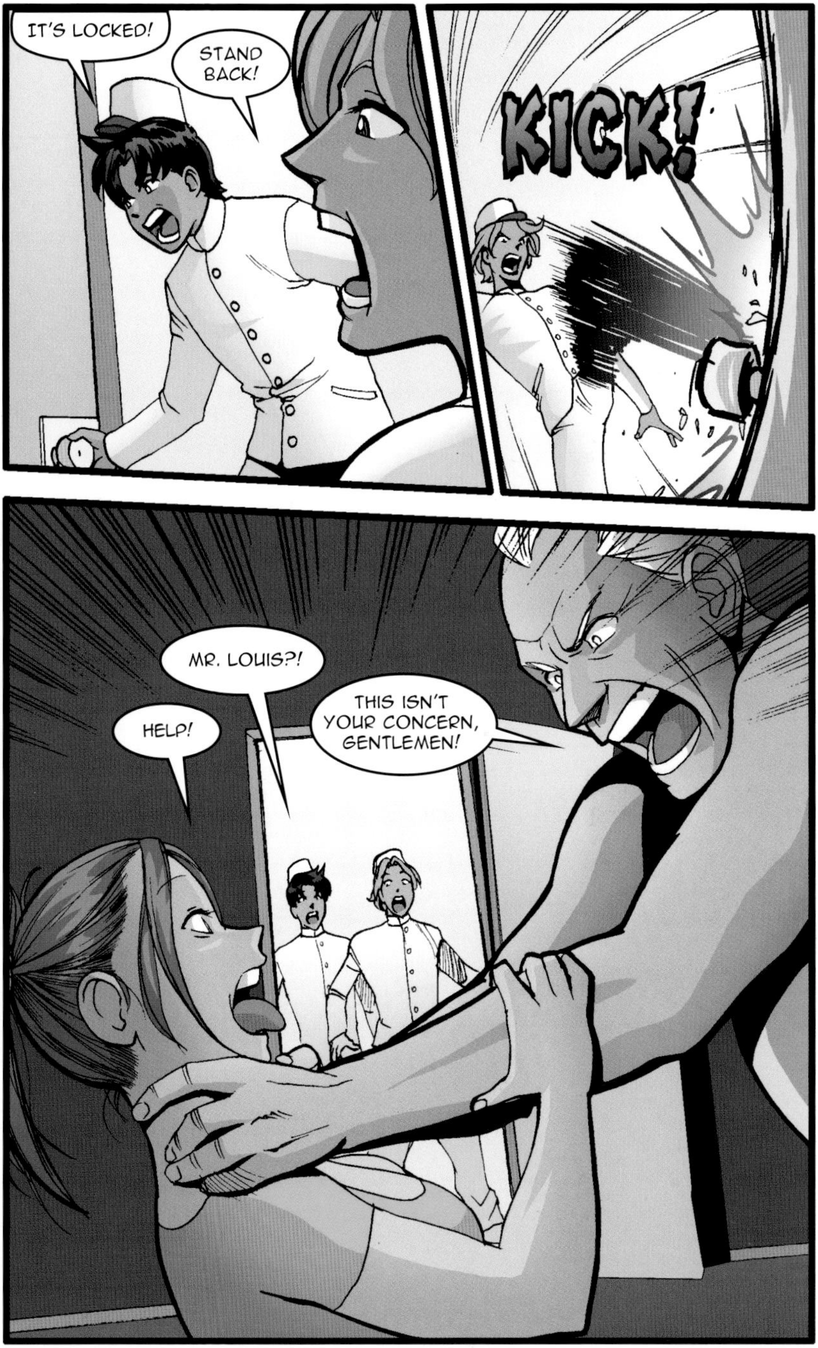
IT'S LOCKED!
STAND BACK!
KICK!
MR. LOUIS?!
HELP!
THIS ISN'T YOUR CONCERN, GENTLEMEN!

CHAPTER EIGHT: "RUNNING OFF THE RAILS"

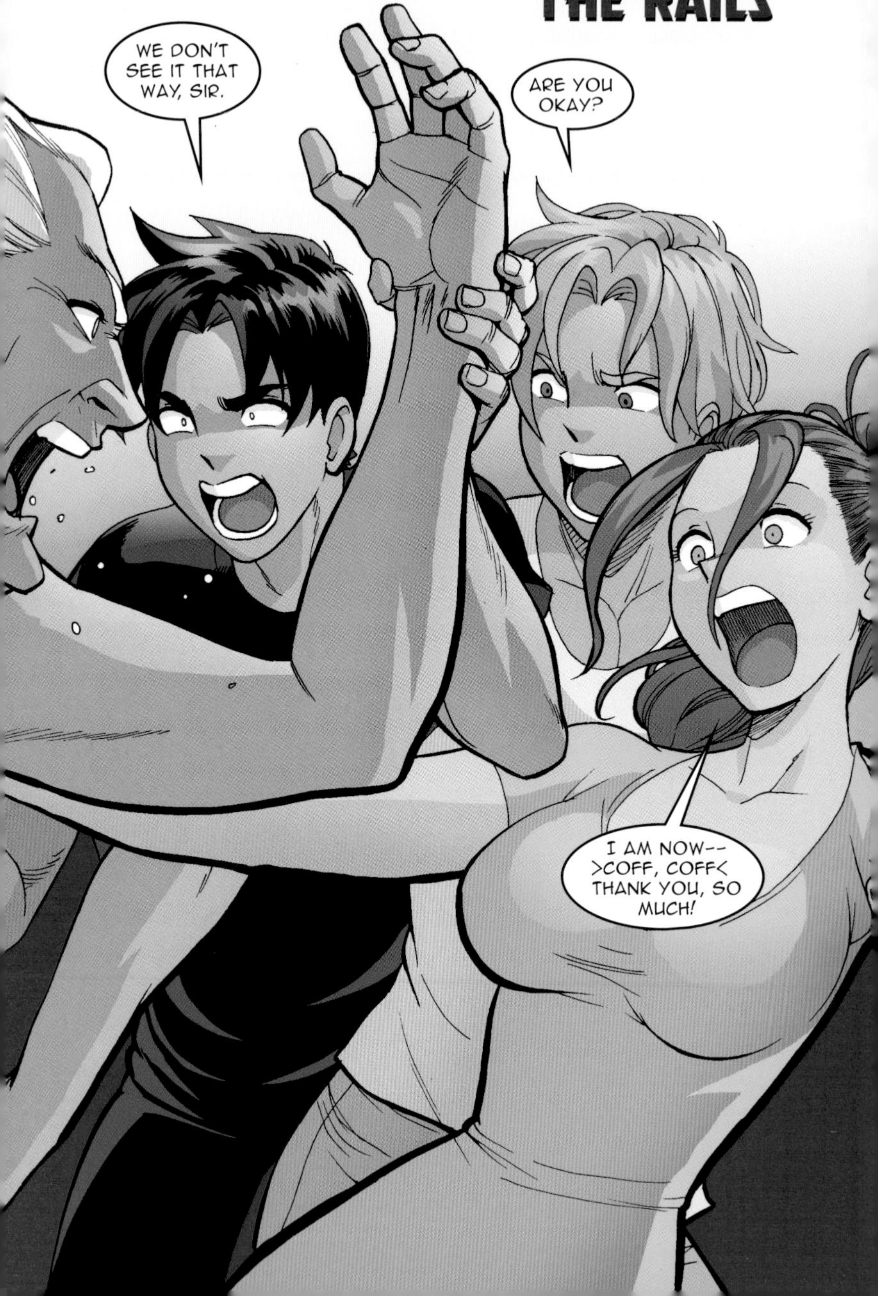
WE DON'T SEE IT THAT WAY, SIR.
ARE YOU OKAY?
I AM NOW-- >COFF, COFF< THANK YOU, SO MUCH!

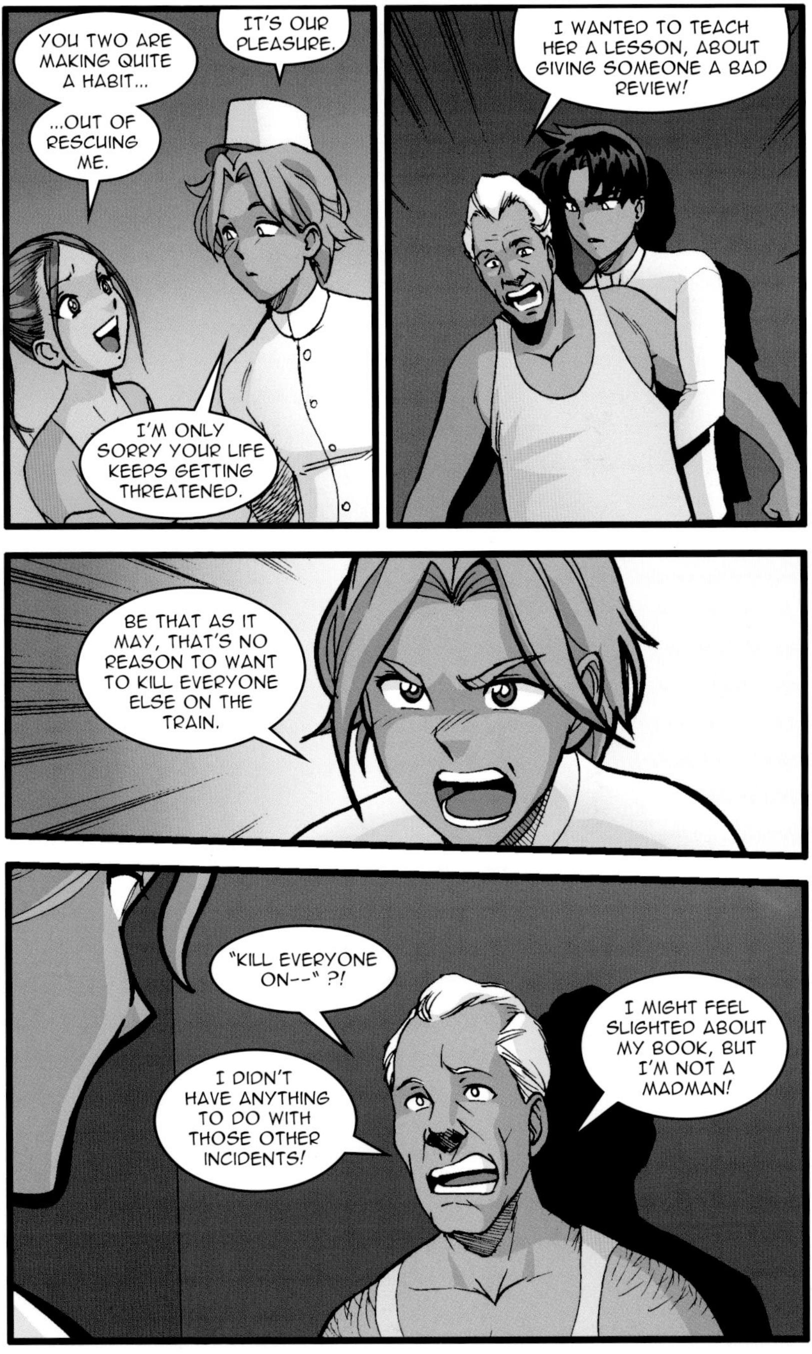
YOU TWO ARE MAKING QUITE A HABIT...
...OUT OF RESCUING ME.
IT'S OUR PLEASURE.
I'M ONLY SORRY YOUR LIFE KEEPS GETTING THREATENED.
I WANTED TO TEACH HER A LESSON, ABOUT GIVING SOMEONE A BAD REVIEW!
BE THAT AS IT MAY, THAT'S NO REASON TO WANT TO KILL EVERYONE ELSE ON THE TRAIN.
"KILL EVERYONE ON--" ?!
I DIDN'T HAVE ANYTHING TO DO WITH THOSE OTHER INCIDENTS!
I MIGHT FEEL SLIGHTED ABOUT MY BOOK, BUT I'M NOT A MADMAN!

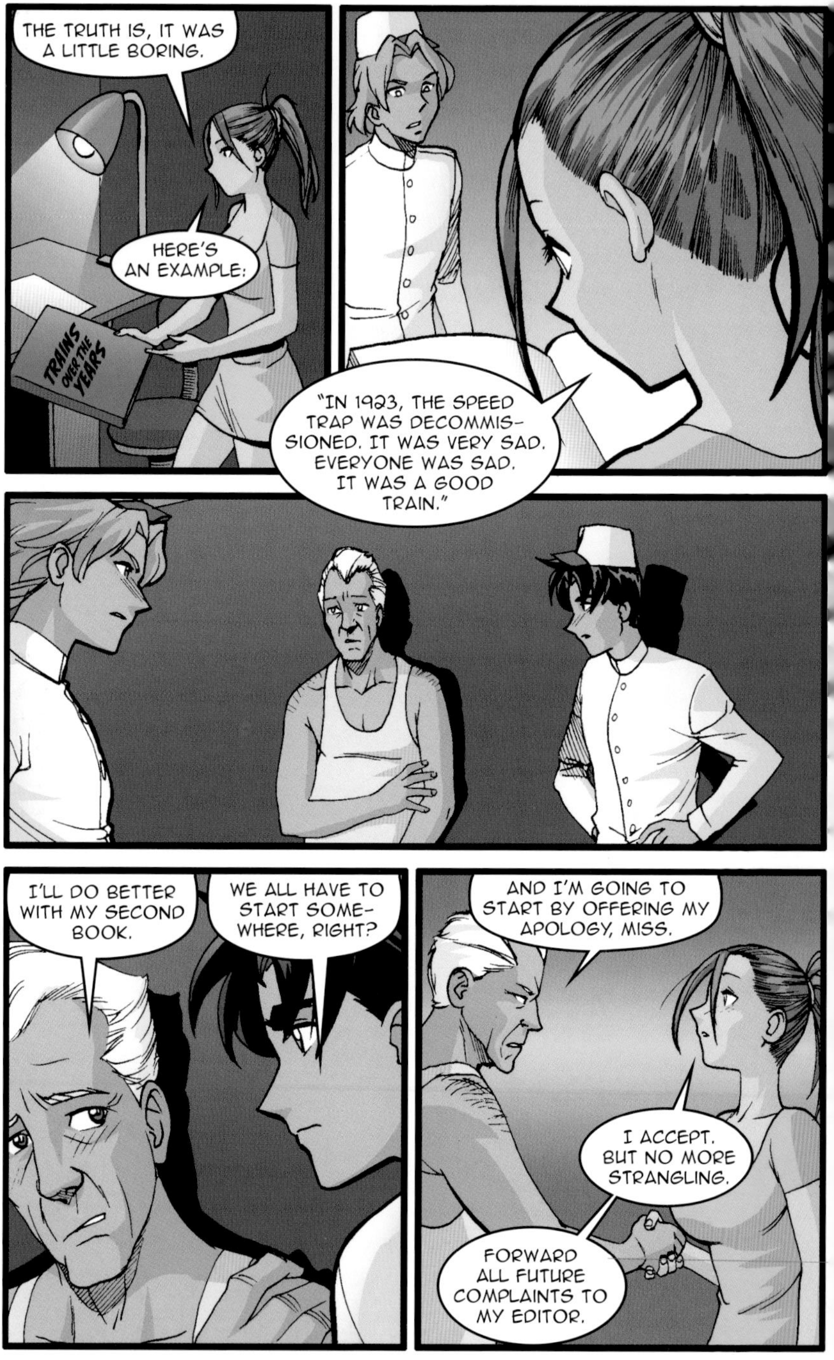
THE TRUTH IS, IT WAS A LITTLE BORING.
HERE'S AN EXAMPLE:
TRAINS OVER THE YEARS
"IN 1923, THE SPEED TRAP WAS DECOMMISSIONED. IT WAS VERY SAD. EVERYONE WAS SAD. IT WAS A GOOD TRAIN."
I'LL DO BETTER WITH MY SECOND BOOK.
WE ALL HAVE TO START SOMEWHERE, RIGHT?
AND I'M GOING TO START BY OFFERING MY APOLOGY, MISS.
I ACCEPT. BUT NO MORE STRANGLING.
FORWARD ALL FUTURE COMPLAINTS TO MY EDITOR.

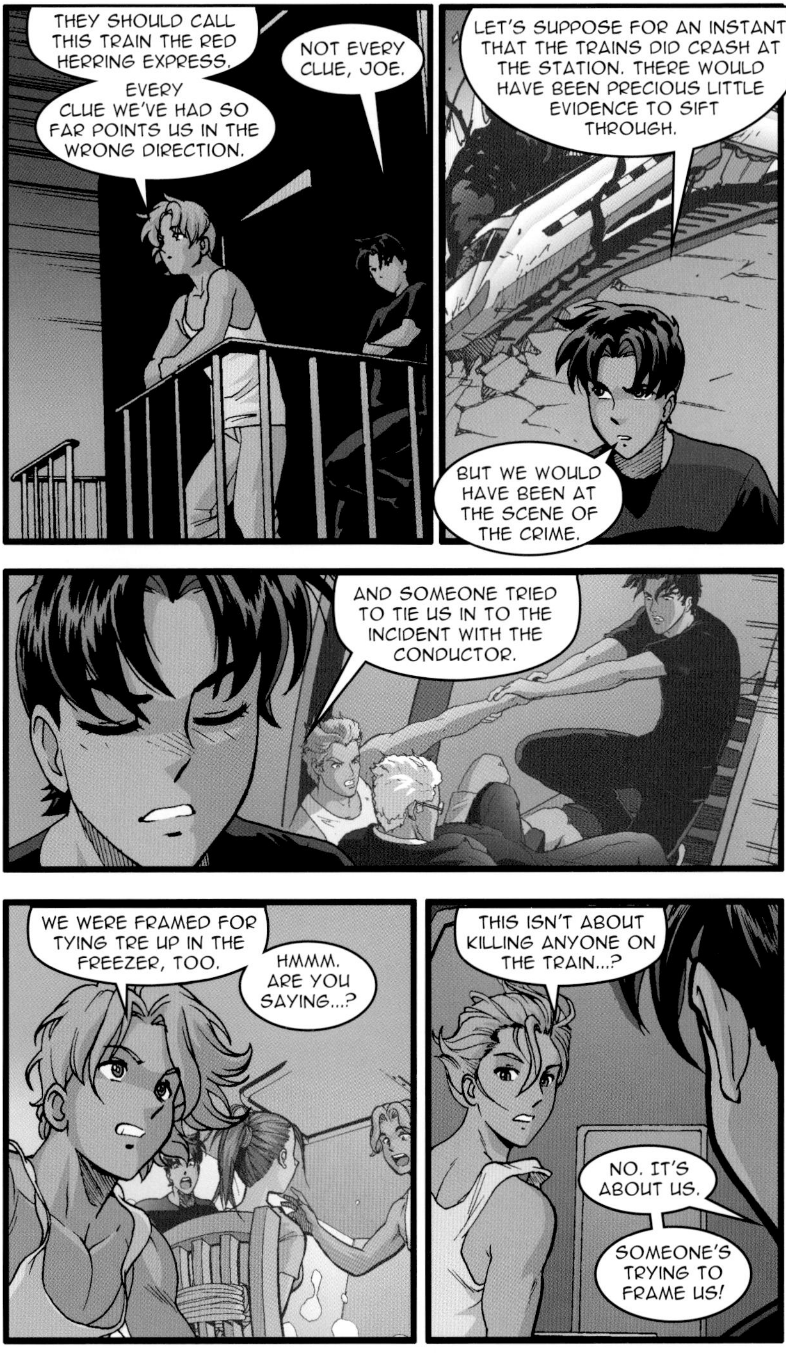
THEY SHOULD CALL THIS TRAIN THE RED HERRING EXPRESS.
EVERY CLUE WE'VE HAD SO FAR POINTS US IN THE WRONG DIRECTION.
NOT EVERY CLUE, JOE.
LET'S SUPPOSE FOR AN INSTANT THAT THE TRAINS DID CRASH AT THE STATION. THERE WOULD HAVE BEEN PRECIOUS LITTLE EVIDENCE TO SIFT THROUGH.
BUT WE WOULD HAVE BEEN AT THE SCENE OF THE CRIME.
AND SOMEONE TRIED TO TIE US IN TO THE INCIDENT WITH THE CONDUCTOR.
WE WERE FRAMED FOR TYING TRE UP IN THE FREEZER, TOO.
HMMM. ARE YOU SAYING...?
THIS ISN'T ABOUT KILLING ANYONE ON THE TRAIN...?
NO. IT'S ABOUT US.
SOMEONE'S TRYING TO FRAME US!

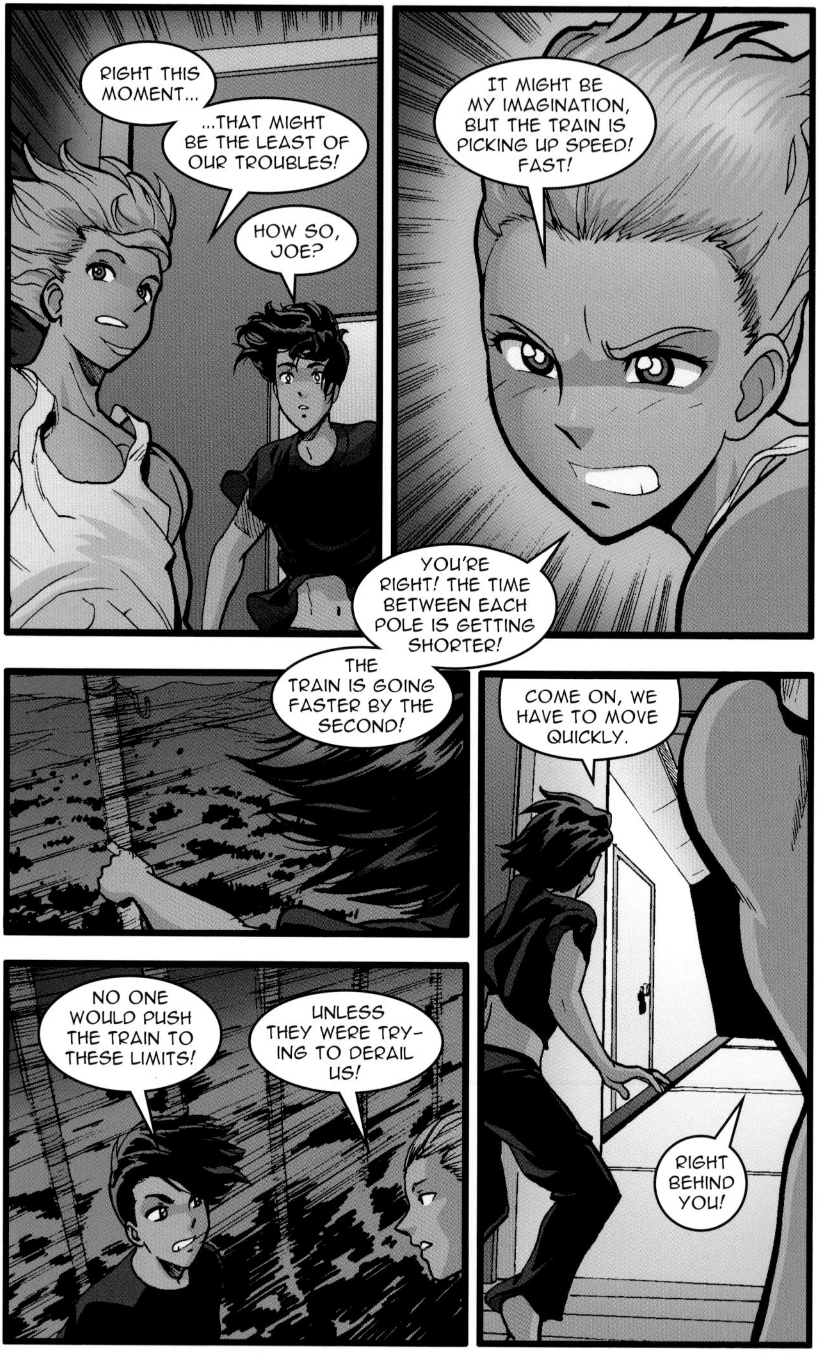
RIGHT THIS MOMENT...
...THAT MIGHT BE THE LEAST OF OUR TROUBLES!
HOW SO, JOE?
IT MIGHT BE MY IMAGINATION, BUT THE TRAIN IS PICKING UP SPEED! FAST!
YOU'RE RIGHT! THE TIME BETWEEN EACH POLE IS GETTING SHORTER!
THE TRAIN IS GOING FASTER BY THE SECOND!
NO ONE WOULD PUSH THE TRAIN TO THESE LIMITS!
UNLESS THEY WERE TRY-ING TO DERAIL US!
COME ON, WE HAVE TO MOVE QUICKLY.
RIGHT BEHIND YOU!

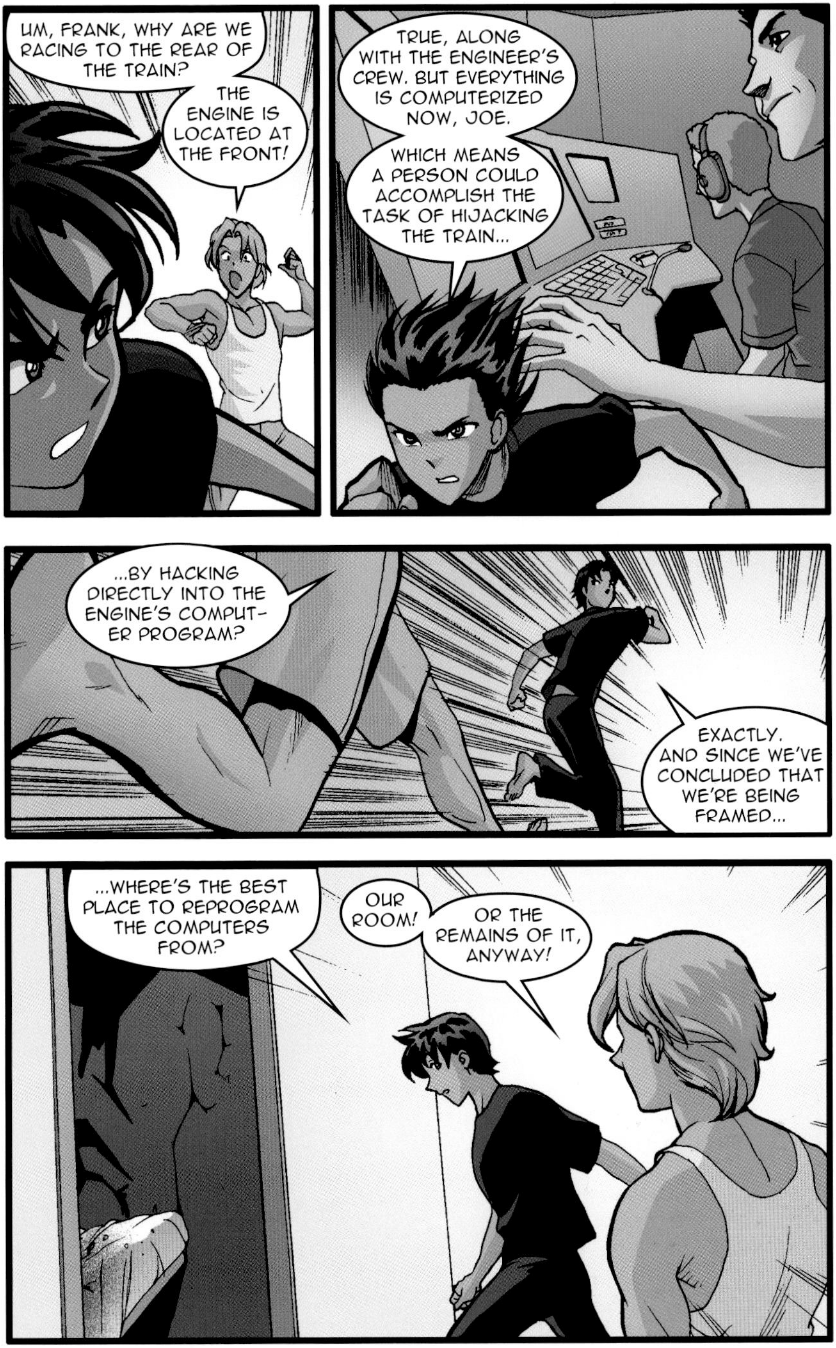
UM, FRANK, WHY ARE WE RACING TO THE REAR OF THE TRAIN?
THE ENGINE IS LOCATED AT THE FRONT!
TRUE, ALONG WITH THE ENGINEER'S CREW. BUT EVERYTHING IS COMPUTERIZED NOW, JOE.
WHICH MEANS A PERSON COULD ACCOMPLISH THE TASK OF HIJACKING THE TRAIN...
...BY HACKING DIRECTLY INTO THE ENGINE'S COMPUT-ER PROGRAM?
EXACTLY. AND SINCE WE'VE CONCLUDED THAT WE'RE BEING FRAMED...
...WHERE'S THE BEST PLACE TO REPROGRAM THE COMPUTERS FROM?
OUR ROOM!
OR THE REMAINS OF IT, ANYWAY!

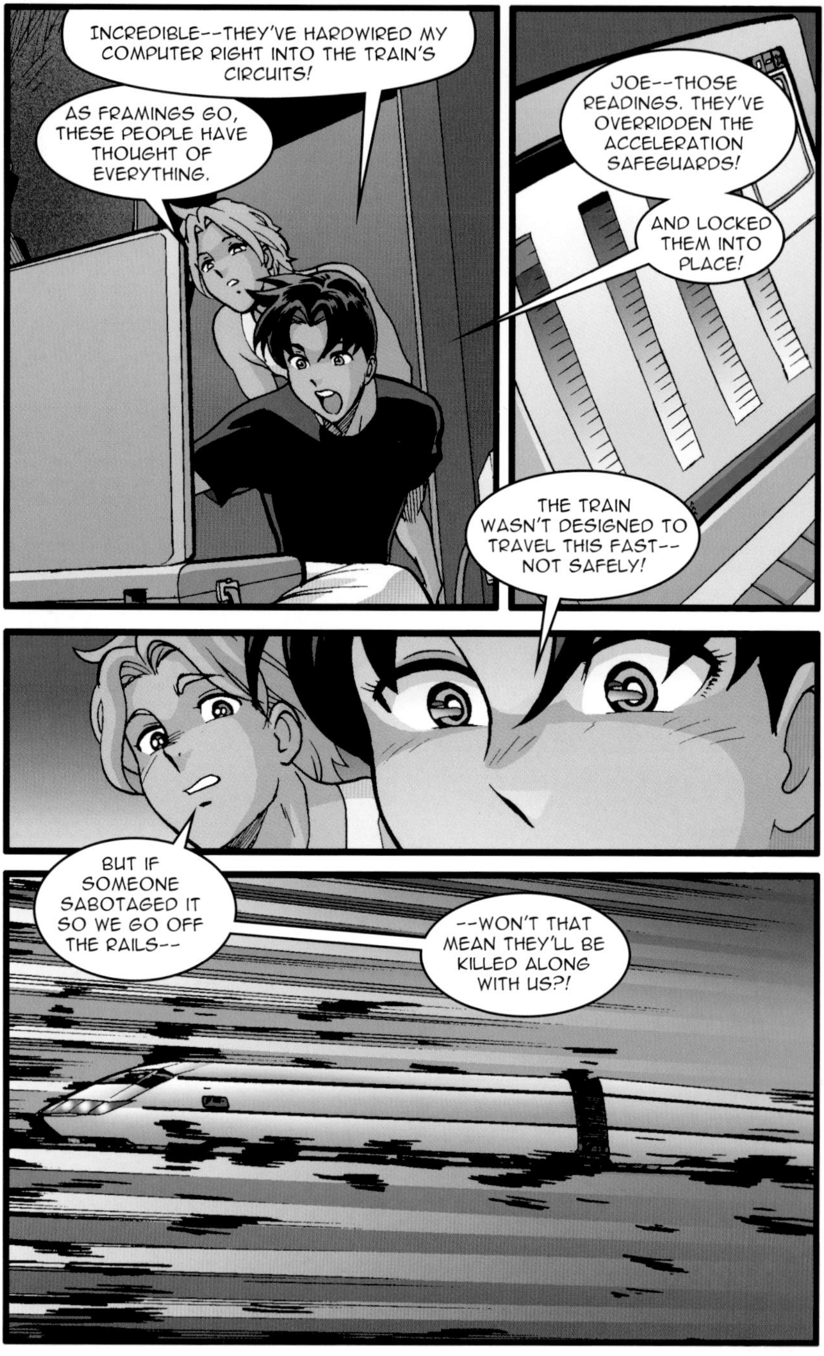
INCREDIBLE--THEY'VE HARDWIRED MY COMPUTER RIGHT INTO THE TRAIN'S CIRCUITS!
AS FRAMINGS GO, THESE PEOPLE HAVE THOUGHT OF EVERYTHING.
JOE--THOSE READINGS. THEY'VE OVERRIDDEN THE ACCELERATION SAFEGUARDS!
AND LOCKED THEM INTO PLACE!
THE TRAIN WASN'T DESIGNED TO TRAVEL THIS FAST--NOT SAFELY!
BUT IF SOMEONE SABOTAGED IT SO WE GO OFF THE RAILS--
--WON'T THAT MEAN THEY'LL BE KILLED ALONG WITH US?!

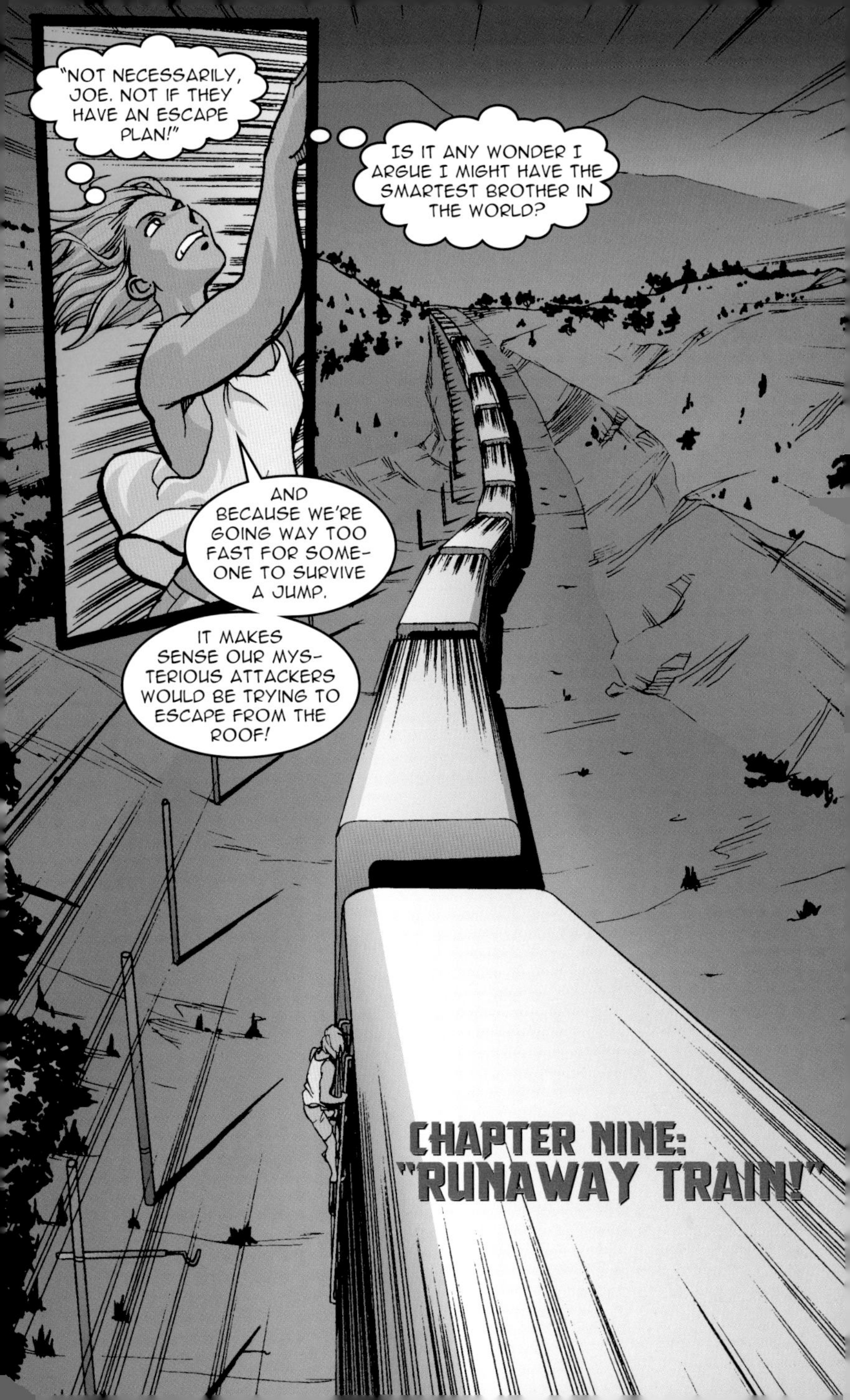
"NOT NECESSARILY, JOE. NOT IF THEY HAVE AN ESCAPE PLAN!"
IS IT ANY WONDER I ARGUE I MIGHT HAVE THE SMARTEST BROTHER IN THE WORLD?
AND BECAUSE WE'RE GOING WAY TOO FAST FOR SOME-ONE TO SURVIVE A JUMP.
IT MAKES SENSE OUR MYS-TERIOUS ATTACKERS WOULD BE TRYING TO ESCAPE FROM THE ROOF!
CHAPTER NINE:
"RUNAWAY TRAIN!"

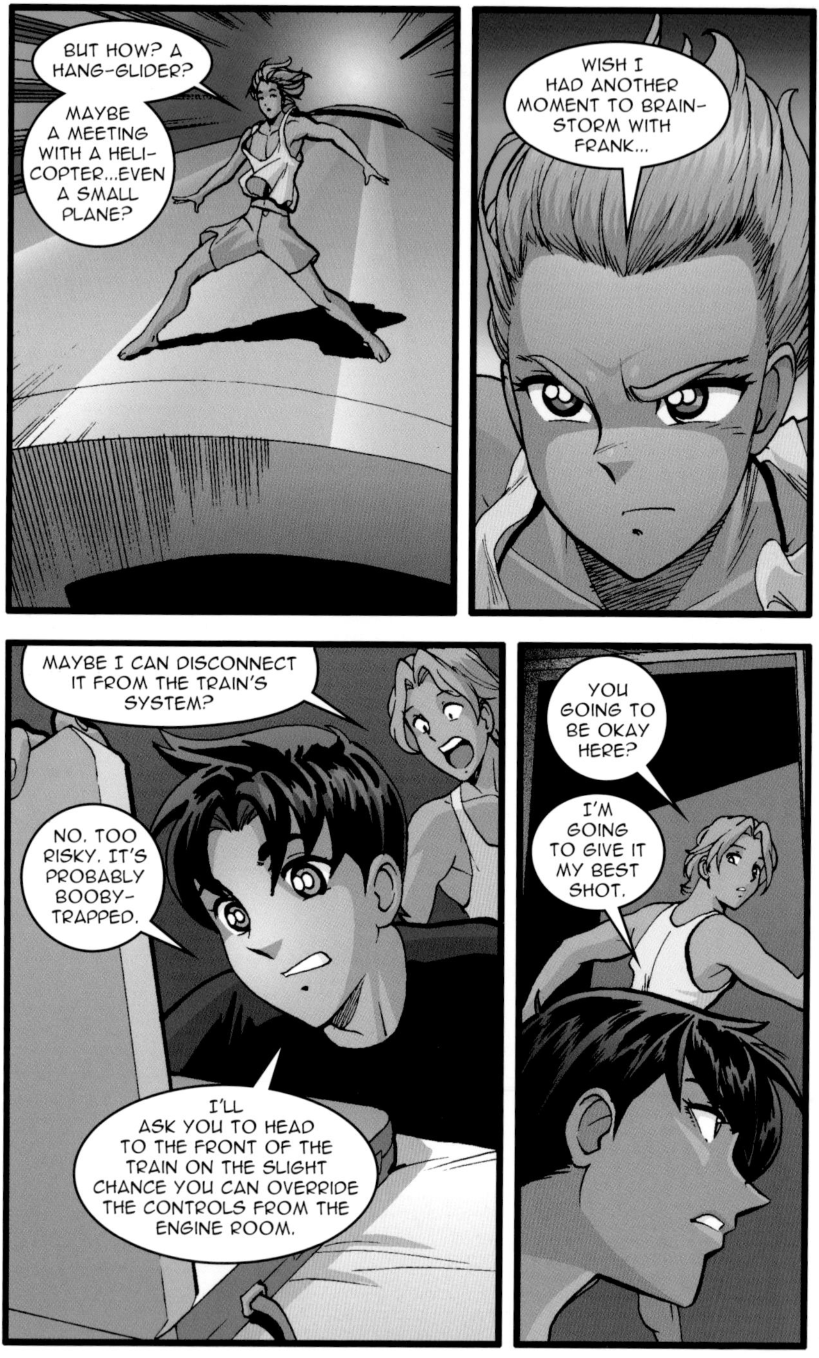
BUT HOW? A HANG-GLIDER?
MAYBE A MEETING WITH A HELI-COPTER...EVEN A SMALL PLANE?
WISH I HAD ANOTHER MOMENT TO BRAIN-STORM WITH FRANK...
MAYBE I CAN DISCONNECT IT FROM THE TRAIN'S SYSTEM?
NO. TOO RISKY. IT'S PROBABLY BOOBY-TRAPPED.
I'LL ASK YOU TO HEAD TO THE FRONT OF THE TRAIN ON THE SLIGHT CHANCE YOU CAN OVERRIDE THE CONTROLS FROM THE ENGINE ROOM.
YOU GOING TO BE OKAY HERE?
I'M GOING TO GIVE IT MY BEST SHOT.

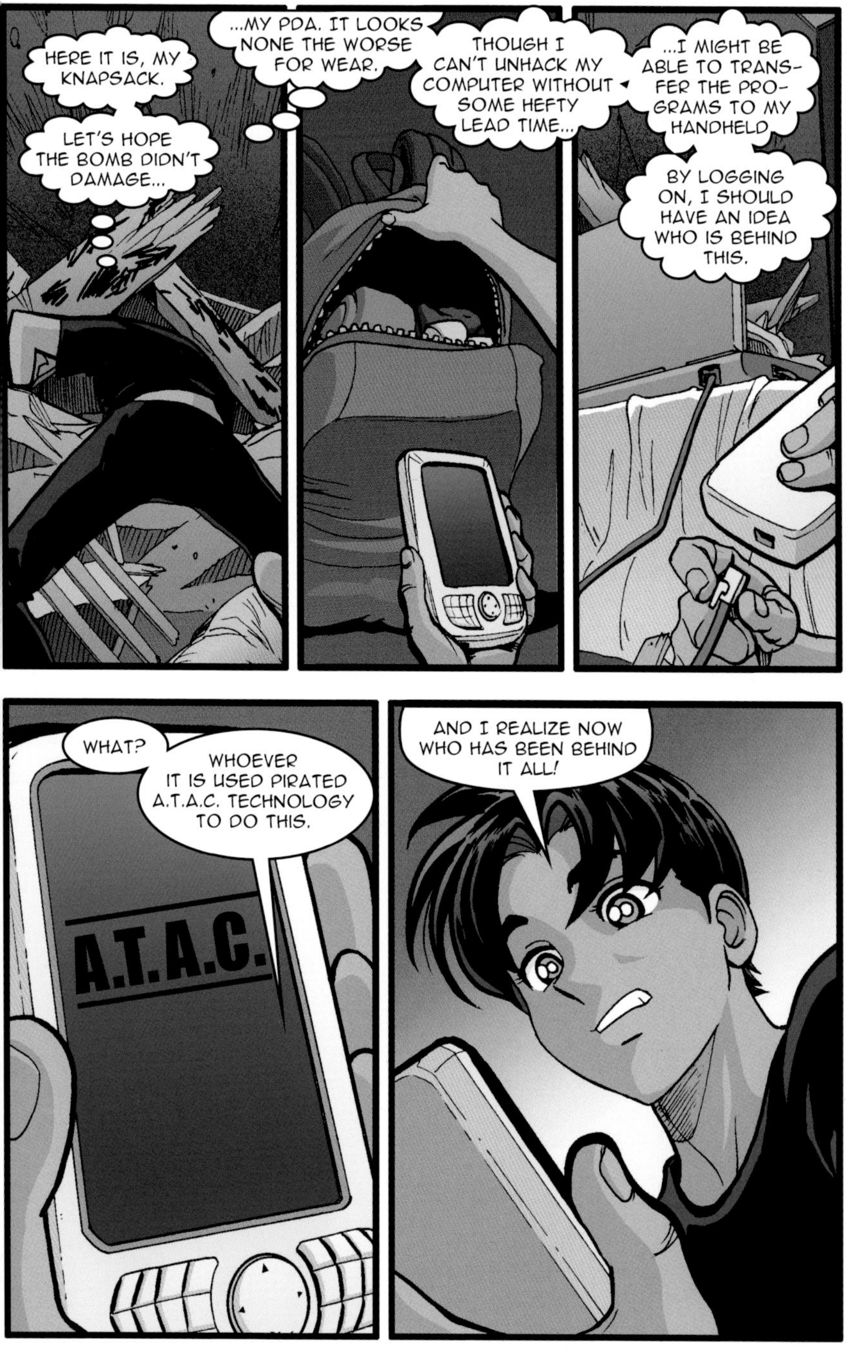
HERE IT IS, MY KNAPSACK.
LET'S HOPE THE BOMB DIDN'T DAMAGE...
...MY PDA. IT LOOKS NONE THE WORSE FOR WEAR.
THOUGH I CAN'T UNHACK MY COMPUTER WITHOUT SOME HEFTY LEAD TIME...
...I MIGHT BE ABLE TO TRANS-FER THE PRO-GRAMS TO MY HANDHELD.
BY LOGGING ON, I SHOULD HAVE AN IDEA WHO IS BEHIND THIS.
WHAT?
WHOEVER IT IS USED PIRATED A.T.A.C. TECHNOLOGY TO DO THIS.
A.T.A.C.
AND I REALIZE NOW WHO HAS BEEN BEHIND IT ALL!

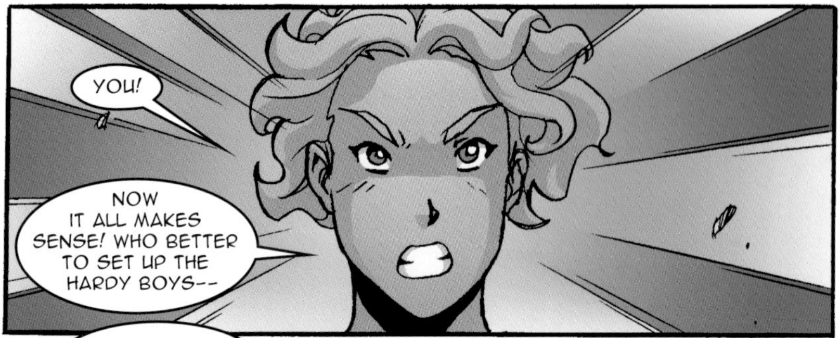
YOU!
NOW IT ALL MAKES SENSE! WHO BETTER TO SET UP THE HARDY BOYS--

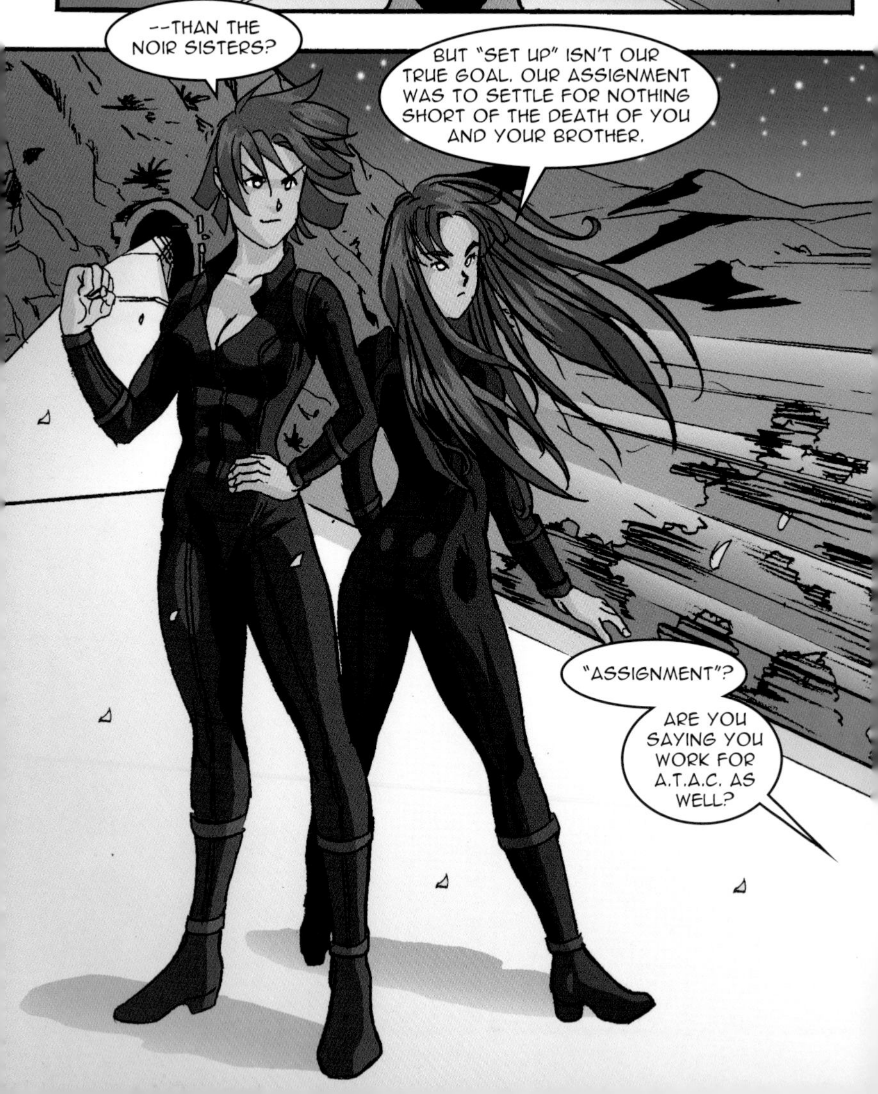
--THAN THE NOIR SISTERS?
BUT "SET UP" ISN'T OUR TRUE GOAL. OUR ASSIGNMENT WAS TO SETTLE FOR NOTHING SHORT OF THE DEATH OF YOU AND YOUR BROTHER.
"ASSIGNMENT"?
ARE YOU SAYING YOU WORK FOR A.T.A.C. AS WELL?

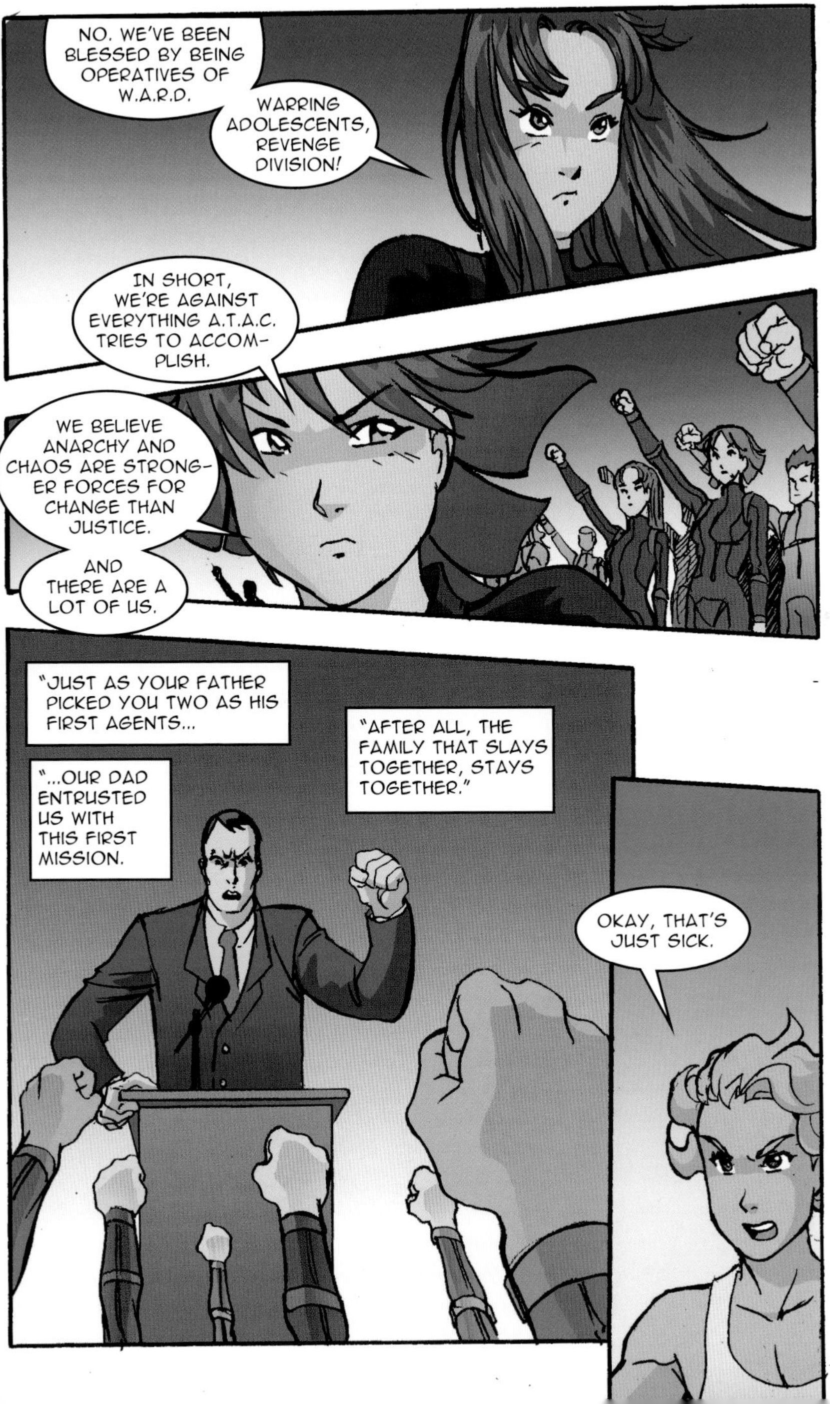
NO. WE'VE BEEN BLESSED BY BEING OPERATIVES OF W.A.R.D.
WARRING ADOLESCENTS, REVENGE DIVISION!
IN SHORT, WE'RE AGAINST EVERYTHING A.T.A.C. TRIES TO ACCOMPLISH.
WE BELIEVE ANARCHY AND CHAOS ARE STRONGER FORCES FOR CHANGE THAN JUSTICE.
AND THERE ARE A LOT OF US.
"JUST AS YOUR FATHER PICKED YOU TWO AS HIS FIRST AGENTS...
"...OUR DAD ENTRUSTED US WITH THIS FIRST MISSION.
"AFTER ALL, THE FAMILY THAT SLAYS TOGETHER, STAYS TOGETHER."
OKAY, THAT'S JUST SICK.

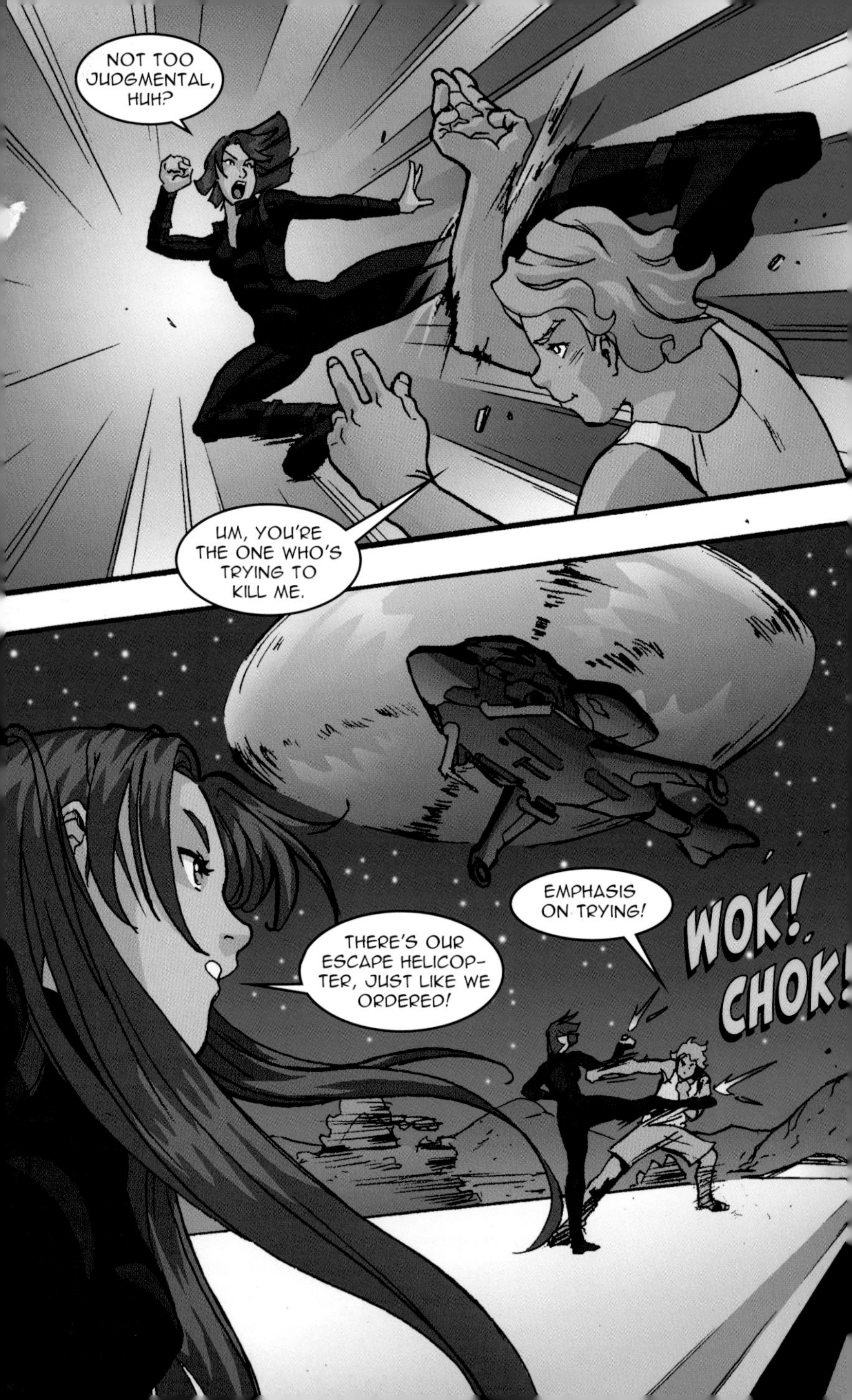
NOT TOO JUDGMENTAL, HUH?
UM, YOU'RE THE ONE WHO'S TRYING TO KILL ME.
EMPHASIS ON TRYING!
THERE'S OUR ESCAPE HELICOP-TER, JUST LIKE WE ORDERED!
WOK!
CHOK!

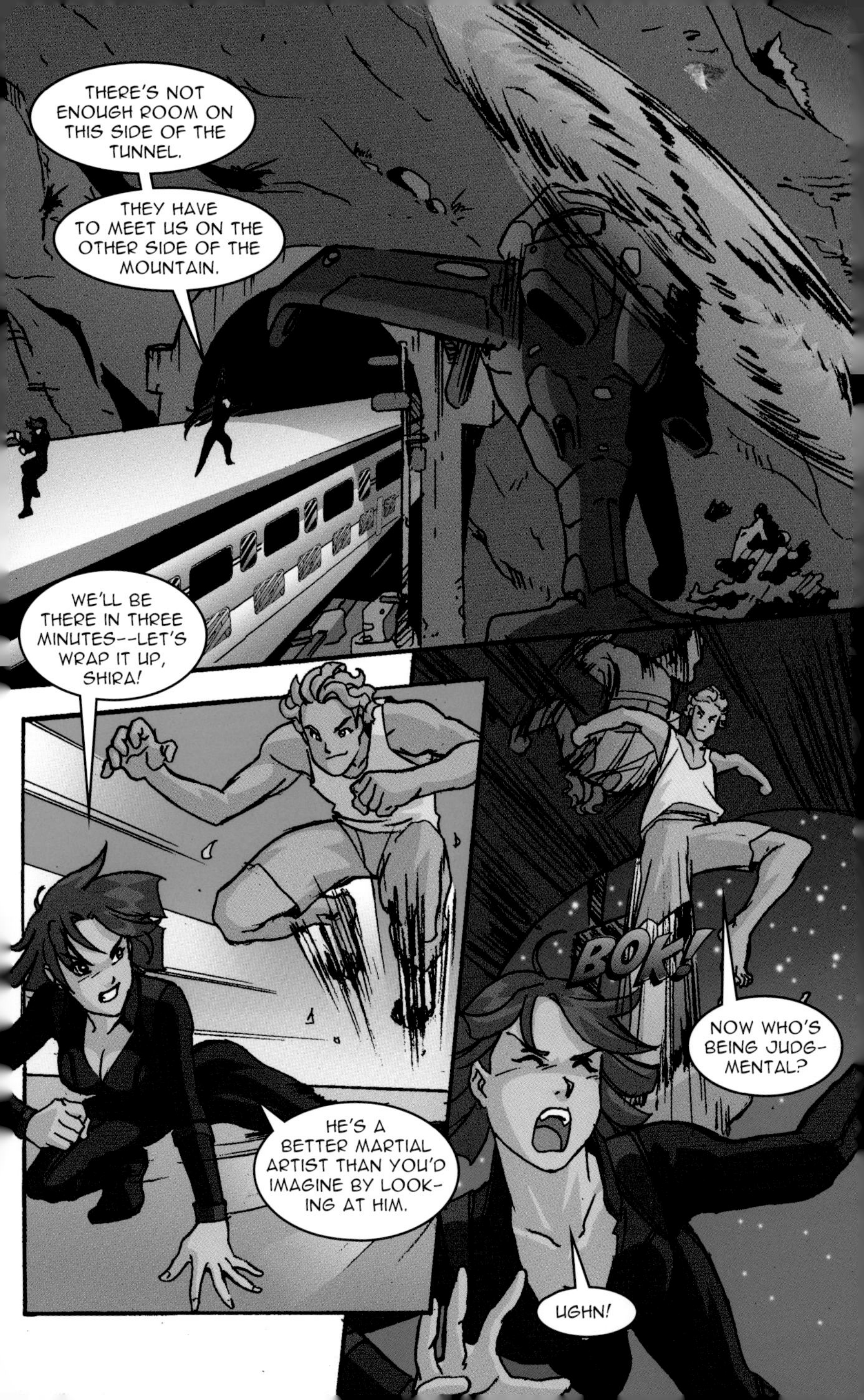
THERE'S NOT ENOUGH ROOM ON THIS SIDE OF THE TUNNEL.
THEY HAVE TO MEET US ON THE OTHER SIDE OF THE MOUNTAIN.
WE'LL BE THERE IN THREE MINUTES--LET'S WRAP IT UP, SHIRA!
HE'S A BETTER MARTIAL ARTIST THAN YOU'D IMAGINE BY LOOK-ING AT HIM.
BOK!
NOW WHO'S BEING JUDG-MENTAL?
UGHN!

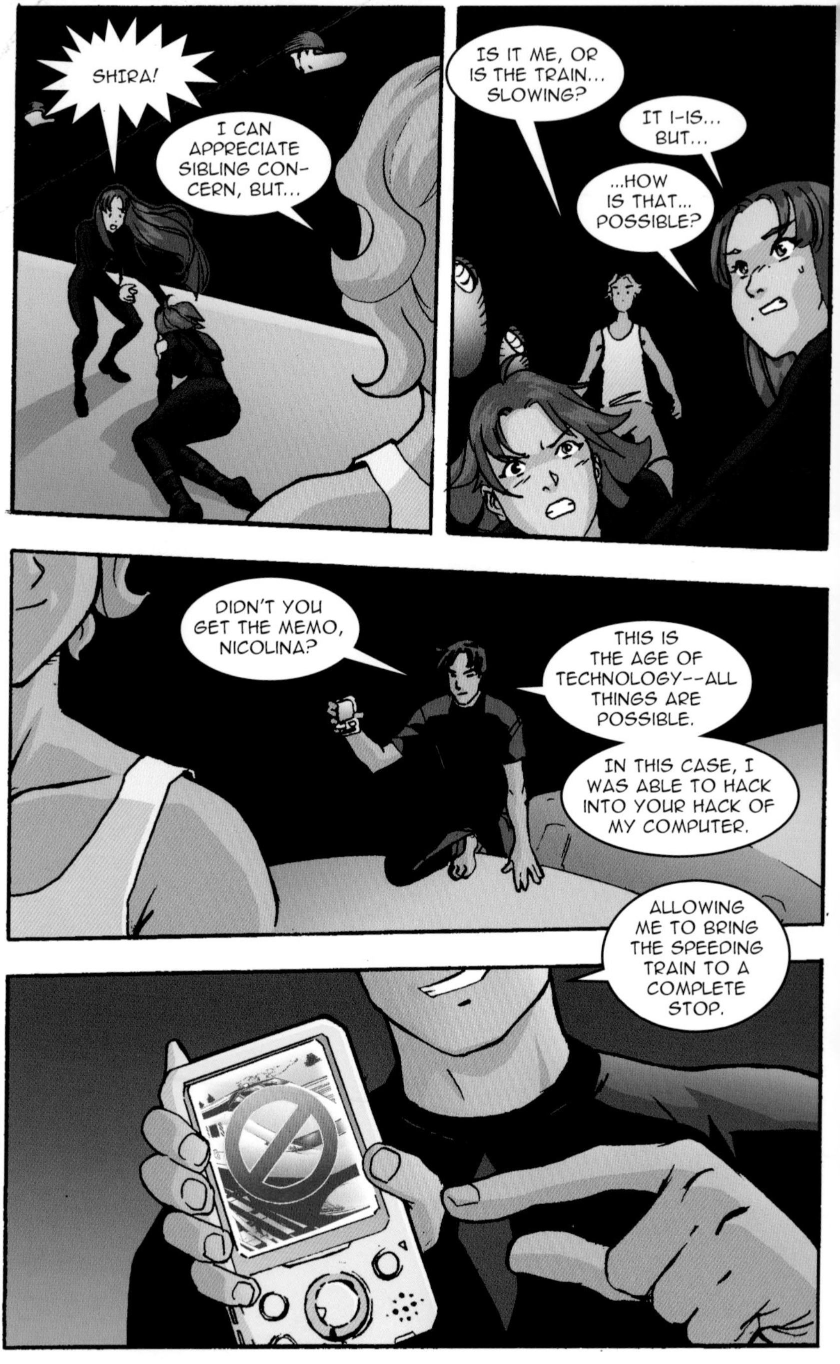
SHIRA!
I CAN APPRECIATE SIBLING CON- CERN, BUT...
IS IT ME, OR IS THE TRAIN... SLOWING?
IT I-IS... BUT...
...HOW IS THAT... POSSIBLE?
DIDN'T YOU GET THE MEMO, NICOLINA?
THIS IS THE AGE OF TECHNOLOGY--ALL THINGS ARE POSSIBLE.
IN THIS CASE, I WAS ABLE TO HACK INTO YOUR HACK OF MY COMPUTER.
ALLOWING ME TO BRING THE SPEEDING TRAIN TO A COMPLETE STOP.

CHAPTER TEN: "THE TUNNEL OF NOT LOVE"

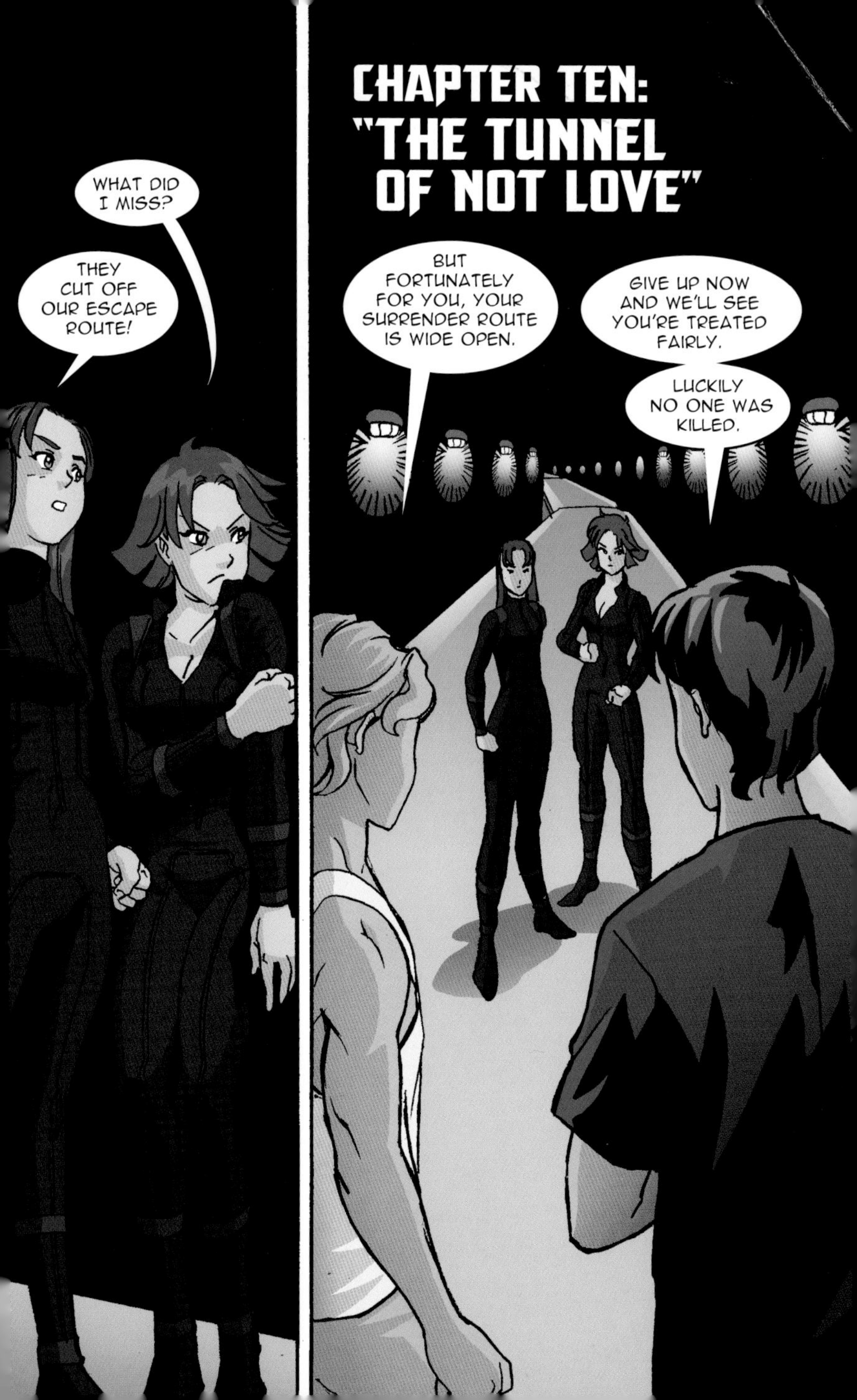
WHAT DID I MISS?
THEY CUT OFF OUR ESCAPE ROUTE!
BUT FORTUNATELY FOR YOU, YOUR SURRENDER ROUTE IS WIDE OPEN.
GIVE UP NOW AND WE'LL SEE YOU'RE TREATED FAIRLY.
LUCKILY NO ONE WAS KILLED.

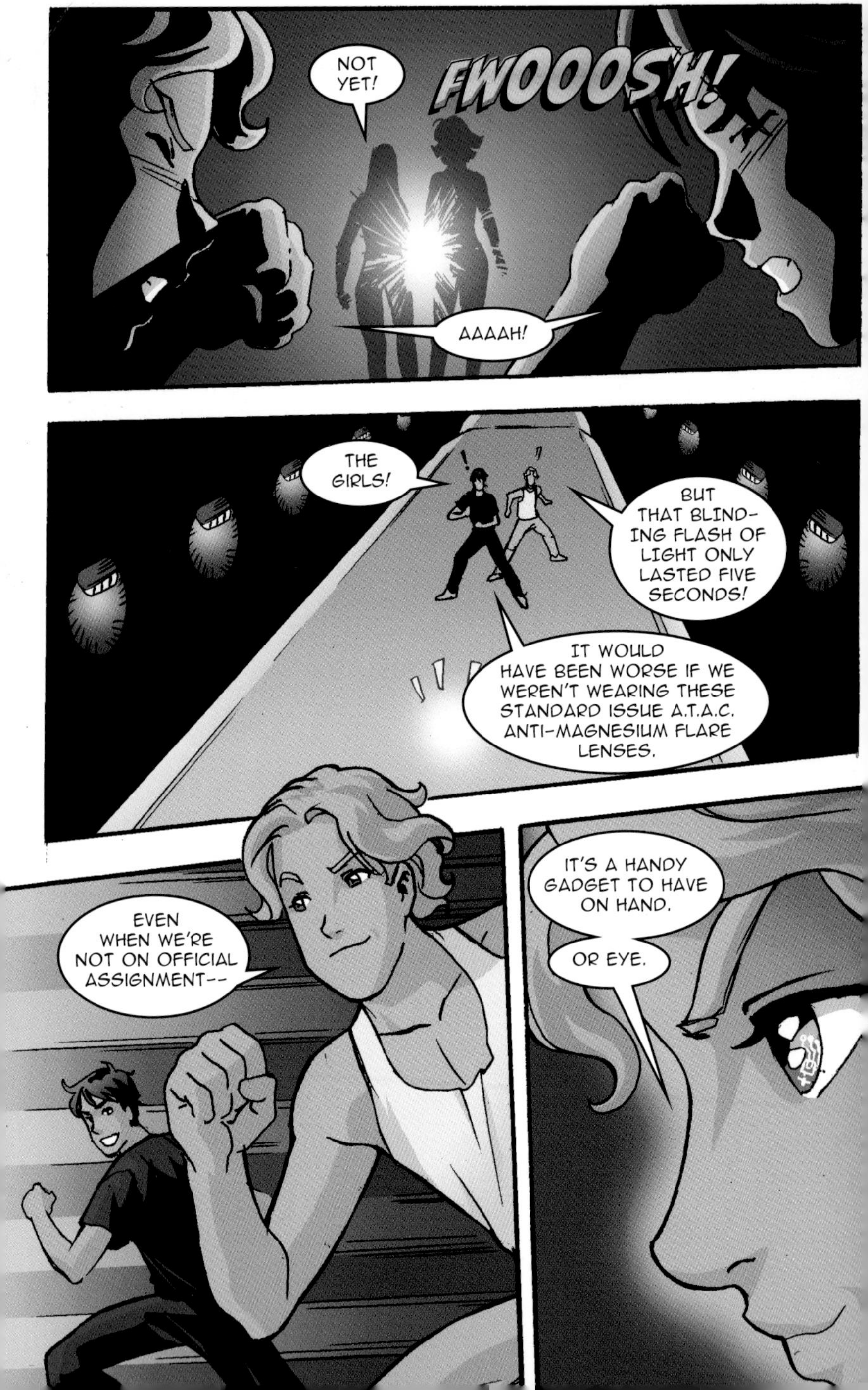
NOT YET!
FWOOOSH!
AAAAH!
THE GIRLS!
BUT THAT BLINDING FLASH OF LIGHT ONLY LASTED FIVE SECONDS!
IT WOULD HAVE BEEN WORSE IF WE WEREN'T WEARING THESE STANDARD ISSUE A.T.A.C. ANTI-MAGNESIUM FLARE LENSES.
EVEN WHEN WE'RE NOT ON OFFICIAL ASSIGNMENT--
IT'S A HANDY GADGET TO HAVE ON HAND.
OR EYE.

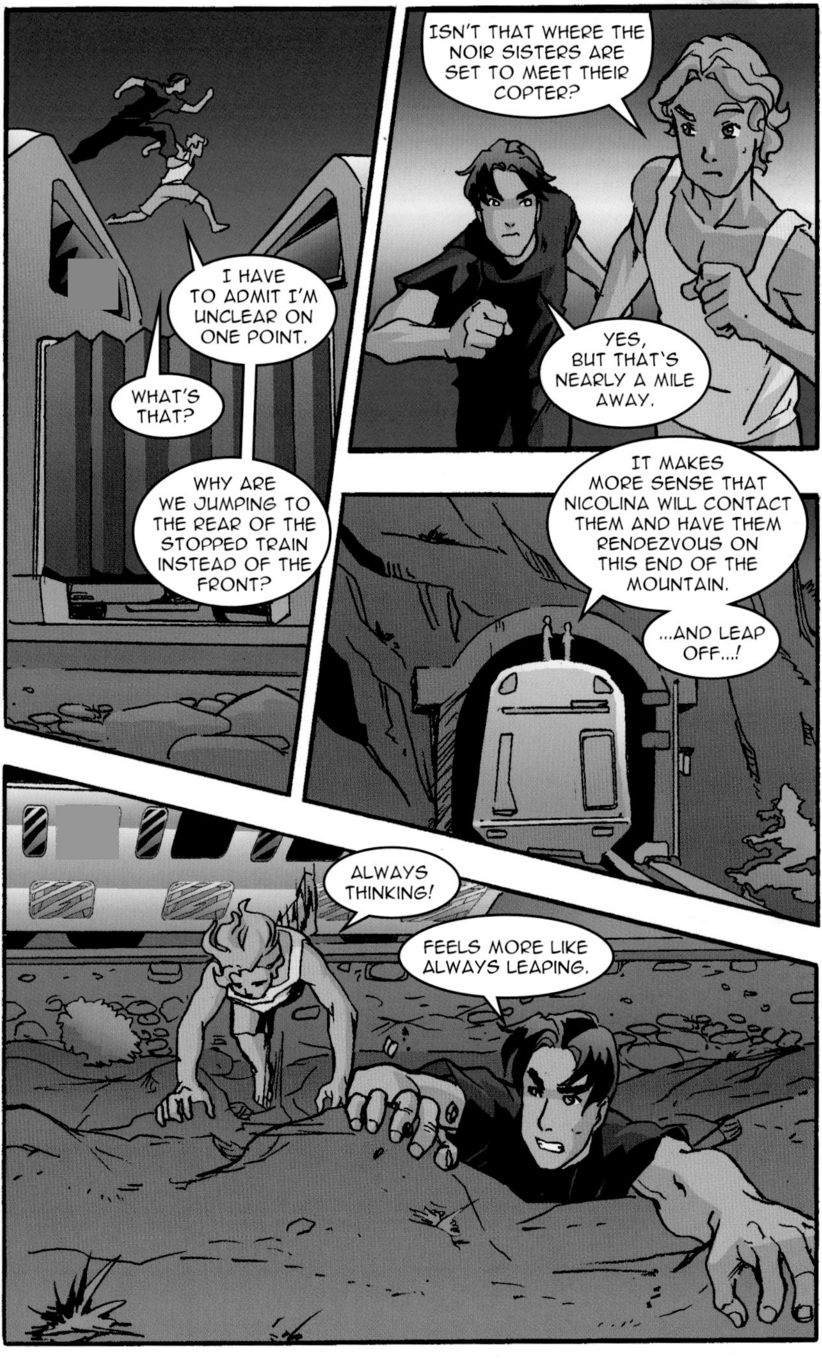
I HAVE TO ADMIT I'M UNCLEAR ON ONE POINT.
WHAT'S THAT?
WHY ARE WE JUMPING TO THE REAR OF THE STOPPED TRAIN INSTEAD OF THE FRONT?
ISN'T THAT WHERE THE NOIR SISTERS ARE SET TO MEET THEIR COPTER?
YES, BUT THAT'S NEARLY A MILE AWAY.
IT MAKES MORE SENSE THAT NICOLINA WILL CONTACT THEM AND HAVE THEM RENDEZVOUS ON THIS END OF THE MOUNTAIN.
...AND LEAP OFF...!
ALWAYS THINKING!
FEELS MORE LIKE ALWAYS LEAPING.

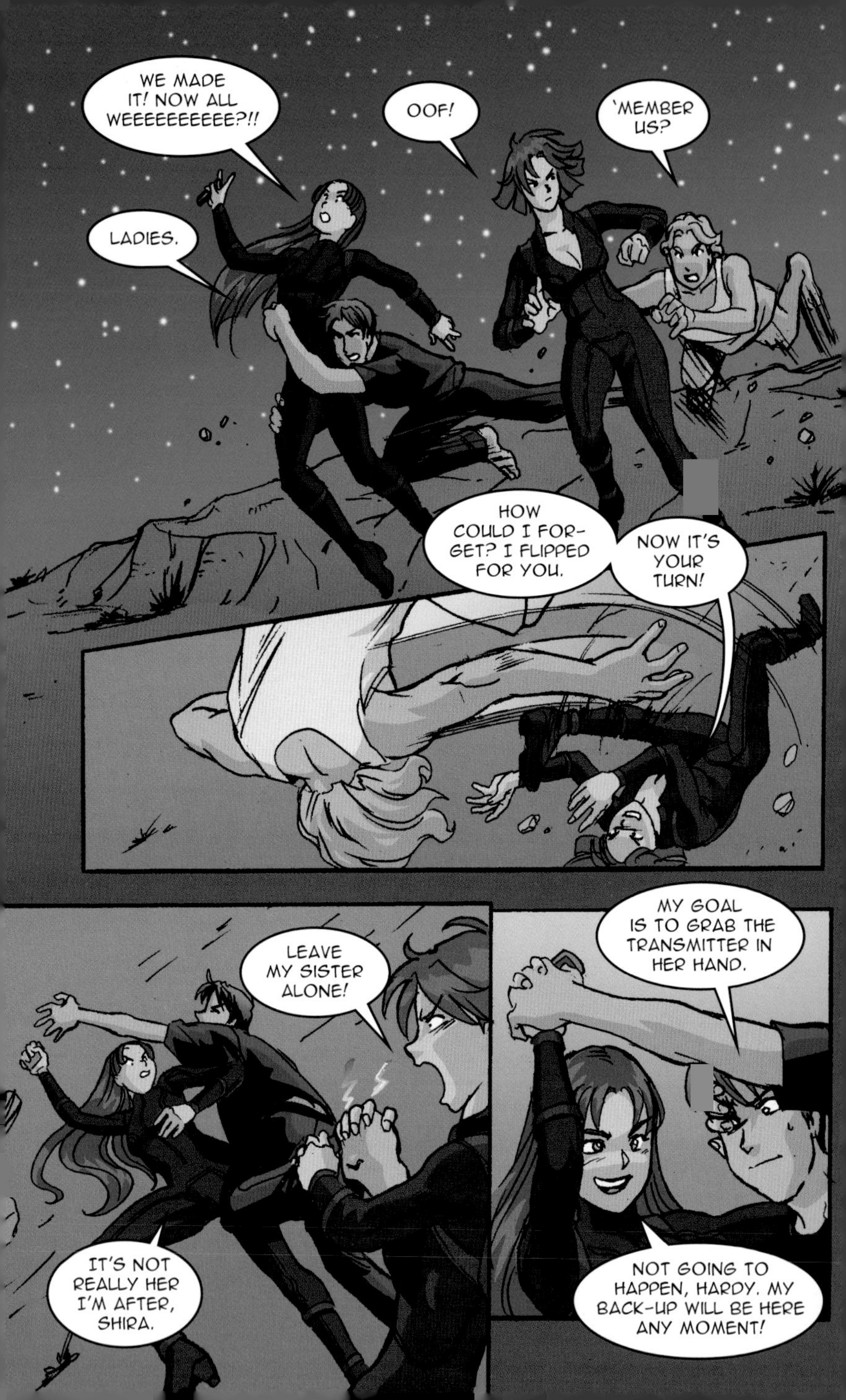
WE MADE IT! NOW ALL WEEEEEEEEEE?!!
OOF!
'MEMBER US?
LADIES.
HOW COULD I FOR-GET? I FLIPPED FOR YOU.
NOW IT'S YOUR TURN!
LEAVE MY SISTER ALONE!
IT'S NOT REALLY HER I'M AFTER, SHIRA.
MY GOAL IS TO GRAB THE TRANSMITTER IN HER HAND.
NOT GOING TO HAPPEN, HARDY. MY BACK-UP WILL BE HERE ANY MOMENT!

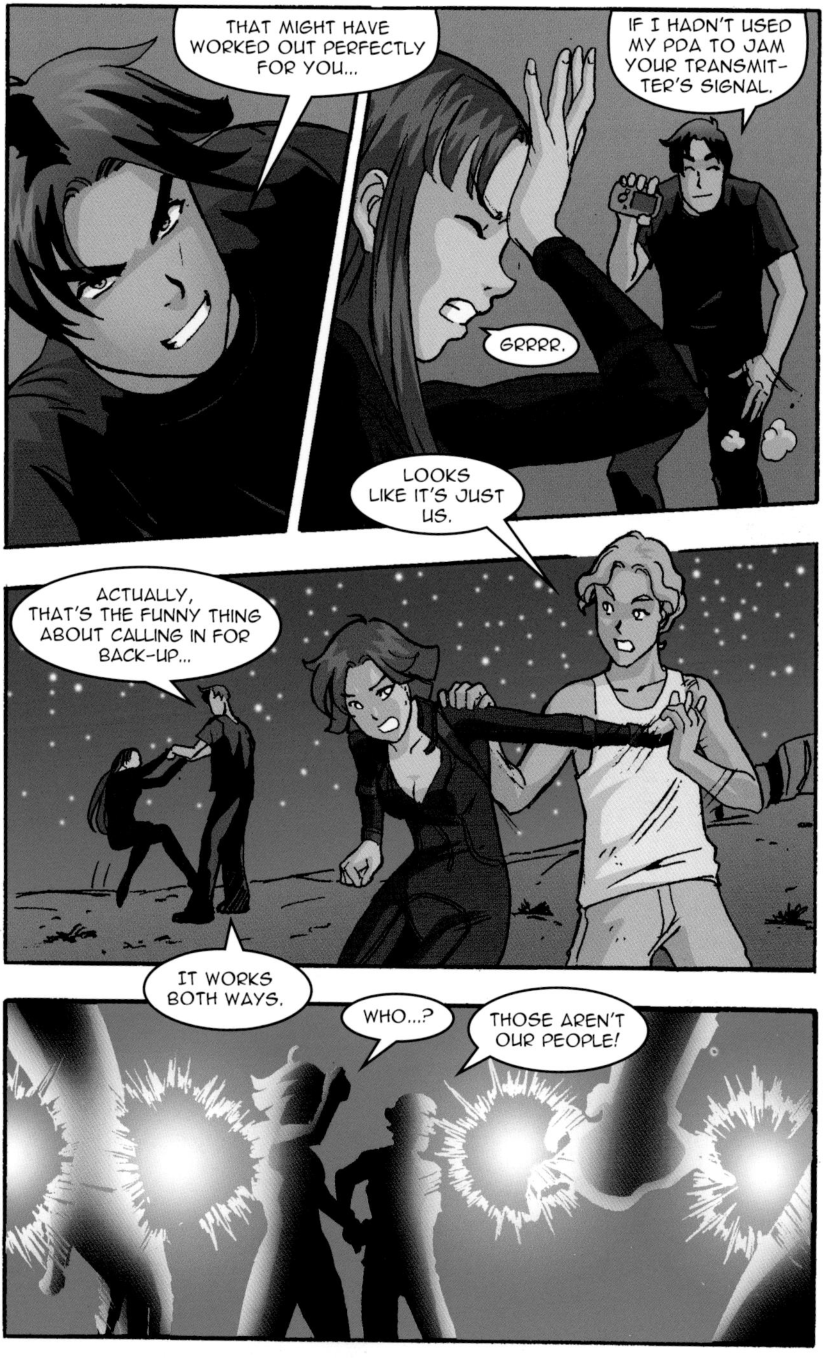
THAT MIGHT HAVE WORKED OUT PERFECTLY FOR YOU...
IF I HADN'T USED MY PDA TO JAM YOUR TRANSMIT-TER'S SIGNAL.
GRRRR.
LOOKS LIKE IT'S JUST US.
ACTUALLY, THAT'S THE FUNNY THING ABOUT CALLING IN FOR BACK-UP...
IT WORKS BOTH WAYS.
WHO...?
THOSE AREN'T OUR PEOPLE!

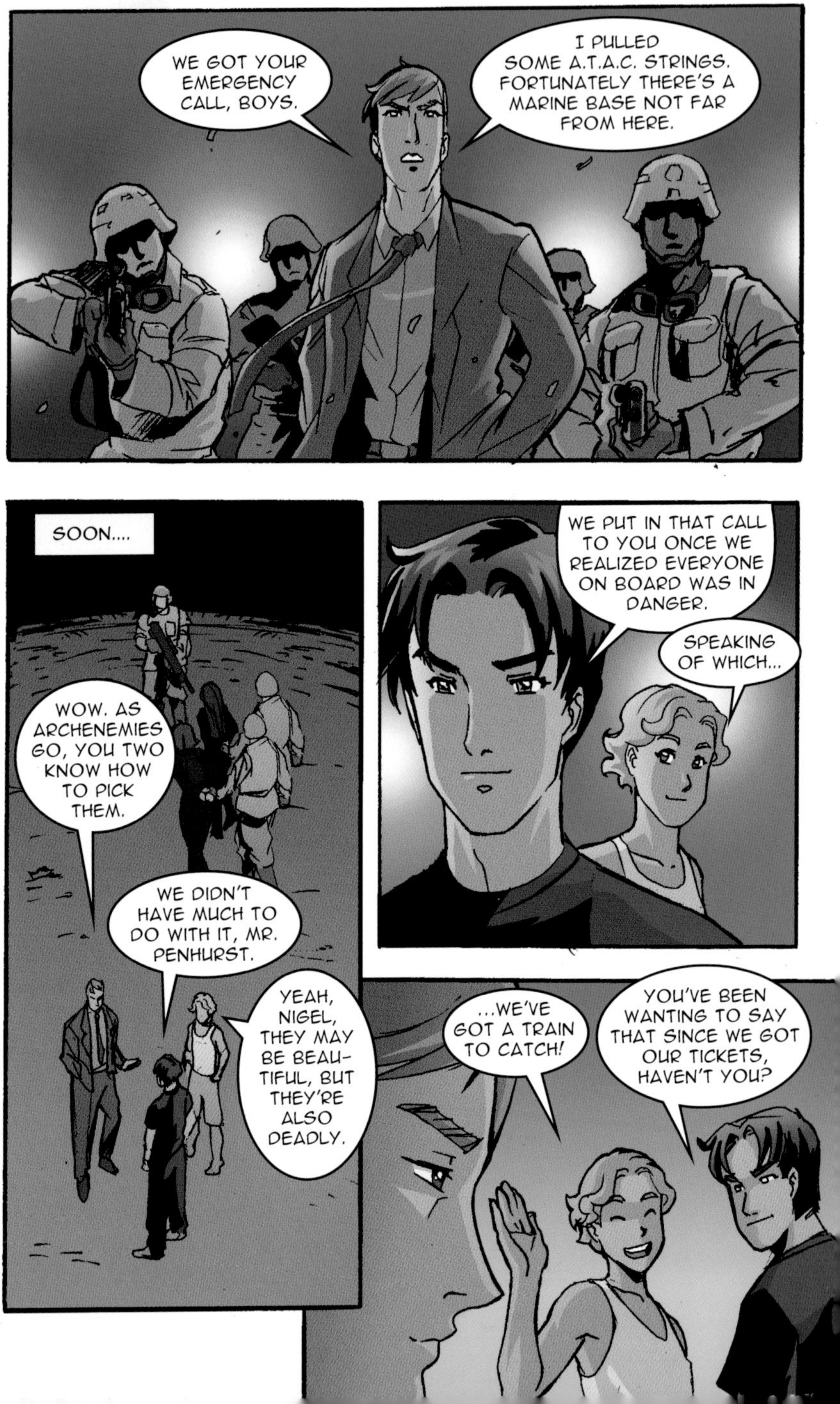
WE GOT YOUR EMERGENCY CALL, BOYS.
I PULLED SOME A.T.A.C. STRINGS. FORTUNATELY THERE'S A MARINE BASE NOT FAR FROM HERE.
SOON....
WOW. AS ARCHENEMIES GO, YOU TWO KNOW HOW TO PICK THEM.
WE DIDN'T HAVE MUCH TO DO WITH IT, MR. PENHURST.
YEAH, NIGEL, THEY MAY BE BEAU-TIFUL, BUT THEY'RE ALSO DEADLY.
WE PUT IN THAT CALL TO YOU ONCE WE REALIZED EVERYONE ON BOARD WAS IN DANGER.
SPEAKING OF WHICH...
...WE'VE GOT A TRAIN TO CATCH!
YOU'VE BEEN WANTING TO SAY THAT SINCE WE GOT OUR TICKETS, HAVEN'T YOU?

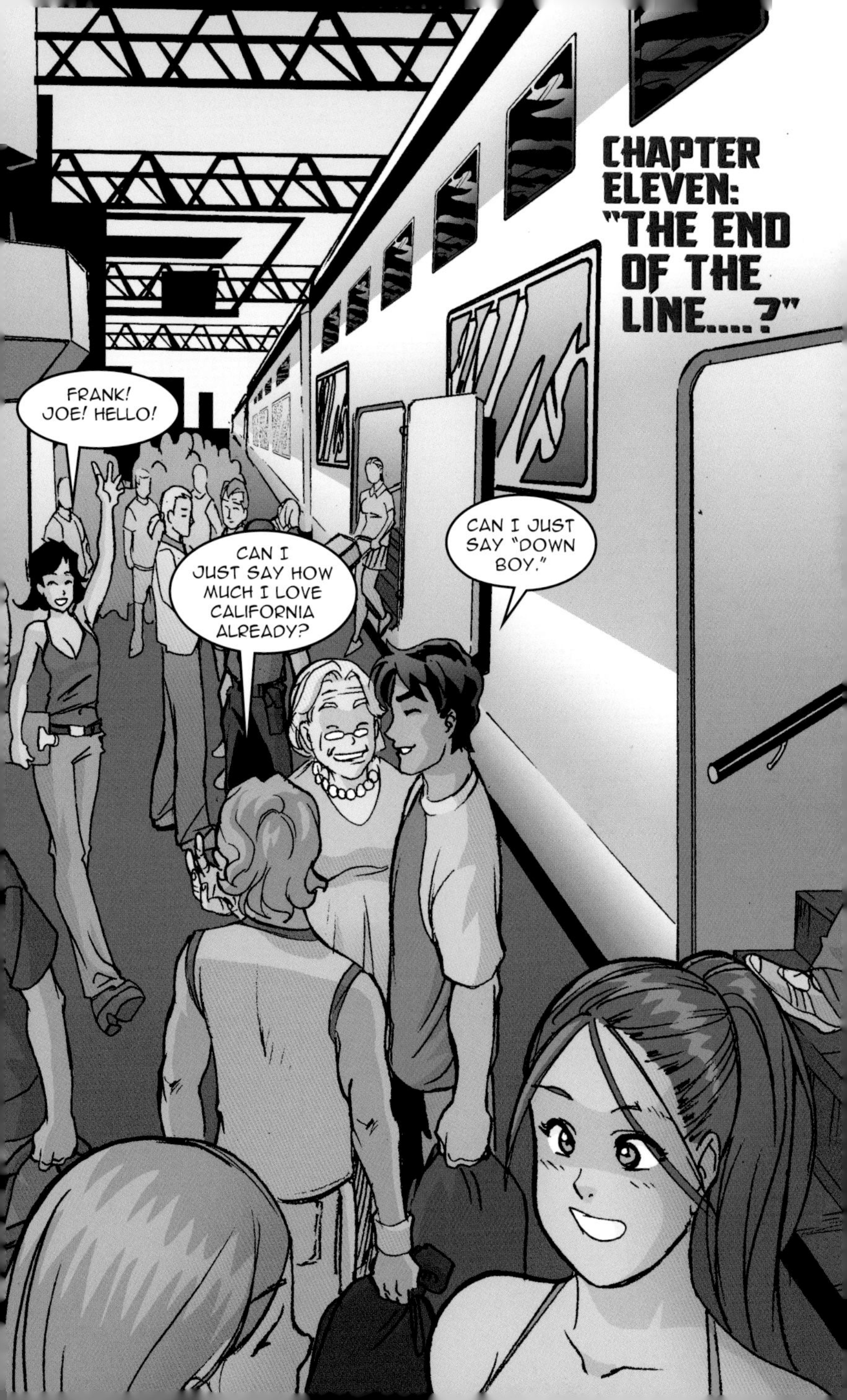
CHAPTER ELEVEN: "THE END OF THE LINE....?"
FRANK! JOE! HELLO!
CAN I JUST SAY HOW MUCH I LOVE CALIFORNIA ALREADY?
CAN I JUST SAY "DOWN BOY."

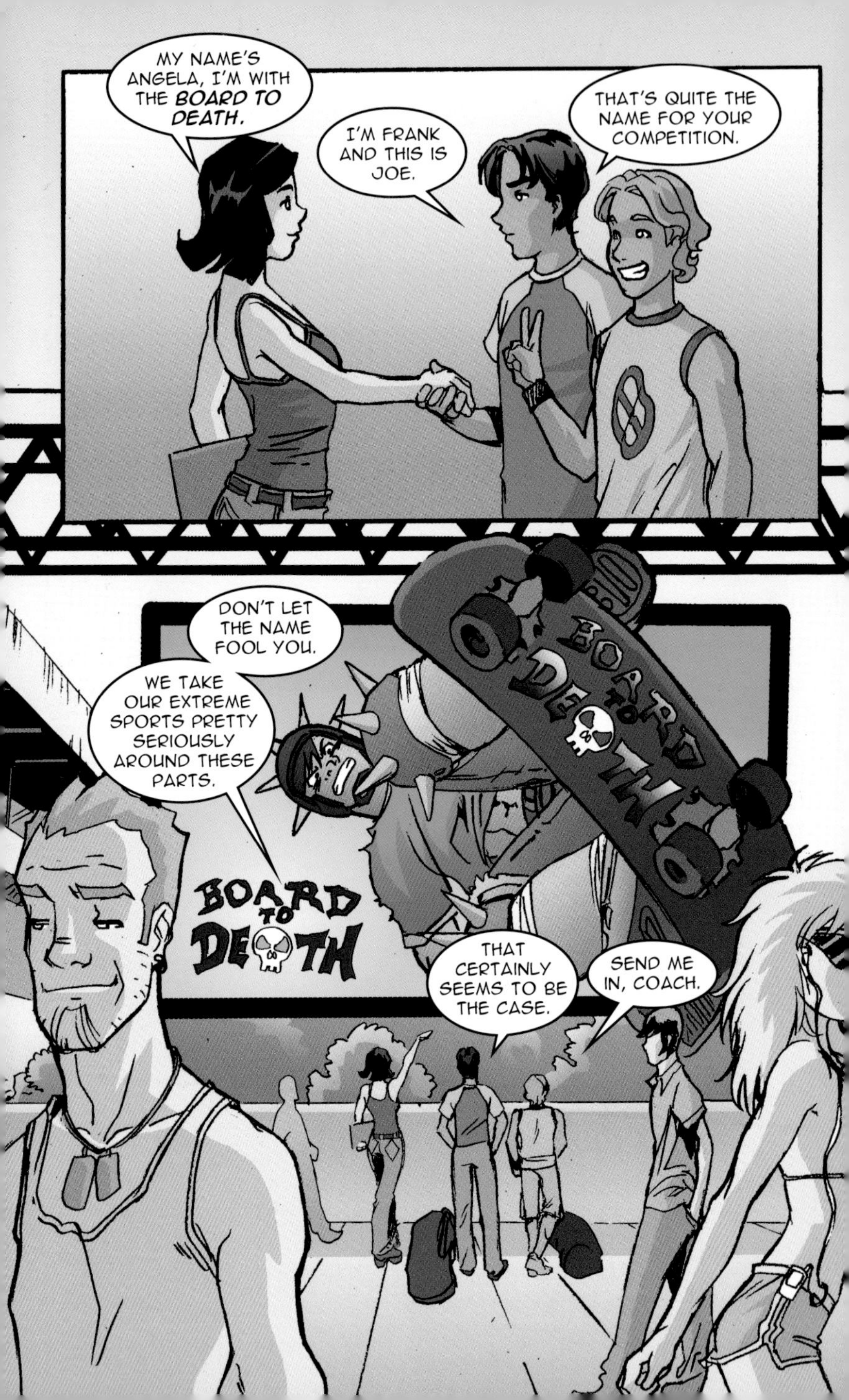
MY NAME'S ANGELA, I'M WITH THE BOARD TO DEATH.
I'M FRANK AND THIS IS JOE.
THAT'S QUITE THE NAME FOR YOUR COMPETITION.
DON'T LET THE NAME FOOL YOU.
WE TAKE OUR EXTREME SPORTS PRETTY SERIOUSLY AROUND THESE PARTS.
BOARD TO DEATH
BOARD TO DEATH
THAT CERTAINLY SEEMS TO BE THE CASE.
SEND ME IN, COACH.

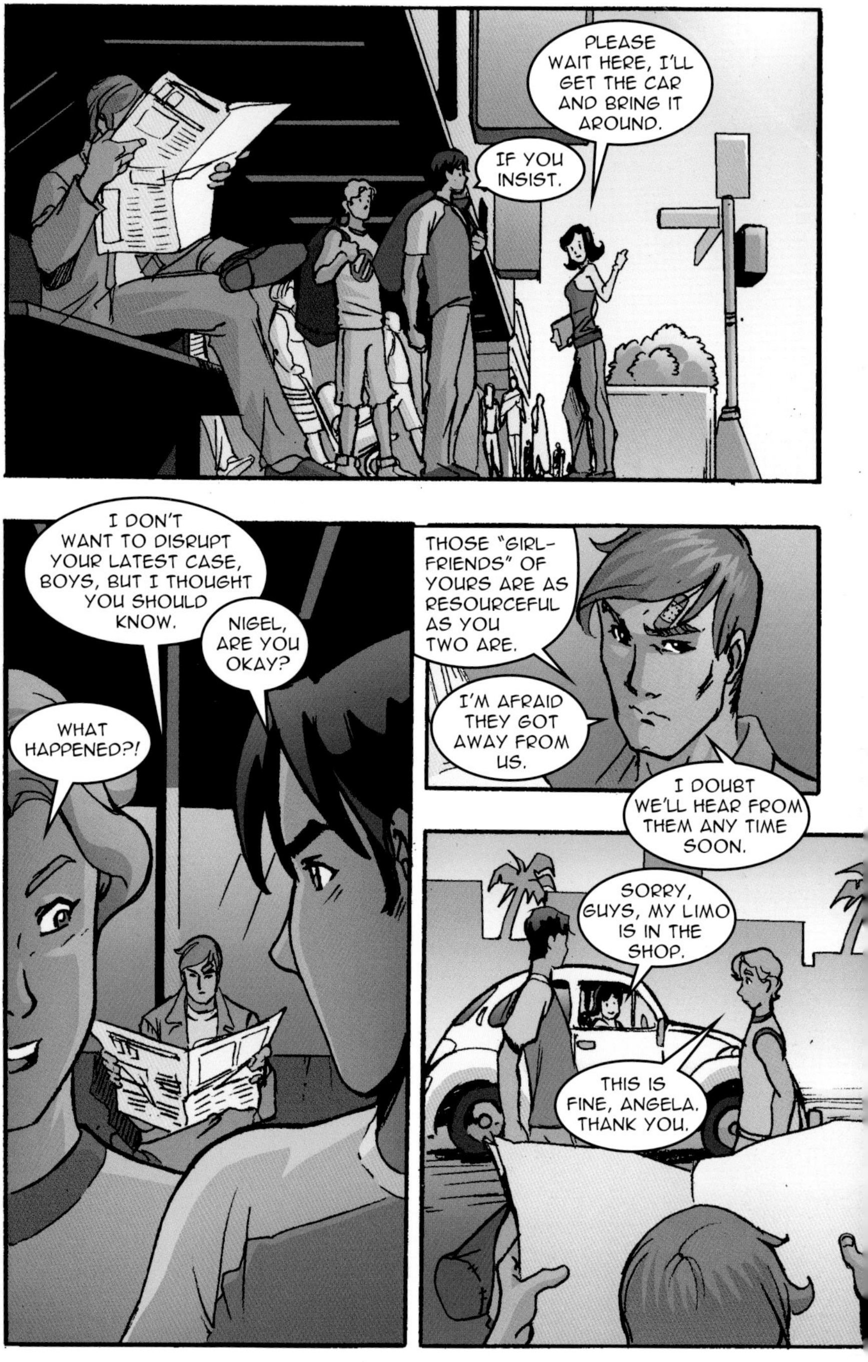
PLEASE WAIT HERE, I'LL GET THE CAR AND BRING IT AROUND.
IF YOU INSIST.
I DON'T WANT TO DISRUPT YOUR LATEST CASE, BOYS, BUT I THOUGHT YOU SHOULD KNOW.
NIGEL, ARE YOU OKAY?
WHAT HAPPENED?!
THOSE "GIRL-FRIENDS" OF YOURS ARE AS RESOURCEFUL AS YOU TWO ARE.
I'M AFRAID THEY GOT AWAY FROM US.
I DOUBT WE'LL HEAR FROM THEM ANY TIME SOON.
SORRY, GUYS, MY LIMO IS IN THE SHOP.
THIS IS FINE, ANGELA. THANK YOU.

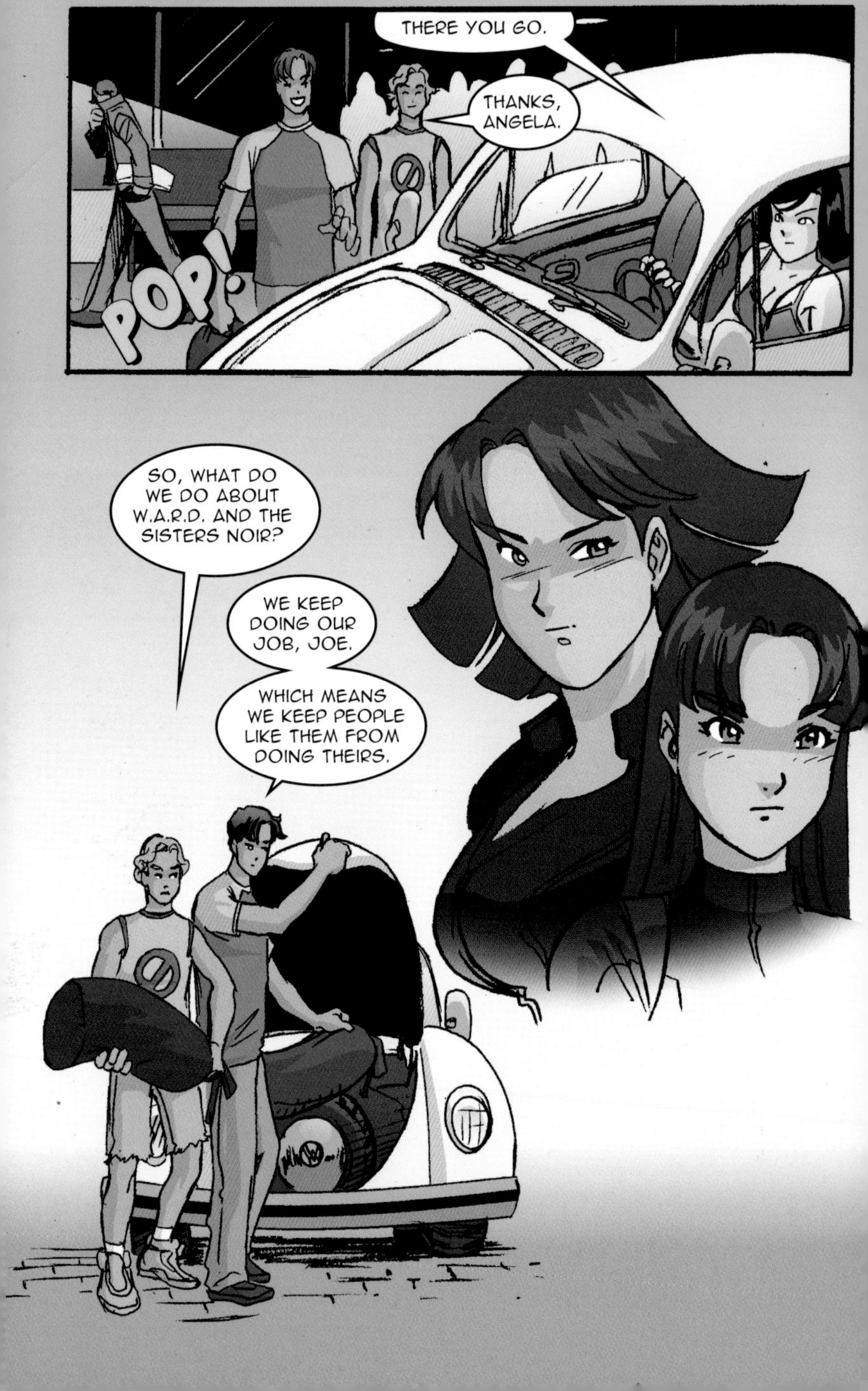
THERE YOU GO.
THANKS, ANGELA.
POP!
SO, WHAT DO WE DO ABOUT W.A.R.D. AND THE SISTERS NOIR?
WE KEEP DOING OUR JOB, JOE.
WHICH MEANS WE KEEP PEOPLE LIKE THEM FROM DOING THEIRS.

Special Advance Preview of THE HARDY BOYS Graphic Novel #8- "Board To Death"

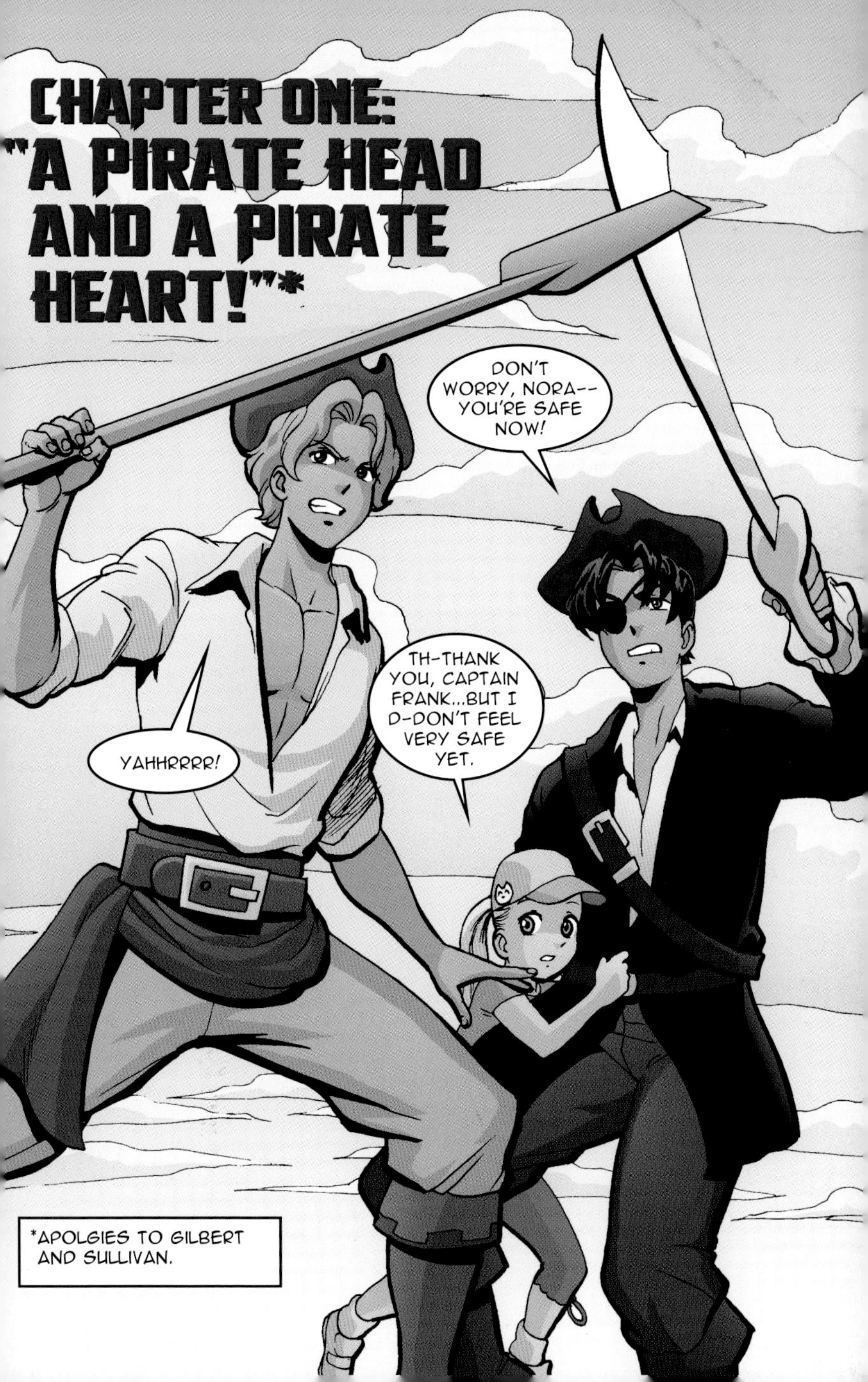
CHAPTER ONE:
"A PIRATE HEAD AND A PIRATE HEART!"*
DON'T WORRY, NORA-- YOU'RE SAFE NOW!
TH-THANK YOU, CAPTAIN FRANK...BUT I D-DON'T FEEL VERY SAFE YET.
YAHHRRRR!
*APOLGIES TO GILBERT AND SULLIVAN.

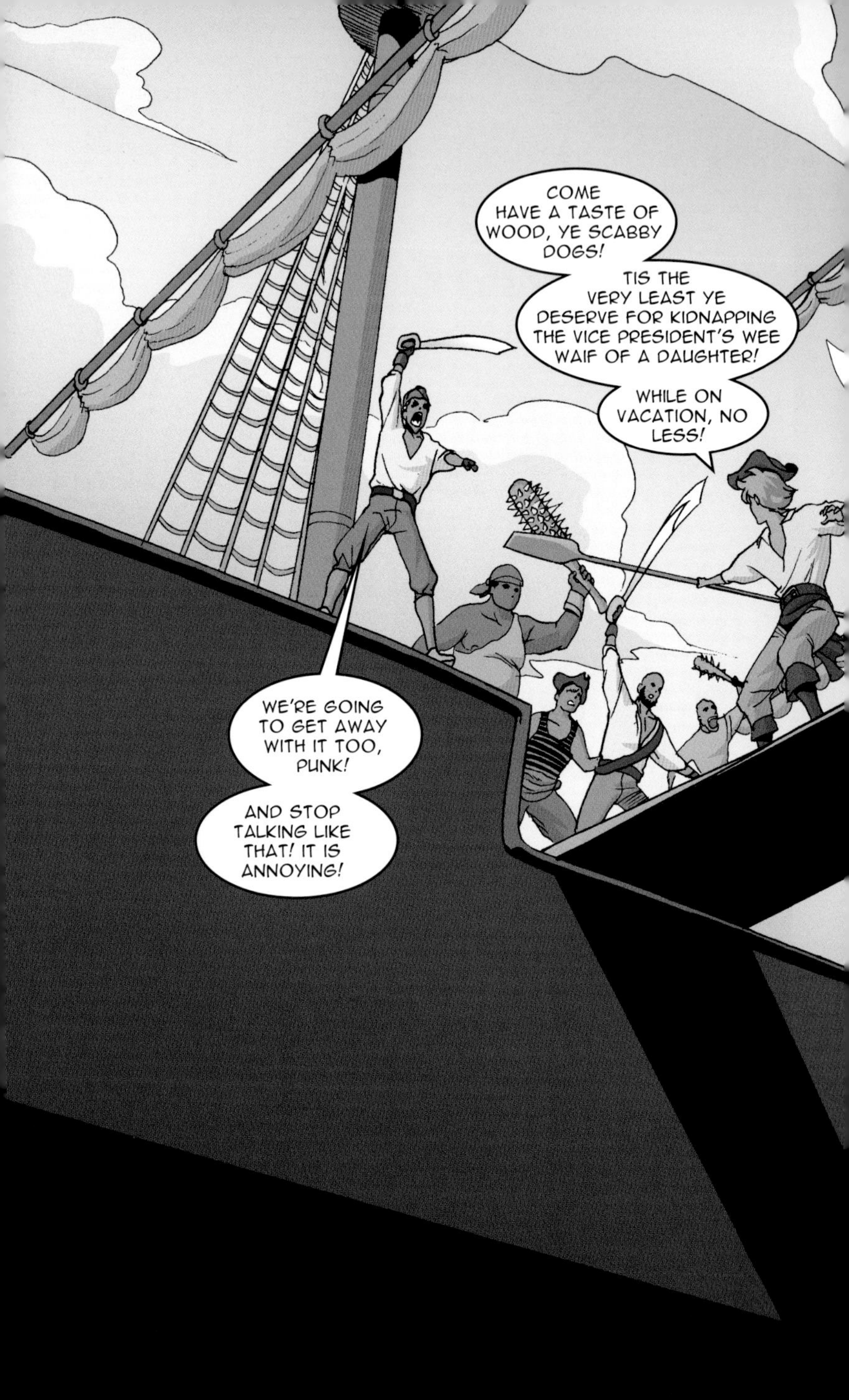
COME HAVE A TASTE OF WOOD, YE SCABBY DOGS!
TIS THE VERY LEAST YE DESERVE FOR KIDNAPPING THE VICE PRESIDENT'S WEE WAIF OF A DAUGHTER!
WHILE ON VACATION, NO LESS!
WE'RE GOING TO GET AWAY WITH IT TOO, PUNK!
AND STOP TALKING LIKE THAT! IT IS ANNOYING!

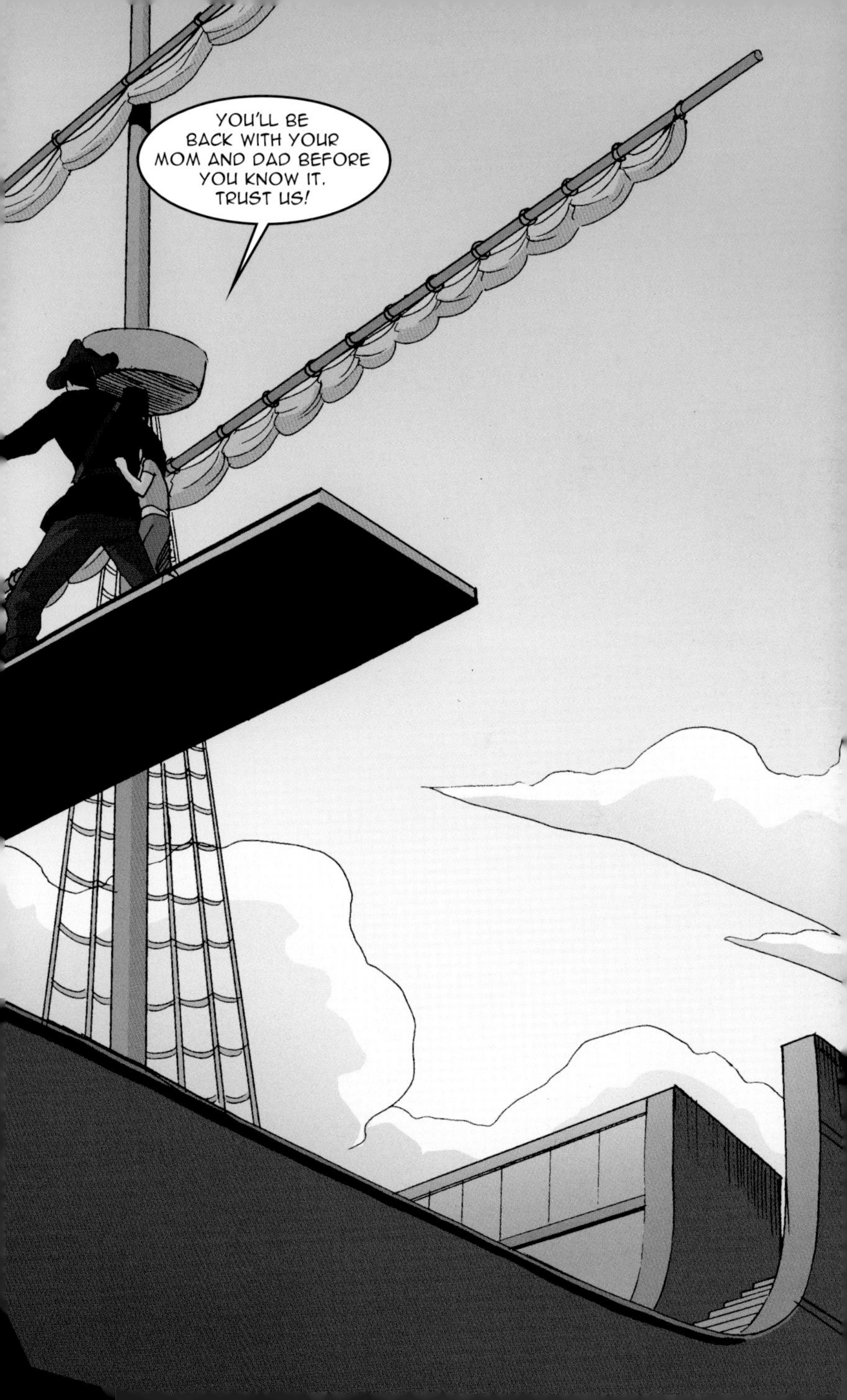
YOU'LL BE BACK WITH YOUR MOM AND DAD BEFORE YOU KNOW IT. TRUST US!

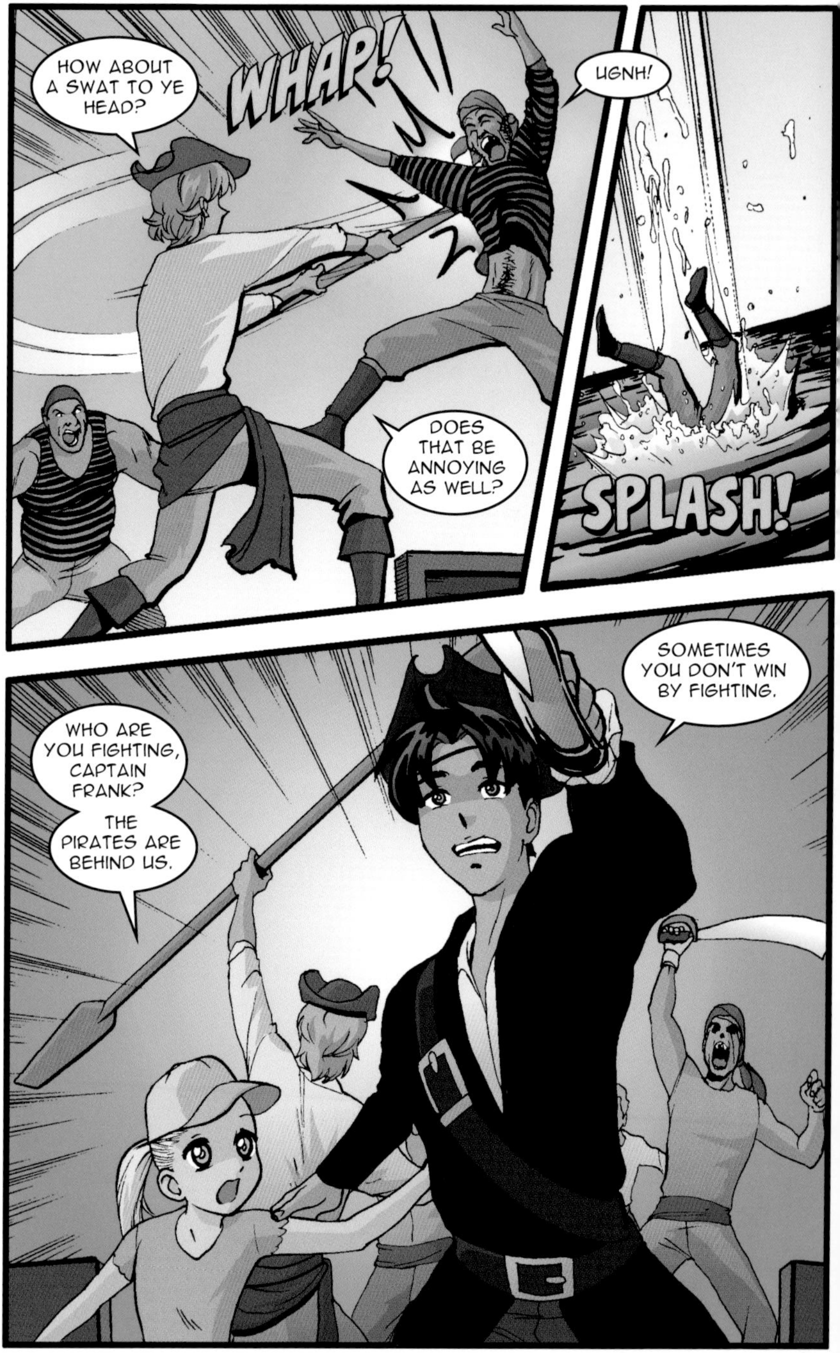
HOW ABOUT A SWAT TO YE HEAD?
WHAP!
UGNH!
DOES THAT BE ANNOYING AS WELL?
SPLASH!
SOMETIMES YOU DON'T WIN BY FIGHTING.
WHO ARE YOU FIGHTING, CAPTAIN FRANK?
THE PIRATES ARE BEHIND US.

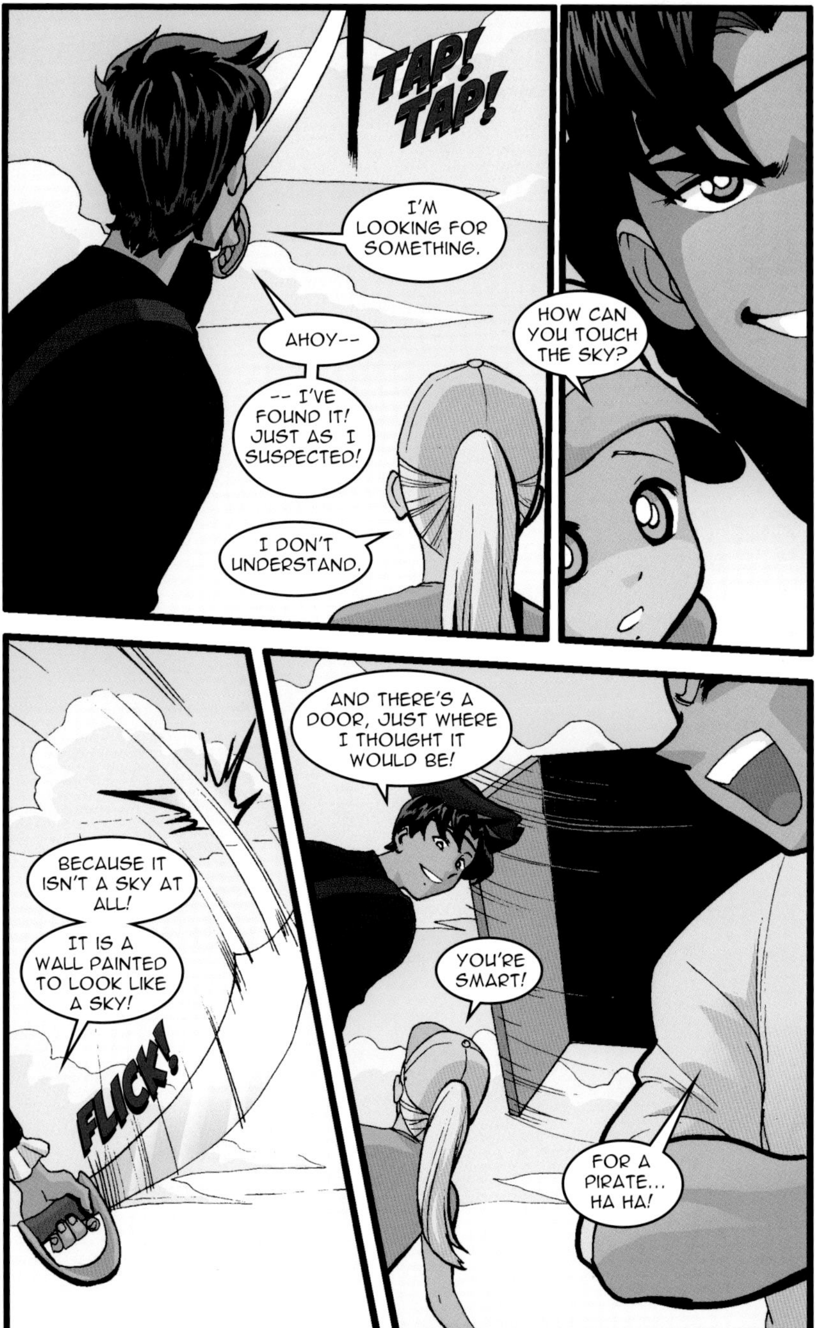
TAP! TAP!
I'M LOOKING FOR SOMETHING.
AHOY--
-- I'VE FOUND IT! JUST AS I SUSPECTED!
I DON'T UNDERSTAND.
HOW CAN YOU TOUCH THE SKY?
BECAUSE IT ISN'T A SKY AT ALL!
IT IS A WALL PAINTED TO LOOK LIKE A SKY!
FLICK!
AND THERE'S A DOOR, JUST WHERE I THOUGHT IT WOULD BE!
YOU'RE SMART!
FOR A PIRATE... HA HA!

Don't miss THE HARDY BOYS Graphic Novel #8- "Board To Death"

NANCY DREW

A NEW ONE EVERY 3 MONTHS!

NEW STORY! FULL-COLOR GRAPHIC NOVEL
NANCY DREW
#12
DRESS REHEARSAL
girl detective
BASED ON THE SERIES BY CAROLYN KEENE
Stefan PETRUCHA
Sho MURASE
ON SALE NOW!
PAPERCUTZ

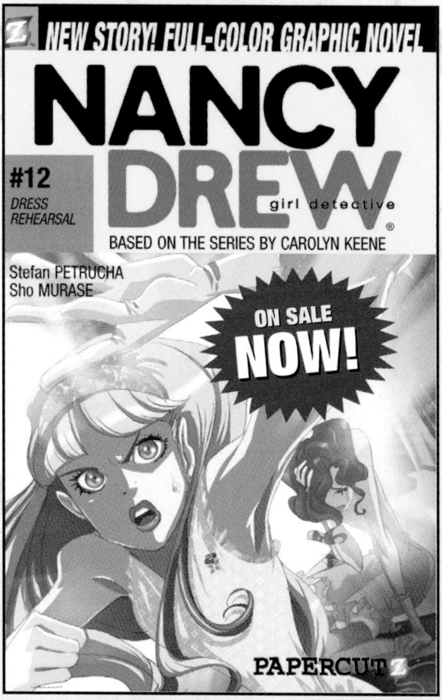

#1 "The Demon of River Heights"
ISBN 1-59707-000-9
#2 "Writ In Stone"
ISBN 1-59707-002-5
#3 "The Haunted Dollhouse"
ISBN 1-59707-008-4
#4 "The Girl Who Wasn't There"
ISBN 1-59707-012-2
#5 "The Fake Heir"
ISBN 1-59707-024-6
#6 "Mr. Cheeters Is Missing"
ISBN 1-59707-030-0
#7 "The Charmed Bracelet"
ISBN 1-59707-036-X
#8 "Global Warning"
ISBN 1-59707-051-3
#9 "Ghost in the Machinery"
ISBN 1-59707-058-0
#10 "The Disoriented Express"
ISBN 1-59707-066-1
#11 "Monkey Wrench Blues"
ISBN 1-59707-076-9
NEW! #12 "Dress Reversal"
ISBN 1-59707-086-9
All: Pocket sized, 96-112pp., full color, $7.95
Also available in hardcover! $12.95 each.

NEW STORIES! FULL-COLOR GRAPHIC NOVELS
NANCY DREW
BASED ON THE SERIES BY CAROLYN KEENE
PAPERCUTZ

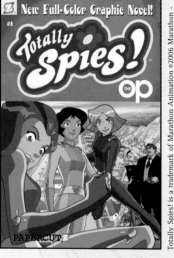

Nancy Drew
Boxed Set, #1-4
384 pages of color comics! $29.95,
ISBN 1-59707-038-6
Nancy Drew
Boxed Set, #5-8
432 pages of color comics! $29.95,
ISBN 1-59707-074-2

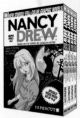

TOTALLY SPIES!

New Full-Color Graphic Novel!
#1
Totally Spies!
THE OP
PAPERCUTZ

#1 "The O.P." ISBN 1-59707-043-2
#2 "I Hate the 80's" ISBN 1-59707-045-9
#3 "Evil Jerry" ISBN 1-59707-047-8
#4 "Spies in Space" ISBN 1-59707-055-6
Each: 5x7 1/2, 112pp., full color paperback: $7.95
Also available in hardcover! $12.95 each

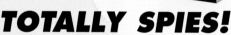

www.papercutz.com

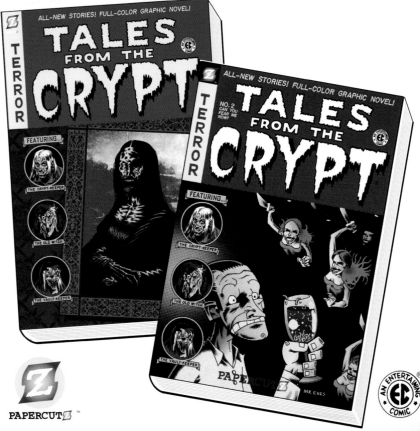

WATCH OUT FOR PAPERCUTZ™

If this is your very first Papercutz graphic novel, then allow me, Jim Salicrup, your humble and lovable Editor-in-Chief, to welcome you to the Papercutz Backpages where we check out what's happening in the ever-expanding Papercutz Universe! If you're a long-time Papercutz fan, then welcome back, friend!

Things really have been popping at Papercutz! In the last few editions of the Backpages we've announced new titles such as TALES FROM THE CRYPT, CLASSICS ILLUSTRATED, and CLASSICS ILLUSTRATED DELUXE. Well, guess what? The tradition continues, and we're announcing yet another addition to our line-up of blockbuster titles. So, what is our latest and greatest title? We'll give you just one hint -- the stars of the next Papercutz graphic novel series just happen to be the biggest, most exciting line of constructible action figures ever created! That's right -- BIONICLE is coming! Check out the power-packed preview pages ahead!

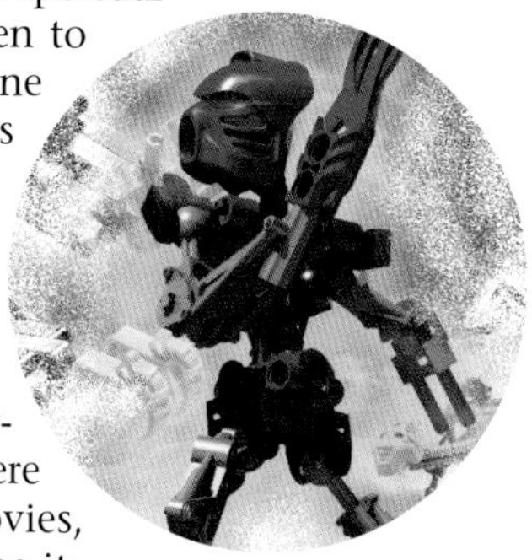

Before I run out of room, let me say that we're always interested in what you think! Are there characters, TV shows, movies, books, videogames, you-name-it, that you'd like to see Papercutz turn into graphic novels? Don't be shy, let's us know! You can contact me at salicrup@papercutz.com or Jim Salicrup, PAPERCUTZ, 40 Exchange Place, Ste. 1308, New York, NY 10005 and let us know how we're doing. After all, we want you to be as excited about Papercutz as we are!

Thanks,

Jim

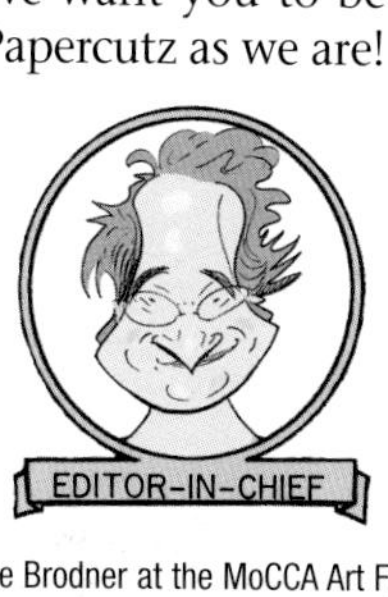
EDITOR-IN-CHIEF

Caricature drawn by Steve Brodner at the MoCCA Art Fest.

TWO DOZEN TEEN DETECTIVE GRAPHIC NOVELS NOW IN PRINT!

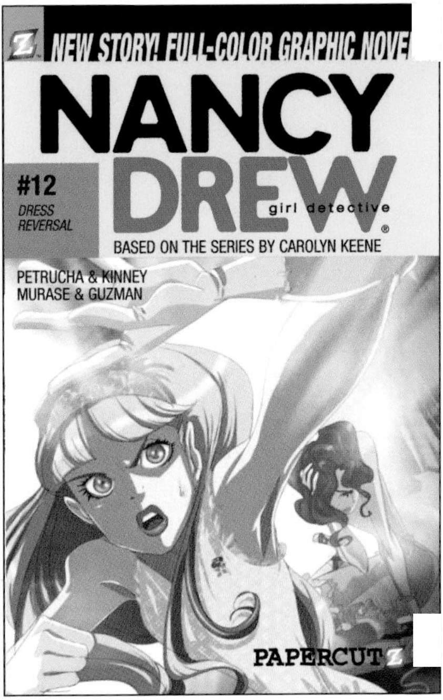
NEW STORY! FULL-COLOR GRAPHIC NOVE
NANCY DREW
girl detective
#12
DRESS REVERSAL
BASED ON THE SERIES BY CAROLYN KEENE
PETRUCHA & KINNEY
MURASE & GUZMAN
PAPERCUTZ

You know, while it's exciting to be adding so many new titles, we don't want anyone to think we've forgotten any of our previous Papercutz publications! For example, can you believe there are now two dozen all-new, full-color graphic novels starring America's favorite teen sleuths?! Let's check out what's happening in the 12th volume of NANCY DREW…

Writers Stefan Petrucha and Sarah Kinney and artists Sho Murase and Carlos Jose Guzman present Nancy's latest case, "Dress Reversal." After showing up at River Height's social event of the year, in the identical dress as the party's hostess, Deirdre Shannon, things get worse for Nancy when she's suddenly kidnapped! That leaves Bess, George, and Ned to solve the mystery of the missing Girl Detective.

That's all in NANCY DREW #12 "Dress Reversal," on sale sale at bookstores everywhere and online booksellers.

Behold. . .

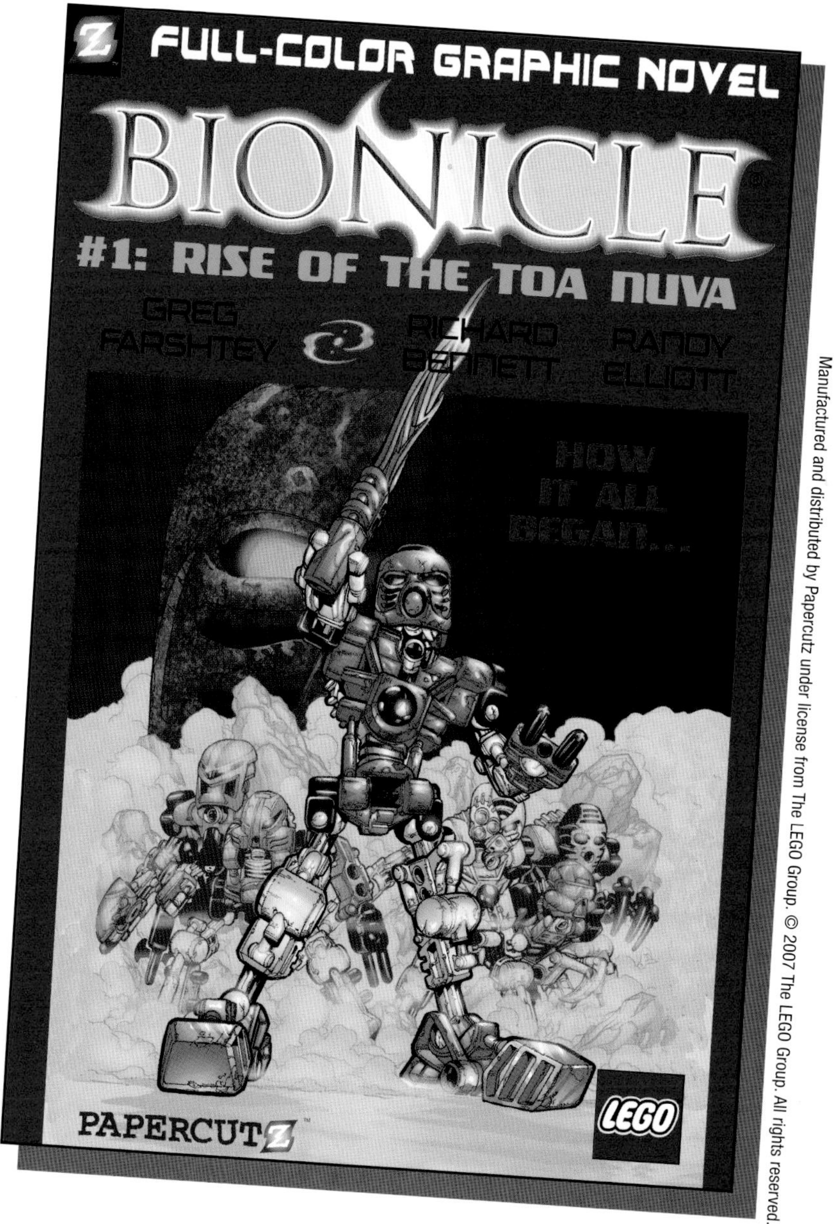
FULL-COLOR GRAPHIC NOVEL
BIONICLE®
#1: RISE OF THE TOA NUVA
GREG FARSHTEY
RICHARD BENNETT
RANDY ELLIOTT
HOW IT ALL BEGAN...
PAPERCUTZ™
LEGO

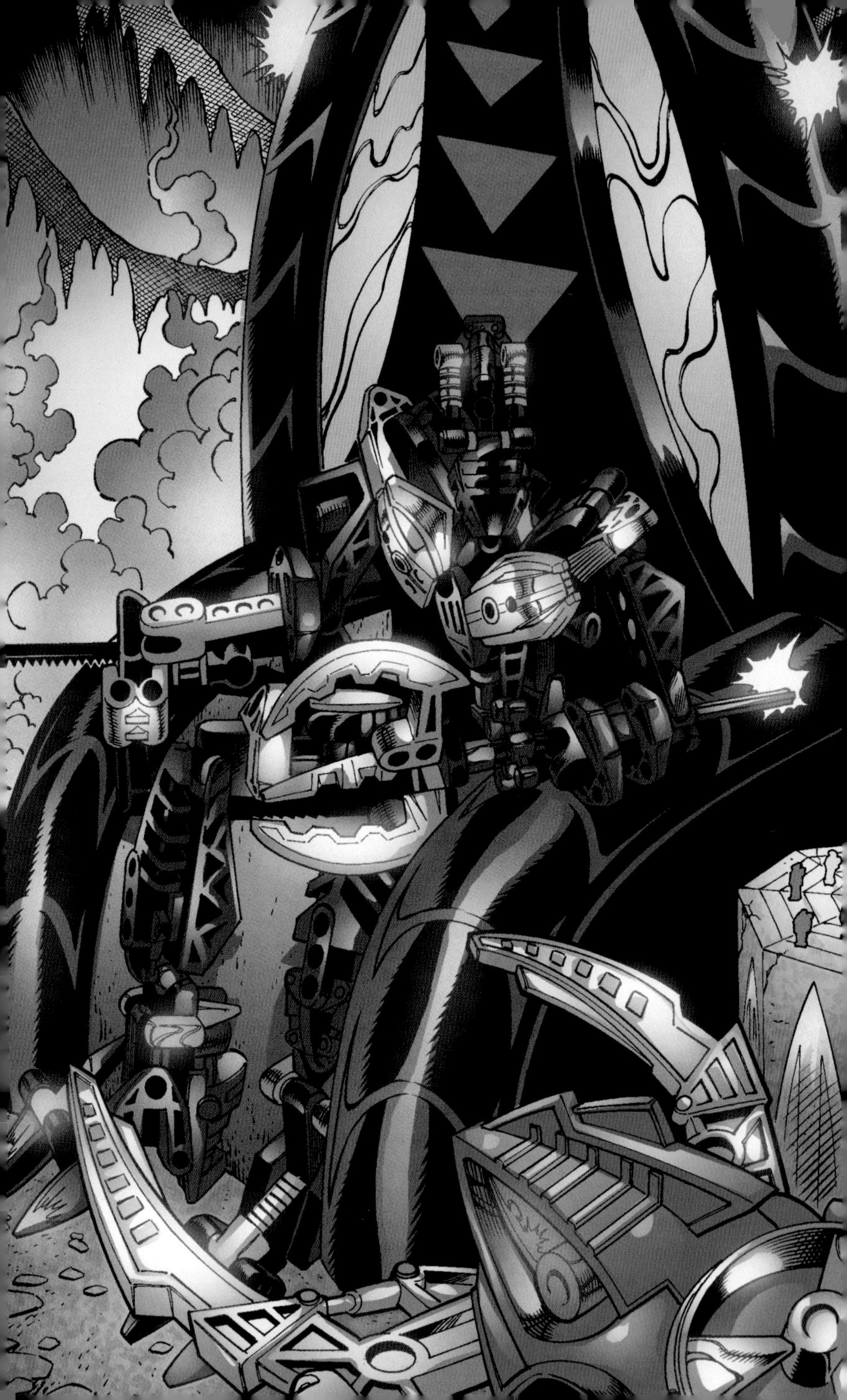

At the start of the new millennium, a new line of toys from LEGO made their dramatic debut. Originally released in six color-coded canisters, each containing a constructible, fully-poseable, articulated character, BIONICLE was an instant hit!

The BIONICLE figures were incredibly intriguing. With their exotic names hinting at a complex history, fans were curious to discover more about these captivating characters. Even now, over six years later, there are still many unanswered questions surrounding every facet of the ever-expanding BIONICLE universe.

A comicbook, written by leading BIONICLE expert and author of most of the BIONICLE novels Greg Farshtey, was created by DC Comics and given away to members of the BIONICLE fan club. The action-packed comics revealed much about these mysterious biomechanical (part biological, part mechanical) beings and the world they inhabited. A world filled with many races, most prominent being the Matoran. A world once protected millennia ago by a Great Spirit known as Mata Nui, who has fallen asleep. A world that has begun to decay as its inhabitants must defend themselves from the evil forces of Makuta.

The first story arc of the comics called "The BIONICLE Chronicles," begins when six heroic beings known as Toa arrive on a tropical-like island which is also named Mata Nui. The Toa may just be the saviors the people of Mata Nui need, if they can avoid fighting with themselves, not to mention the Bohrok and the Rahkshise early comics are incredibly hard-to-find, and many new BIONICLE fans have never seen these all-important early chapters in this epic science fantasy. But soon, those comics will be collected as the first two volumes in the Papercutz series of BIONICLE graphic novels.

These early comics are incredibly hard-to-find, and many new BIONICLE fans have never seen these all-important early chapters in this epic science fantasy. But soon, those comics will be collected as the first two volumes in the Papercutz series of BIONICLE graphic novels.

In the following pages, enjoy a special preview of BIONICLE graphic novel #1...

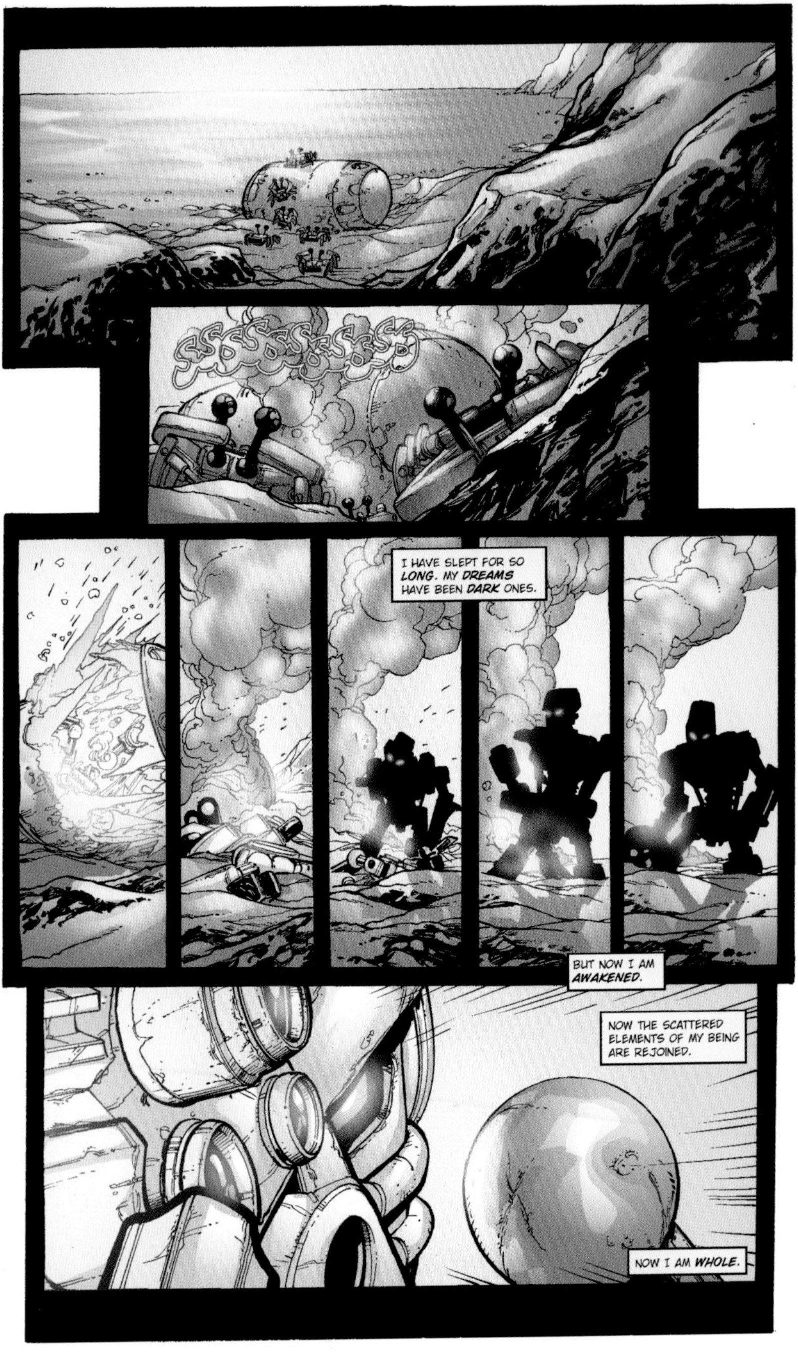
SSSSSSSSSSSSS
I HAVE SLEPT FOR SO LONG. MY DREAMS HAVE BEEN DARK ONES.
BUT NOW I AM AWAKENED.
NOW THE SCATTERED ELEMENTS OF MY BEING ARE REJOINED.
NOW I AM WHOLE.

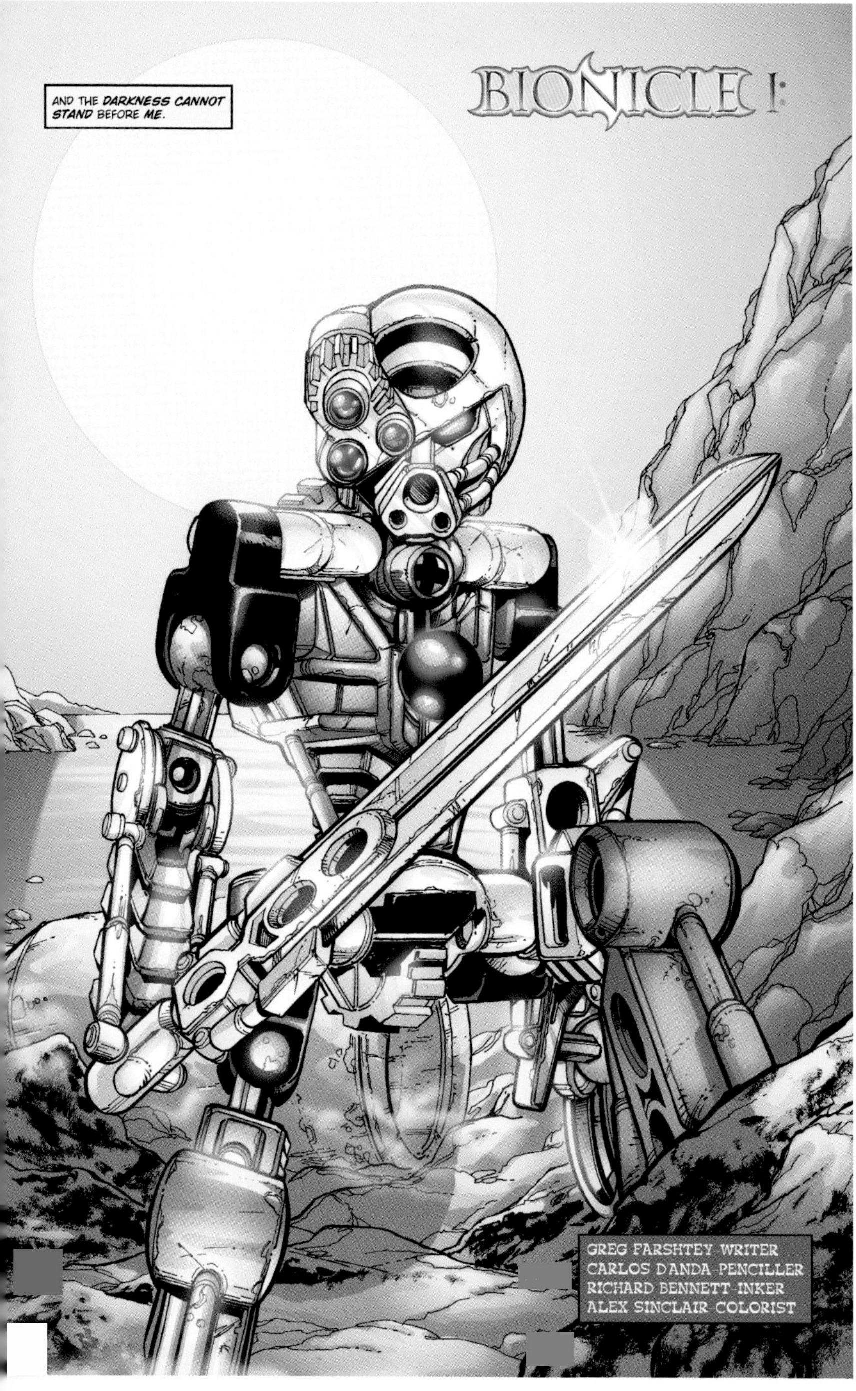
BIONICLE 1:
AND THE DARKNESS CANNOT STAND BEFORE ME.
GREG FARSHTEY-WRITER
CARLOS D'ANDA-PENCILLER
RICHARD BENNETT-INKER
ALEX SINCLAIR-COLORIST

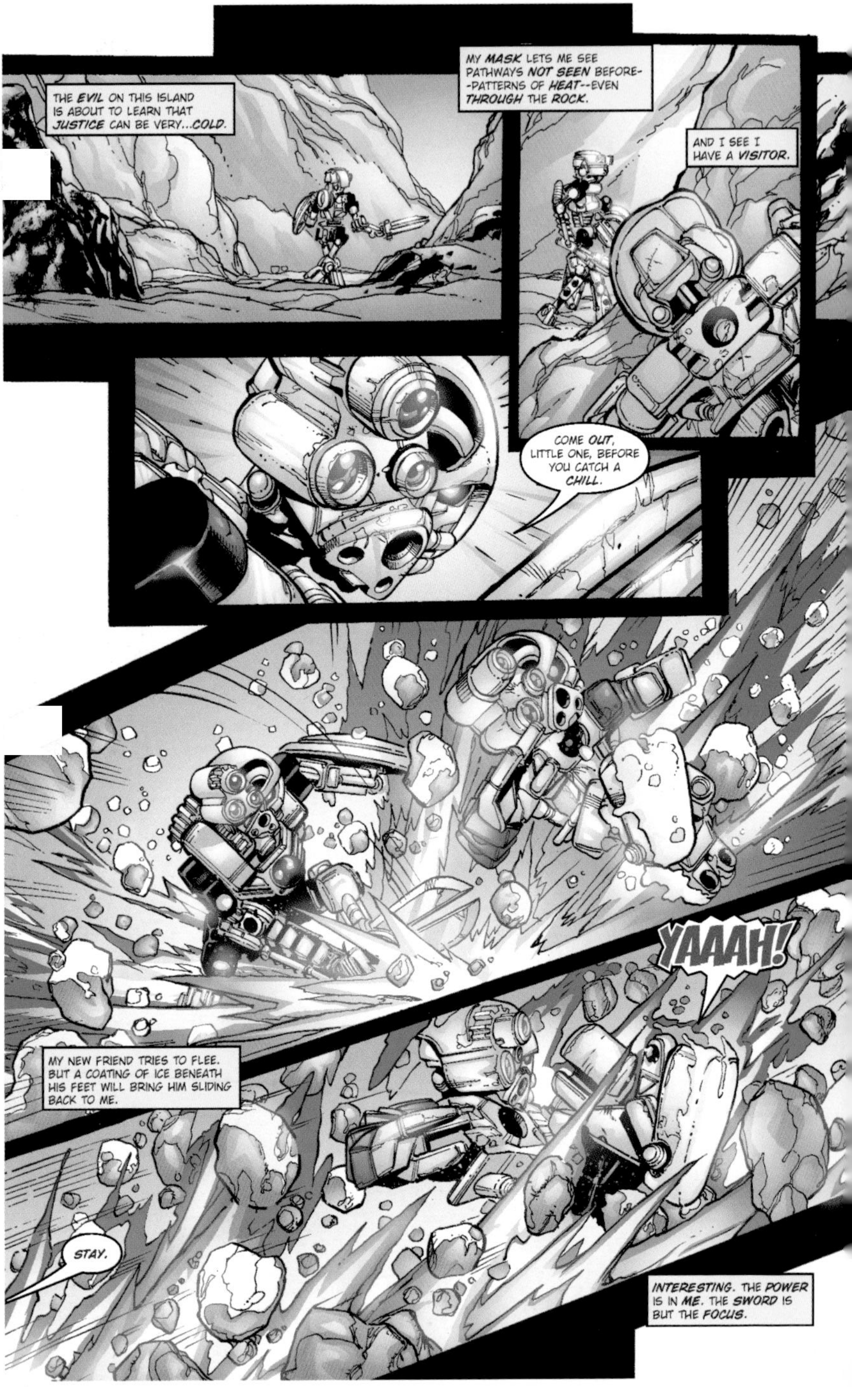
THE EVIL ON THIS ISLAND IS ABOUT TO LEARN THAT JUSTICE CAN BE VERY...COLD.
MY MASK LETS ME SEE PATHWAYS NOT SEEN BEFORE--PATTERNS OF HEAT--EVEN THROUGH THE ROCK.
AND I SEE I HAVE A VISITOR.
COME OUT, LITTLE ONE, BEFORE YOU CATCH A CHILL.
YAAAH!
MY NEW FRIEND TRIES TO FLEE. BUT A COATING OF ICE BENEATH HIS FEET WILL BRING HIM SLIDING BACK TO ME.
STAY.
INTERESTING. THE POWER IS IN ME. THE SWORD IS BUT THE FOCUS.

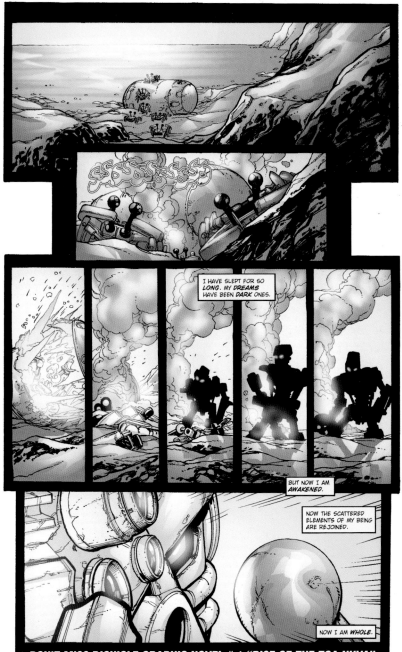

DON'T MISS BIONICLE GRAPHIC NOVEL # 1 "RISE OF THE TOA NUVA"

CLASSICS Illustrated

Featuring Stories by the World's Greatest Authors

Returns in two new series from Papercutz!

The original, best-selling series of comics adaptations of the world's greatest literature, CLASSICS ILLUSTRATED, returns in two new formats--the original, featuring abridged adaptations of classic novels, and CLASSICS ILLUSTRATED DELUXE, featuring longer, more expansive adaptations-from graphic novel publisher Papercutz. "We're very proud to say that Papercutz has received such an enthusiastic reception from librarians and school teachers for its NANCY DREW and HARDY BOYS graphic novels as well as THE LIFE OF POPE JOHN PAUL II...*IN COMICS!*, that it only seemed logical for us to bring back the original CLASSICS ILLUSTRATED comicbook series beloved by parents, educators, and librarians," explained Papercutz Publisher, Terry Nantier. "We can't thank the enlightened librarians and teachers who have supported Papercutz enough. And we're thrilled that they're so excited about CLASSICS ILLUSTRATED."

Upcoming titles include The Invisible Man, Tales from the Brothers Grimm, and Robinson Crusoe.

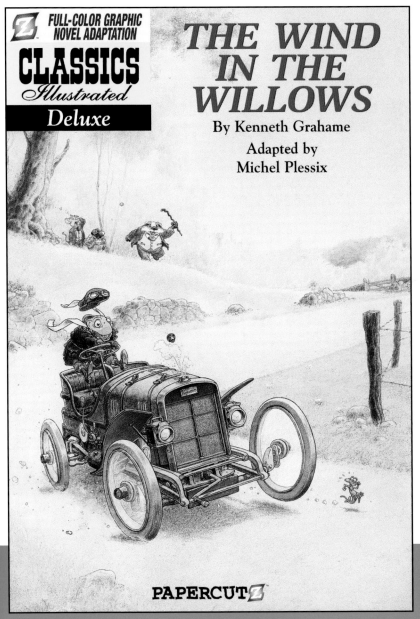

FULL-COLOR GRAPHIC NOVEL ADAPTATION

CLASSICS Illustrated
Deluxe

THE WIND IN THE WILLOWS

By Kenneth Grahame

Adapted by
Michel Plessix

PAPERCUTZ

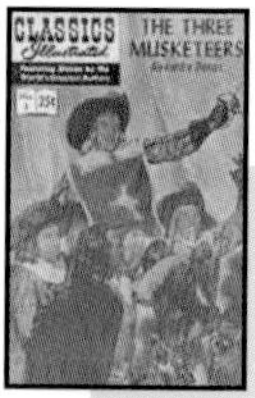
CLASSICS Illustrated
THE THREE MUSKETEERS
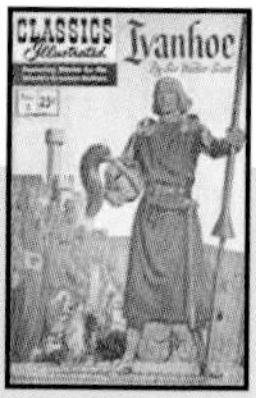
CLASSICS Illustrated
Ivanhoe
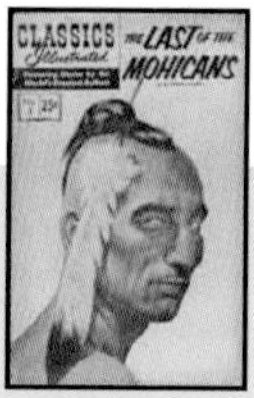
CLASSICS Illustrated
THE LAST OF THE MOHICANS
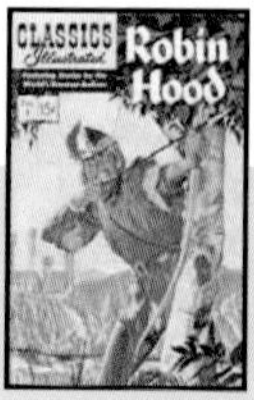
CLASSICS Illustrated
Robin Hood
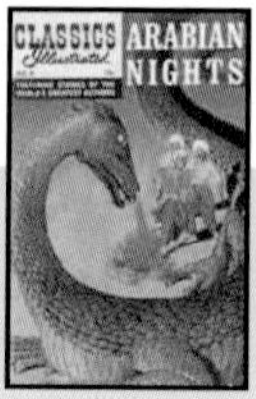
CLASSICS Illustrated
ARABIAN NIGHTS
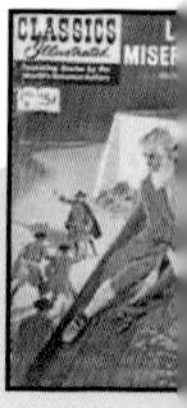
CLASSICS Illustrated
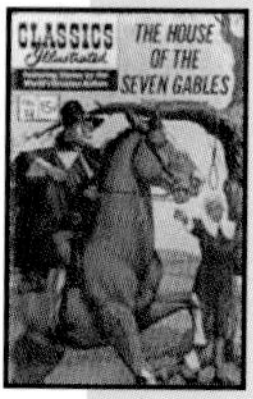
CLASSICS Illustrated
THE HOUSE OF THE SEVEN GABLES

A Short History of CLASSICS ILLUSTRATED...

William B. Jones Jr. is the author of Classics Illustrated: A Cultural History, which offers a comprehensive overview of the original comic-book series and the writers, artists, editors, and publishers behind-the-scenes. With Mr. Jones Jr.'s kind permission, here's a very short overview of the history of CLASSICS ILLUSTRATED adapted from his 2005 essay on Albert Kanter.

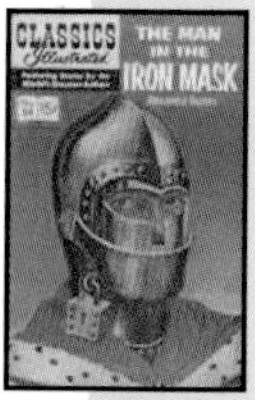
CLASSICS Illustrated
THE MAN IN THE IRON MASK
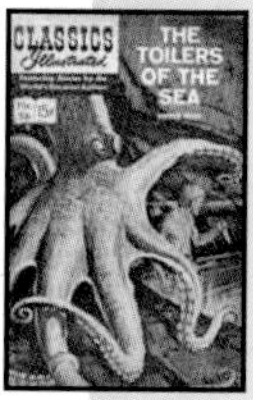
CLASSICS Illustrated
THE TOILERS OF THE SEA
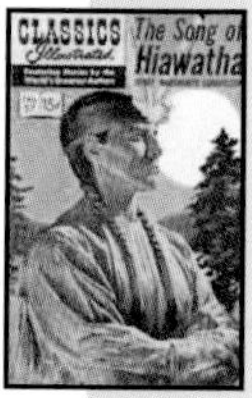
CLASSICS Illustrated
The Song of Hiawatha

CLASSICS ILLUSTRATED was the creation of Albert Lewis Kanter, a visionary publisher, who from 1941 to 1971, introduced young readers worldwide to the realms of literature, history, folklore, mythology, and science in over 200 titles in such comicbook series as CLASSICS ILLUSTRATED and CLASSICS ILLUSTRATED JUNIOR. Kanter, inspired by the success of the first comicbooks published in the early 30s and late 40s, believed he

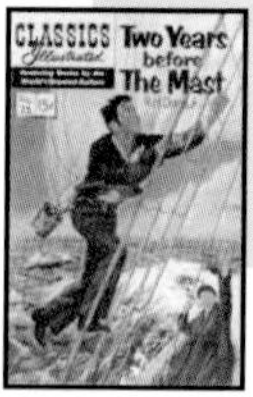
CLASSICS Illustrated
Two Years before The Mast
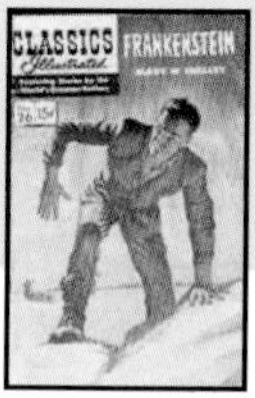
CLASSICS Illustrated
FRANKENSTEIN
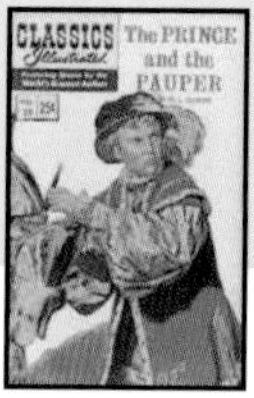
CLASSICS Illustrated
The PRINCE and the PAUPER
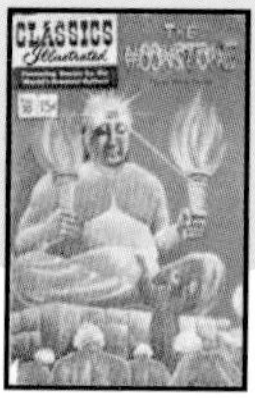
CLASSICS Illustrated
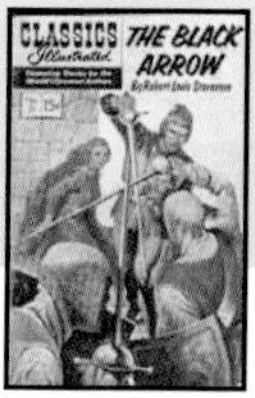
CLASSICS Illustrated
THE BLACK ARROW
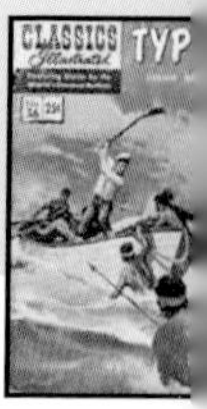
CLASSICS Illustrated

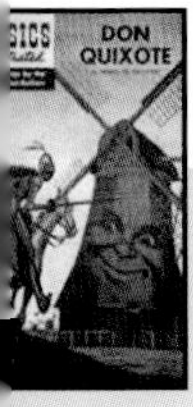
DON QUIXOTE
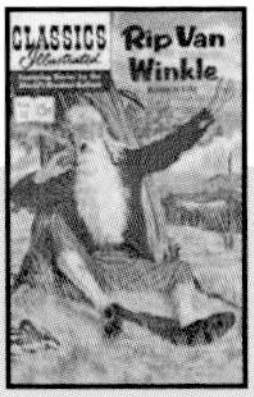
CLASSICS Illustrated
Rip Van Winkle
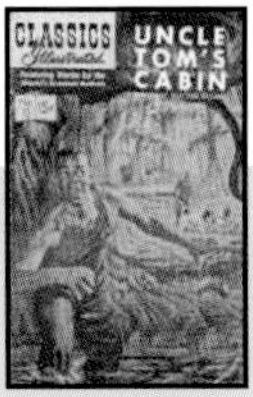
CLASSICS Illustrated
UNCLE TOM'S CABIN
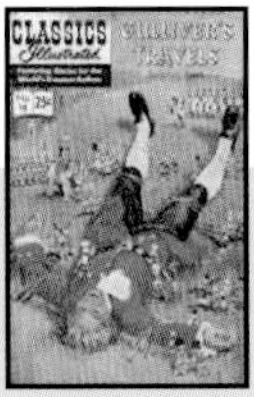
CLASSICS Illustrated
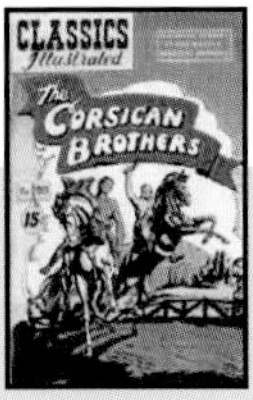
CLASSICS Illustrated
The CORSICAN BROTHERS
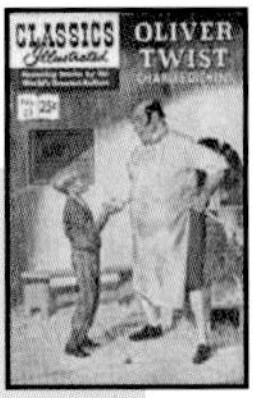
CLASSICS Illustrated
OLIVER TWIST

could use the same medium to introduce young readers to the world of great literature. CLASSIC COMICS (later changed to CLASSICS ILLUSTRATED in 1947) was launched in 1941, and soon the comicbook adaptations of Shakespeare, Stevenson, Twain, Verne, and other authors, were being used in schools and endorsed by educators.

CLASSICS ILLUSTRATED was translated and distributed in countries such as Canada, Great Britain, the Netherlands, Greece, Brazil, Mexico, and Australia. The genial publisher was hailed abroad as "Papa Kassiker." By the beginning of the 1960s, CLASSICS ILLUSTRATED was the largest childrens publication in the world. The original CLASSICS ILLUSTRATED series adapted into comics 169 titles; among these were Frankenstein, 20,000 Leagues Under the Sea, Treasure Island, Julius Caesar, and Faust.

Albert L. Kanter died, March 17, 1973, leaving behind a rich legacy for the millions of readers whose imaginations were awakened by CLASSICS ILLUSTRATED.

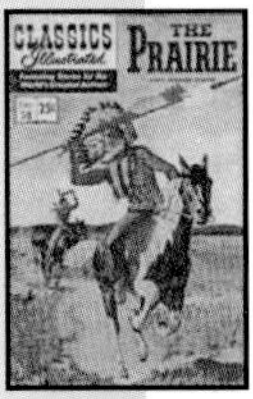
CLASSICS Illustrated
THE PRAIRIE
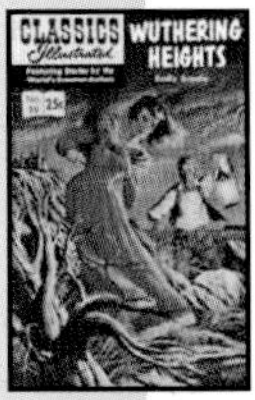
CLASSICS Illustrated
WUTHERING HEIGHTS
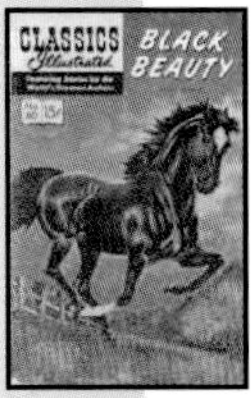
CLASSICS Illustrated
BLACK BEAUTY
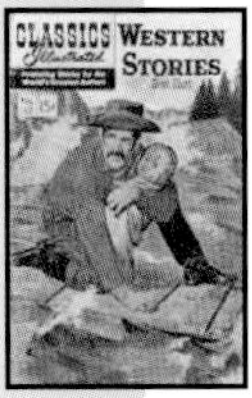
CLASSICS Illustrated
WESTERN STORIES

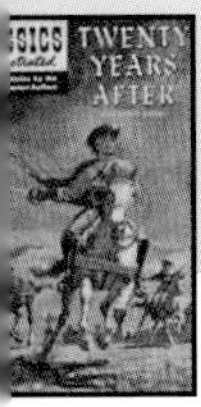
TWENTY YEARS AFTER
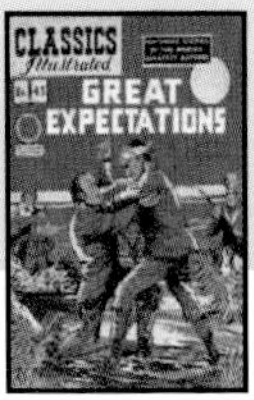
CLASSICS Illustrated
GREAT EXPECTATIONS
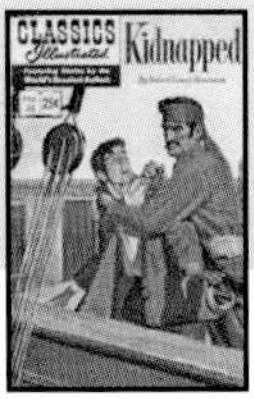
CLASSICS Illustrated
Kidnapped
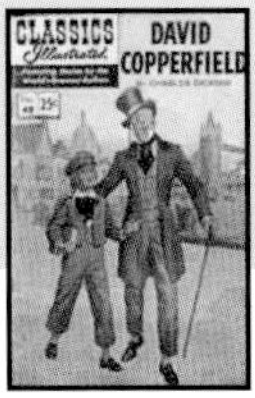
CLASSICS Illustrated
DAVID COPPERFIELD
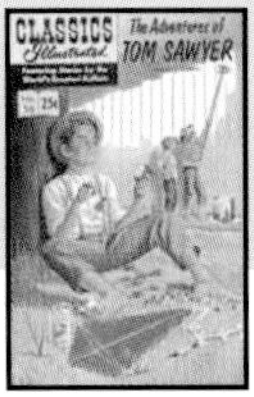
CLASSICS Illustrated
The Adventures of TOM SAWYER
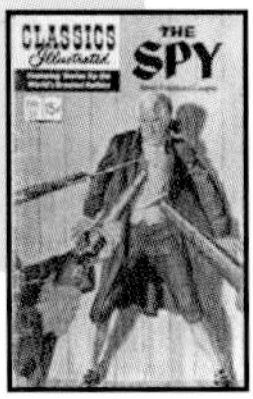
CLASSICS Illustrated
THE SPY

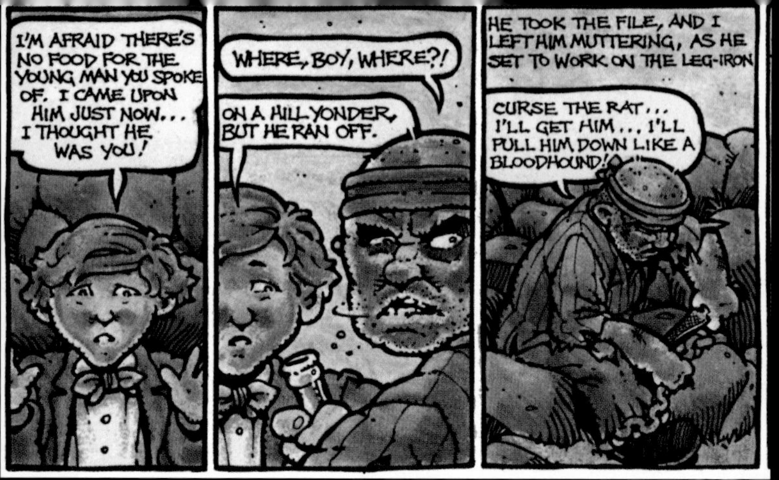
I'M AFRAID THERE'S NO FOOD FOR THE YOUNG MAN YOU SPOKE OF. I CAME UPON HIM JUST NOW... I THOUGHT HE WAS YOU!
WHERE, BOY, WHERE?!
ON A HILL YONDER, BUT HE RAN OFF.
HE TOOK THE FILE, AND I LEFT HIM MUTTERING, AS HE SET TO WORK ON THE LEG-IRON
CURSE THE RAT... I'LL GET HIM... I'LL PULL HIM DOWN LIKE A BLOODHOUND!

CLASSICS ILLUSTRATED was re-launched in 1990 in graphic novel/book form by the Berkley Publishing Group and First Publishing, Inc. featuring all-new adaptations by such top graphic novelists as Rick Geary, Bill Sienkiewicz, Kyle Baker, Gahan Wilson, and others. "First had the right idea, they just came out about 15 years too soon. Now bookstores are ready for graphic novels such as these," Jim explains. Many of these excellent adaptations have been acquired by Papercutz and will make up the new series of CLASSICS ILLUSTRATED titles.

The first volume of the new CLASSICS ILLUSTRATED series presents graphic novelist Rick Geary's adaptation of "Great Expectations" by Charles Dickens, the bittersweet tale of one boy's adolescence, and of the choices he makes to shape his destiny. Into an engrossing mystery, Dickens weaves a heartfelt inquiry into morals and virtues-as the orphan Pip, the convict Magwitch, the beautiful Estella, the bitter Miss Havisham, the goodhearted Biddy, the kind Joe and other memorable characters entwine in a battle of human nature. Rick Geary's delightful illustrations capture the newfound awe and frustrations of young Pip as he comes of age, and begins to understand the opportunities that life presents.

FULL-COLOR GRAPHIC NOVEL ADAPTATION

CLASSICS *Illustrated*®

Featuring Stories by the World's Greatest Authors

GREAT EXPECTATIONS

By Charles Dickens

Adapted by Richard Geary

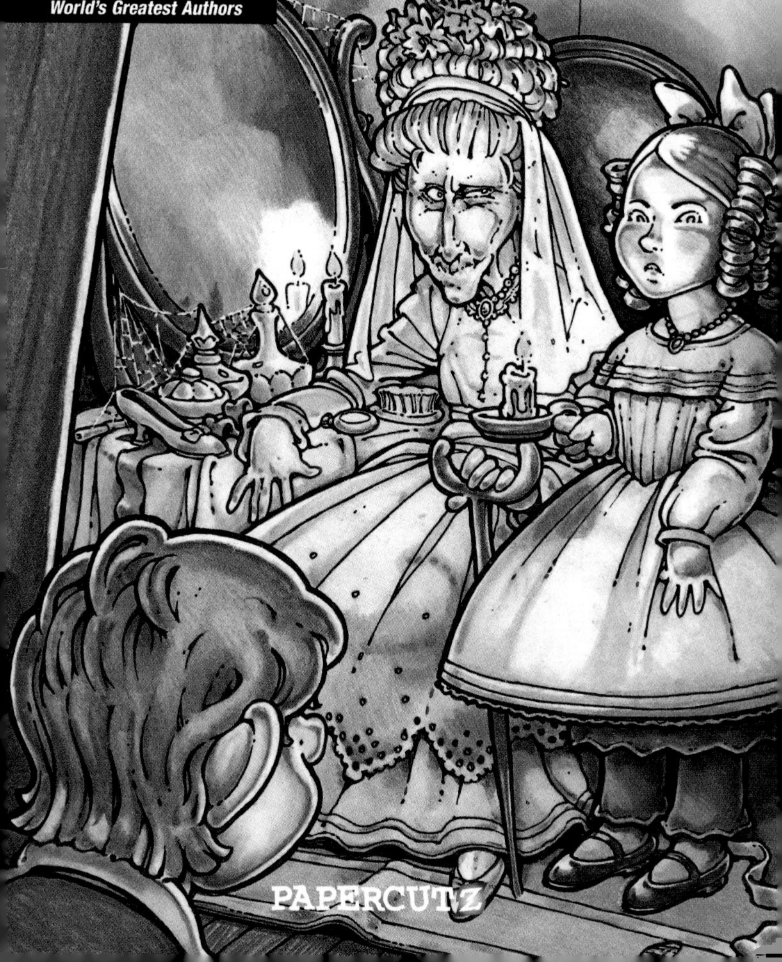

PAPERCUTZ

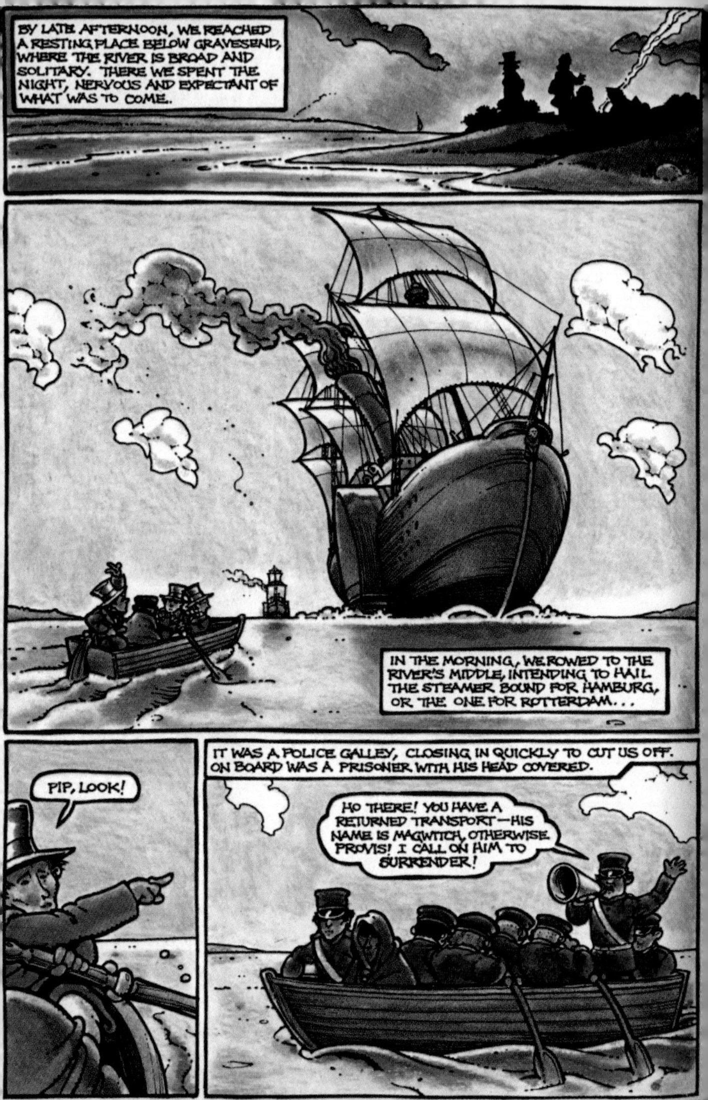
BY LATE AFTERNOON, WE REACHED A RESTING PLACE BELOW GRAVESEND, WHERE THE RIVER IS BROAD AND SOLITARY. THERE WE SPENT THE NIGHT, NERVOUS AND EXPECTANT OF WHAT WAS TO COME.
IN THE MORNING, WE ROWED TO THE RIVER'S MIDDLE, INTENDING TO HAIL THE STEAMER BOUND FOR HAMBURG, OR THE ONE FOR ROTTERDAM...
PIP, LOOK!
IT WAS A POLICE GALLEY, CLOSING IN QUICKLY TO CUT US OFF. ON BOARD WAS A PRISONER WITH HIS HEAD COVERED.
HO THERE! YOU HAVE A RETURNED TRANSPORT—HIS NAME IS MAGWITCH, OTHERWISE PROVIS! I CALL ON HIM TO SURRENDER!

Iere is one preview page of CLASSICS ILLUSTRATED #1 "Grea xpectations" by Charles Dickens, as adapted by Rick Geary. (CLA ICS ILLUSTRATED will be printed in a larger 6 1/2" x 9" format, s he art will be bigger than what you see here.)